REVISING HERSELF

REVISING

The Story of
Women's
Identity
from College
to Midlife

HERSELF

Ruthellen
Josselson

New York   Oxford
Oxford University Press
1996

Oxford University Press

Oxford   New York
Athens   Auckland   Bangkok   Bogotá   Bombay
Buenos Aires   Calcutta   Cape Town   Dar es Salaam
Delhi   Florence   Hong Kong   Istanbul   Karachi
Kuala Lumpur   Madras   Madrid   Melbourne
Mexico City   Nairobi   Paris   Singapore
Taipei   Tokyo   Toronto

and associated companies in
Berlin   Ibadan

Published by Oxford University Press, Inc.
198 Madison Avenue, New York, New York 10016

Oxford is a registered trademark of Oxford University Press

Library of Congress Cataloging-in-Publication Data
Josselson, Ruthellen.
Revising herself : the story of women's identity
from college to midlife / Ruthellen Josselson.
p.   cm.   Includes bibliographical references and index.
ISBN 0-19-510839-6
1. Women—United States—Psychology—Longitudinal studies.
2. Women—United States—Identity—Longitudinal studies.
3. Identity (Psychology)—United States—
Longitudinal studies. I. Title
HQ1206.J67   1996
155.6'33—dc20   96-10380

The author gratefully acknowledges the use of interview material from
Find Herself: Pathways to Identity Development in Women, San Francisco: Jossey-Bass Publishers, 1987.

Excerpt from "East Coker" in FOUR QUARTETS, copyright 1943 by T.S. Eliot
and renewed 1971 by Esme Valerie Eliot, reprinted by permission of Harcourt Brace & Company.

Excerpt from "East Coker" in FOUR QUARTETS, copyright 1943 by T.S. Eliot
and renewed 1971 by Esme Valerie Eliot, reprinted by permission of Faber and Faber Ltd.

1 3 5 7 9 8 6 4 2

Printed in the United States of America
on acid-free paper

For Jaimie—
May she become
all that she is

Home is where one starts from. As we grow older
The world becomes stranger, the pattern more complicated
Of dead and living. Not the intense moment
Isolated, with no before and after,
But a lifetime burning in every moment

T.S. Eliot, East Coker

PREFACE

In this book, I follow a group of women as they grow from their college years to midlife. *Revising Herself* differs from other books about women because I meet and revisit these women over time, over twenty-two years, as they are in the process of developing and reworking their identity. Retrospective accounts are always distorted. What we remember about how we were always differs from how we experienced ourselves at the time.

The challenge in doing this book has been to grapple with the complexity of these women, a complexity I know well because it is mine, too. I rarely find myself in what I read about women. Certainly, I have loved too much and made foolish choices, I have feared success and silenced my inner voice for fear of disapproval and loss of love. But these are aspects of me, episodes or moments of my life—they are not the whole of me.

I want to paint a more holistic psychological portrait of women—a portrait that will fit women who are not necessarily remarkable in any way—who are not disturbed or victimized or uncommonly successful. I'm interested in ordinary women, women like me, women I see at the grocery store going about their lives. All the women I have been studying are educated, and this is a group that society has largely ignored recently—after all, they have received the bounty and, unless they have been abused, have no grounds for complaint. As a society, we have begun to notice only those who have a claim to outrage.

I have had the unique opportunity over the last twenty years to follow closely the unfolding of thirty women's lives—to look at their lives as works in progress. These are women I did not know when I began my study and women I would never have gotten to know because our paths would not likely have crossed. I have been trying to grasp, from a psychological point of view, how they have formed themselves in this ever-changing world. I have wanted to know how they created—and then revised—their identity.

In this book, I try to do verbally what Michael Apted did visually in his *35 UP* series—and from a more psychological point of view. I observe the metamorphosis of identity as women age from 21 to 43. I focus on what has felt essential to them in their lives, and how the stake they claim in life has changed over time.

I have spent hours, months, years—poring over these lives and the more I know them, the more questions arise. We can never grasp other people in their entirety. Yet there are some truths that I have abstracted from what these women have told me about themselves and about their discoveries in living life—and these I try to share with my readers.

I mean this book to be an antidote for any simplified formulations, which are all too widespread in psychology. My test of any psychological exposition I read is: Does it help me understand these women? And I want this book to add to a conversation that we have been having in our society—and within psychology—about who women are, how they got that way, and where they think they are going. I take these women for who they think they are. I do not require them to be more like me or more like some idea of how I think women ought to be.

This book is a meditation on women's lives, and I do not intend it as the last word. If it does nothing more than get people talking—adding their own observations to mine, extending my comments into new areas, disagreeing with me—then I will consider this a successful project. Everyone will find truth in some of the biographies in this book and be critical of others—depending on their own identity history. In some ways, the life stories in this book are a projective test for the reader. Everyone will read these life histories through the lens of her (or his) own life experience and will respond to different aspects—and that is quite all right. I want only to say: think about these people, think about the different ways in which women take up their lives, and think about yourself and how you have become who you are. And to my colleagues, I also want to say, now how are we going to contain all this in a theory of women's development?

What have I found out about women? That they are enormously complicated and, even if they have superficial similarity, they are astonishingly diverse. Behind each face is an intricate story—a tale of becoming, and then revising, herself.

But who am I to comment on these women's lives? I come to this study as a psychologist who has been thinking about women's development for many years. I have worked with women as patients and guided women as students. And I have been thinking about how women grow at closer range—as the mother of a daughter. Even more deeply, I, too, have grown up a woman in this society at the same time as my participants and I, too, have struggled with the same questions as the women I write about. In other words, I bring some intellectual tools and some firsthand experience, but I try not to judge. If doing intensive, longitudinal work teaches a researcher anything, it teaches humility.

As much as possible, I try to present enough material about the women I discuss so that my readers may come to their own conclusions. I try to present whole lives in progress rather than snippets that confirm some point I want to make (although I do some of that as well). At the same time, I recognize that it is I who have digested hours of interviews and have decided what to tell and what to leave out—I control the narrative here. So I do not pretend that any of the life story summaries are in any way complete. In addition, to many questions, especially those about feelings or meanings, the women themselves, being frank, often do not have clear answers about themselves. Experience is never linear or categorical: If someone were to ask me, Were you close to your mother?, how could I answer except to say, yes and no, and anyway, what do you mean by close? I don't ask questions like that, and I don't expect—indeed, I am mistrustful of—unequivocal answers.

My stance in regard to my work is less to find answers and more to describe the questions these women are posing to themselves and how they go about making peace with them. I am equally interested in how they have changed and how they have stayed the same.

I bring, of course, my own biases to this work. As a developmental psychologist, I believe that the present has roots in the past but is influenced by unforeseen events as well. As a clinical psychologist, I believe everyone struggles with internal conflict, but some people cope better than others. But this is not a self-help book. I never expected to find a "best way" to live that I could market to others. All choices have their rewards and their costs. None of the women in this book, and no one I know, including myself, has it all figured out. That is our strength. That is why we continue to grow.

R. J.

March 1996
Baltimore, Maryland

ACKNOWLEDGMENTS

This book owes its existence to the honesty, good faith, and cooperation of thirty extraordinary women. I have been an unusual sort of apparition in their lives, appearing every ten years to ask them to give an accounting of themselves. But they have greeted me warmly and opened the deepest recesses of themselves to me—for no apparent return. I have come to care deeply about each of them, but have no way of expressing this, for I come to them as a "scientist," there only to observe. Here, at the very least, I would like to say publicly, "Thank you."

Over the twenty years of this project, a great many people have taken part and assisted me in various ways. Here I express my gratitude to those who have been most immediately involved in this recent work. I began this twenty-year followup during a year I spent as a visiting professor at the Harvard Graduate School of Education. There I was blessed with a very talented and enthusiastic group of graduate students. I thank, first of all, Mary Casey, who was my research assistant, my "right hand" in the work, who did a superb job of organizing material, searching for the participants, and then interviewing several of them and conferring with me on making sense of the interviews.

Without her commitment to this work and her thoughtful ideas about carrying it out, I could not have seen it through. Other very skilled students conducted some of the interviews and shared with me their comments and insightful analysis. I thank them heartily: Joan Dolamore, Suzanne Cook-Greuter, Kathy Johnson, MaryBeth Kent, Carlene Larsson, and Vicki Magee. Sarah Hanson was also enormously helpful in getting the work arranged. I also thank Carol Gilligan for having made it possible for me to be there working with such able people.

Many people have read drafts of this book and helped me through the process of figuring out how to present such masses of material in an intelligible way. My daughter, Jaimie Baron, always did the first edit—and, only age fifteen at the time, showed an unerring sense of language and cadence. Thanks to her, this book is free of jargon.

I wrote this book while on sabbatical at the Hebrew University of Jerusalem. The second response was from a group of wonderful, brilliant, highly critical graduate students who entered into an unusual bargain with me: I conducted a course for them in exchange for their detailed comments on what I was writing. I hope they liked the course. I profited immensely from their reactions: they are Tali Kaufman, Yael Oberman, Tamar Portnoy, and Moshe Wurgaft.

I am also grateful for careful, thoughtful, and sensitive readings from my colleagues and friends: Judith Armstrong, Tirza Assor, Mary Casey, Ravenna Helson, Tova Halbertal, Amia Lieblich, Beverley Mizrachi, Anat Ninio, Beverly Palmer, June Price, Annie Rogers, and Ada Zohar. My husband, Hanoch Flum, not only read the chapters but was also willing to think through with me, over many hours, the roadblocks to conceptualization.

My editor, Joan Bossert, was exceptionally helpful and supportive as was my agent and friend, Katinka Matson. I also thank Towson State University, Harvard University, and the Hebrew University for their institutional support.

Both my daughter, Jaimie, and my husband, Hanoch, have provided the love and connection which, as we will see in this book, is what makes it possible for women to do their work.

CONTENTS

WOMEN IN
SEARCH OF
THEMSELVES

We all begin with the natural equipment to live a thousand kinds of life
but end in the end having lived only one.

Clifford Geertz, The Interpretation of Cultures

1 INTRODUCTION

After milling around at my twenty-fifth college reunion, a group of us—the former 8th-floor back corner of South Quad—go off to have some "real talk." We catch each other up on what we've done, what we've suffered, what life has turned out to be. The ghost of those old late-night sessions is with us— the times that we used to crowd our pillows and blankets into one dorm room and talk into the early morning about how we would live our lives. Having grown up in the fifties, we were schooled to the idea that "success" was graduating with an engagement ring, but many of us felt that there must be more to life than that. And as we took our diplomas in 1968, everything we had ever learned about what was "feminine," what was expected of women, was open to question. Our mandate was to break new ground. As I look around this small group of now middle-aged women, I marvel at our differences. We, who had struggled to define our uniqueness in college, who were determined to live an interesting life of our own choosing, had become—but not as we had imagined.

Margery seems bored with the more philosophical talk, with our shared recognition of compromises, with our affectionate ruefulness about our idealistic adolescent selves. She wants to tell us about the joys of her houses. She is a Wall Street lawyer and has made a fortune, which she enjoys spending on houses in various parts of the world. She invites us all to visit, but bemoans ever having enough money to build the house she has always dreamed of on Nantucket. These are rough economic times for lawyers.

Linda is animated, telling us of her children and her struggles to figure out how to respond to their adolescent antics. When she relates a long story about her son getting picked up by the police for driving after curfew and how comical she looked reclaiming him at the station, we remind her that she had more "late points" in the college dorm than the rest of us put together. Absorbed in the foibles of her three children, she regards Margery, who does not have children, sadly, and can't imagine what childless life could be like. Linda is an interior designer, or used to be, or maybe will be again—she's not sure.

Jane had been the wildest among us in college—she was the first to have sex. She came back one Saturday night and we were up all night extracting details. Then we spent the rest of the month trying to decide if we believed she had really done it. Now she is celebrating her twenty-fourth wedding anniversary, has been a teacher since she graduated, is raising two adopted children, and stays pretty quiet while we talk. She says life has been fine, she has no complaints, but we miss her spark and mischievousness.

We had always taken our troubles to Susan, who was serious and intense. We could depend on her good sense. She had wanted to be a doctor and became one. She had a very reliable, attentive boyfriend in college, which we all envied. Just after graduation, they got married but fifteen years later she divorced him, and has raised their daughter pretty much on her own. She hadn't ever really dated until her early forties and we all enjoy her lampooning the men she's been meeting. (I didn't remember her as being so funny!) Susan felt she hadn't ever really discovered herself until she turned 40; she had always spent her life taking care of other people. Linda joins in on this, seems to know just what she means. Margery and Jane think Susan and Linda have bought into a lot of feminist psychobabble and politely change the subject.

And I? I feel my own story to be so layered and changing, so full of starts and new starts, epochs, and travels that I can't tell it except as vignettes. I became a psychologist, a wife, and a mother, but how I have been a psychologist and to whom I have been a wife have changed dramatically. Only mothering has been constant, but then mothering is never the same from one year to the next. The others regard me as having led a life of excitement and aren't too interested in the anguish, which, in any case, is hard for me to put into words that fit such an occasion.

I don't mind—I prefer to observe tonight. I am filled with wonder: How had we become what we are?

Perhaps I have always been mesmerized by trying to figure out how some people take one path while others pursue another. As a graduate student in psychology, I was troubled that so much of the theory I was learning didn't seem to take enough account of how people differ from one another. There was, for example, supposed to be a sequence of steps toward identity in adolescence, exploration followed by commitment. Erik Erikson described it brilliantly (but only for men), but this fit just some of the people I knew. Others, like Susan, just "always knew" how they would live their lives and never questioned what seemed so self-evident. Still others, like Vicki, who didn't come to the reunion, seemed to live from day to day and not make any choices at all. (Last anyone heard, she was still trying to figure out a life for herself and having a hard time doing it.) Beyond that, society was changing and making the challenge of carving out an identity different as well. Now Margery could have professional success that women could not even have dreamed of just a few years earlier.

Troubled by the absence of what seemed to be real people's real experiences in the literature of psychology, I set out, for my doctoral dissertation, to explore how and why young women, women just a few years younger than I was (and am), chose one path or another in their lives. Over the years, I have followed these women, interviewing them again at age 33 and then at age 43 to learn how their choices or nonchoices have unfolded, what new obstacles and opportunities have emerged along the way, and what has contributed both to their changes and their continuity. I have made myself an observer to the process of women revising themselves.

REVISIONS

Two revisions concern me in this book. One is the way in which women revise their lives as they grow from late adolescence to mature adulthood. The second is how the late 1960s–early 1970s revision of social ideas about what is possible and desirable for women affected the lives of women who were coming of age in the midst of such wrenching changes.

In those late-night talkfests, we conjured and dissected the identities we might live. But we didn't call it that. We probed and argued about what we each believed or planned, wondering together where happiness and fulfillment might lie. We wondered about who we might take into our lives, as partners and friends, and what sort of commitment we would make to them. Did we want a life in the work world and, if so, what kind and with how much devotion? And what price might we have to pay to do it? And what of our spiritual and ethical lives—was there something larger than ourselves, and, if so, what was it and what was our relation to it? We learned by how others contemplated these questions. But always we thought through these questions against the template of our mothers' lives. As young women in the late 1960s, we knew—at least, most of us did—that we wanted something different from the powerlessness and marginality that we saw in most of our mother's lives. Betty Friedan had recently named the syndrome, but we had grown up in its shadow and knew it well. Many of us had come to college in hopes of having lives in which we felt more a part of the world that counted. But what and how—those were the thornier dilemmas. Defining our identity was a way of plotting how we would live our lives.

Although the college dorm was the place where I breathed the turbulent air of identity in the making, the library was where I began my formal study. In search of conceptual guides to plan an organized way to research the growth and unfolding of identity, I read all the works of Erik Erikson, the premier theorist of identity. He understood and wrote about the tangles and distresses of such decision-making, the wrenching reworking of self that allows us to reinvent ourselves, the inner trembling that goes with taking a stand. But he wrote only about men, as though only men have odysseys of self-discovery worth recording or analyzing. Women in our society, he said in one of his papers, are limited to declaring themselves by choosing the men they wish to be sought by.[1]

But I knew from my late-night dorm experiences that Erikson was mistaken about women's identity. Women are perhaps less overt in their search for identity; they may seek in ways that are invisible to men. Their self-searching and experimentation is often less dramatic and apparent (at least it was in those days), but it is no less anguishing and, in the end, no less important. And, in any case, the rumbling of social change in women's roles was growing to a roar, and the rapidity of this change itself was making the riddle of identity even more perplexing for women. I set out to study how women create and choose identity—even though, in 1969, my professors thought this a somewhat hopeless and frivolous dissertation project. Women, after all, were not then a serious topic for academic psychologists. Those times have changed as well.

Through interviewing women who were just about to graduate from college in 1972, I learned much about how women construct identity and the extreme variability among them as they come to terms with the past they were born into. With the scrutiny of my psychological training, I watched them bring the elements of the girls they were into internal conversation with new influences and social possibility. What does it mean, for example, for an Irish Catholic to contemplate having an abortion? How does the woman whose parents thought education was wasted on a daughter orient herself to apply to medical school? What does a woman who always thought of her future in terms of motherhood imagine that she will do with the rest of her life? And what of the women who were not paying attention to identity questions at all—those who were living each day, not asking that the days fit together into any sort of pattern or add up to a life plan? I wrote about these matters twenty years ago, documenting the personality patterns and early influences that seemed to permit a young woman to explore possibilities of being and belief, and then to commit herself to a set of choices (Josselson, 1973). I thought I had figured out some things about why some women took one path while others chose another.

I, like the academic developmental psychology I had been schooled in, felt finished with my work at this point. Developmental psychology presumes that people are "formed" by the end of adolescence and tends not to look beyond—into adulthood. It was the curiosity of my students, impatient with people's lives fixed on a page, that impelled me to find these women and discover what "ever happened to them" as they continued into their adult lives. Indeed, at the close of adolescence, these women were only beginning a journey that would lead them through socially uncharted waters. What became of them? How did they continue to become? I have been able to follow many of them for twenty years. This book is an effort to share what I have learned about these women as they followed their paths from adolescence to midlife.

TELLING A WOMAN'S LIFE

How can we portray a woman's life? How can we frame it without stumbling into stereotypes, clichés, or sentimentality? Our culture offers us certain myths and stories that provide the pattern against which we project a life. In the case of women, the archetypal tale is one of courtship leading to marriage. Snow White and Cinderella get the Prince through various misadventures, Sleeping Beauty is awakened by the Prince and marries him, Beauty discovers that the Beast is really a Prince, and so on. Then they "live happily ever after," whatever that may mean. All our great women heroines of literature are similarly occupied with getting or getting rid of their Princes. Jane Eyre and Jo March find their prince after a journey of adventure, self-discovery, and renunciation. Emma Bovary and Anna Karenina can't live happily ever after with the men they marry or the princes they want and end up killing themselves. What Carolyn Heilbrun has called "the erotic plot" has dominated our cultural conception of a woman's life.

With the change in women's roles in the last third of the twentieth century, we might try to tell a woman's life much as we do a man's, making use of the "quest plot." In this tale, a hero has a mission and sets out to achieve it, and the narrative is of his trials and perils along the way. We make this a woman's story by changing the pronoun. Cinderella decided to finish law school before she married and became a trial attorney where she prepared herself to run for the Senate, was too involved with professional success to have children, and lived happily ever after. To modern ears, this is a little better, but not much. We still know little of what her life was like, how she experienced herself.

Besides, the quest plot is a Procrustean bed for all but a very few women. Most don't articulate clearly defined dreams and try to achieve them.[2] Unlike Odysseus, women do not leave all behind and go off in pursuit. More likely, women, like Penelope, weave. The shuttle moves back and forth, the threads merge, sometimes tightly, sometimes not fitting well together. Sometimes a portion must be undone for something lovelier to replace it, sometimes layers are crafted on top of other older patterns. The parts form a whole, but the whole is more than the sum of the parts. As Carolyn Heilbrun points out, we are never told what Penelope was weaving.[3] This is one of the great silences of literature. What women weave into their identities has similarly been one of the major silences in the psychological literature—at least until recently.

As a culture, no less than the Greeks, we have occupied ourselves with mythologizing women. Bookstore shelves are filled with works trying to understand women's lives in terms of goddesses or ancient heroines. Simone de Beauvoir cautions us, however, that only by demythologizing women can we come to an understanding of their real nature and complexity. Instead of being able to contain in our consciousness the infinitely varied weavings of real living women, we have occupied ourselves as a society with stereotype, another form of mythology. We have been possessed with trying to "fix" women in both senses of that term—to photograph and to repair.

In our quest for a clear image of women, we have tried to "fix" them in terms of our representation of them—as though we can configure womanhood into one image. How shall we picture women? Do we imagine Venus coming forth from her seashell, naked and sensual, clothed only in her hair? Or the Mona Lisa full of secrets? Or do we see the fast-track investment analyst, in a suit, with glasses, carrying a briefcase made of excellent leather? Or a mother, nursing an infant or comforting a toddler? Or Margaret Thatcher depicted as a man in female dress? Or is Woman the quintessential victim of social (i.e., male) oppression? And is it possible to imagine that she could be all of these at once—or none of them? Each society spurts forth these images for us to venerate and denigrate. Yet these are stereotypical images—they caricature instead of characterize. And while there is a bit of Venus, a bit of the financier, a bit of the nurturing, comforting Earth Mother, and a bit of the iron-willed leader in all women, these images codify but do not illuminate.

Once we have these images, we set about trying to "fix" women in another way, by "repairing" their deficiencies so that they will fit the patterns of our imaginings. We are quick, as a society, to point a scolding finger at women and then to offer them advice. Women still make up the vast majority of psychotherapy patients, in the past because they were chafing at their assigned roles as wives and mothers (or because they didn't have "vaginal" orgasms), at present because they have an often-vague awareness that they aren't as they "ought" to be.

Identity in women cannot be simply named, for it resides in the pattern that emerges as a woman stitches together an array of aspects of herself and her investments in others. A woman is, then, *not* a "this" or a "that" (mother, lawyer, wife, secretary, etc.), for these can only be pieces of herself. A woman is how she weaves it all into a whole, articulating herself in the world with others and simultaneously making private sense of it.

Psychology has no adequate theory of women's development, particularly development in adulthood.[4] Within developmental psychology, women tend to be regarded as potential mothers, then as actual mothers who eventually confront an empty nest—and little else about their lives is articulated. More recently, psychologists have paid some attention to whether or not women "work," painting with only a very broad brush women's engagement in the world outside the family. But most of women's emotional and life experience remains invisible. Sometimes, psychology has lingered at the menopause as a significant psychological watershed for women, but this has been largely shown to be overrated. Terri Apter (1995), following her extensive study of midlife women, commented that it is as absurd to make menopause the central event of a woman's middle life as it is to make menstruation the hallmark event of her adolescence.[5] Consequently, women are unlikely to find their selves or their concerns reflected in official psychology.

I am interested in grappling with the realities of women's identity at the end of this century, with identity that is sculpted in lives hidden by the wayside, in towns, offices, houses, and meeting places, in the daily engagements of ordinary life. I learn through the stories of others' lives.

I am not trying to prove a thesis in this book. Nor do I wish to hold forth ideal types. I haven't sought the privileged or the special. Other studies of women's development have selected women from elite colleges and universities, women identified as gifted in some way or women who were, in Gail Sheehy's term, Pathfinders, who did something unusual or were likely to do so. I chose to follow women whom I selected randomly from state universities in Illinois and New York and one selective (but not exceptionally so) women's college in

New York. They became part of this study only because theirs was the fiftieth or hundredth name on a list. As a result, great variability exists among them.

Admittedly, they do not represent all women. For one thing, they all completed college degrees; a great many women do not. They are all white (originally there was one black woman, but she died shortly after college) and therefore they do not represent the experience of racial minorities.

Despite the diversity within this fairly homogeneous group, there are many experiences that are not represented. Most were fortunate enough to have the luxury of choice. Unlike some of their parents who, raised during the Depression, had to forgo their dreams to keep families from hunger, the women of my study were privileged to be able to try to become the people they wished to be. And it is the very existence of this possibility to choose that affords us the opportunity to investigate the pathways by which women take up and encounter that choice, how they sort through what they might become, and how they realize what they are.

While I acknowledge the distinctiveness of these women from those less privileged, it is also clear to me that the lives of middle-class white women have been overgeneralized and homogenized as though they were all cut with the same cookie cutter. Or their lives have been analyzed according to the often-trivializing distinction between those who work for pay and those who don't—as if "having a career" fully names a woman's identity. Among educated white middle-class women are vast differences—of desire, of experience, of psychic fortitude, of conviction, and of styles of arranging a life. My work is an effort to find deeper markers of difference having to do with how past, present, and future are joined, how relationships are taken up and dealt with in juxtaposition to the self, how meaning is created and sometimes lost. Despite differences in opportunity and resources, I hope that the lives of the women I discuss here might nevertheless have something in common with all women.

In this tale, women are the heroines of their own lives, although others may often play central roles. Consciously or not, they create their own plots even as they are influenced and bent by what they encounter.

And in this narrative, women define themselves in their own terms; we must refrain from evaluating them in light of the prevailing social prejudices. This is perhaps the most difficult part. We feel as a society the right to ask women to live out some ideal. I try here not to be judgmental about these lives. (I can't say, for example, who is "in denial" and who is not. Denial of what? Of what I believe or what you hold dear?) I recognize the truth of the maxim that most people get what they want in life. I haven't the right to ask that other people want something other than what they do.

Most of these women regard themselves as happy enough. They are happy often despite the disappointments they have endured and the compromises they have made. Theirs are, by and large, not tales of victimization and oppression. Most feel that they did get what they had wanted or, at least, can want what they got. Should we believe them if they claim contentment? Or should we discount them, pointing out that women are often unaware of the circumstances that oppress them?

I remember in the early days of the women's movement, back in the late 1960s, the tremendous resentment women who were living traditional lives directed at those of us who seemed to be rocking their boat. I was married to a medical student in those days, working on my Ph.D. At medical school parties, where all the medical students were men and all the women were wives who were working to send them to medical school, I was usually the only wife in graduate school, planning, however uncertainly, a career of my own. The women liked to discuss having a baby as soon as possible, their envy and curiosity about those really fortunate wives who already had a baby, and their eagerness to quit work and begin real life. These women had little to say to me and I had little to say in return. If we did talk, the underlying conversation was often along the lines of why we "feminists" assumed that women wanted something other than the traditional forms—they could not be happier. They liked having doors opened for them, getting flowers, and so on. Who was I to tell them they were not happy?

At my dissertation party celebrating my Ph.D. (I was 25), a rite of great professional meaning for me, the wife of one of my professors hugged me and whispered, "So—*now* you can have a baby." I'll never forget that moment. Her assumption was that I had been depriving myself of that joy. In her mind, I expect, she was offering me a gift. She was a woman of considerable academic accomplishment (though never up to her potential). For her—like the medical school wives—having babies was what was central to a woman's happiness. Nothing at that time could have seemed more alien to me. But I was incomprehensible to them—and always feeling vaguely defensive.

Today, twenty-three years later, neither of these events would be likely to happen. More probably, women would be wont to defend themselves for not having a career—or, in some circles, for working in a female-dominated occupation. Intentionally or not, the values expressed in how some women choose to live their lives imply some value judgment on others. We haven't yet reached true tolerance of diversity.

THE PLAN OF THIS BOOK

The genre of this work is psychobiography—multiple psychobiography, in fact.[6] I present, explore, and analyze the life courses of the thirty women I interviewed when they were seniors in college, when they were in their early thirties, and then again when they were in their early forties. I did not select them to "fit" anything—they are a random group. And I've tried to understand them all, not just the ones who fit a convenient social or psychological prototype.

When they were in college, I divided them into four groups according to the pathway they seemed to be taking toward identity—a pathway of decision-making rather than one defined by content. Using a psychological framework that regards identity formation as a dynamic process, I assessed whether or not these young women were exploring alternatives for themselves and if they were making commitments—a set of distinctions I will discuss in detail later. I wanted to know what difference it would make for a woman's life how she began drafting it—in other words, to what extent adult identity was affected by a woman's late adolescent effort to part from her childhood and form her own way of being. The four identity paths served as gateways into adulthood which, in turn, gave a distinct cast to each developing life.

In Part Two, I look at the women who entered adulthood through each of these four identity gateways and explore the conflicts, triumphs, and challenges that marked the next two decades of these women's lives. In Part Three, I reassemble the group and analyze the themes that unify them as women growing up, getting educated, and living their adult lives in this particular social-historical age. I ask about which issues or concerns form the bedrock of their adult identities, and I reflect on the process of revision over time. I look at what these women have in common as they remake, rewrite, and reconsider themselves from age 21 to 43, from college to midlife.

In writing about what I learned from studying these women over such a long time, I enter the throes of what Carolyn Heilbrun has called the problem of writing a woman's life. There are no preexisting plots that will do. We have to create new ones. What to tell, what to omit? What is central and what peripheral? And at what level of analysis—the surface or my hunches about the deep unconscious? And do I tell only what is easy to put into language when so much of what often matters most is beyond words?

Where do I stand to write about these lives? I inhabit the same society, but the world of each of these women is both mine and different from mine. I write also from twenty-two years of professional experience as a psychologist, which guides my insight but sometimes involves its own set of blinders. At the very least, it has given me the skills to listen and to try to understand and organize others' experience.

Over these twenty-two years, I have developed a relationship with each one of these women. Millie said she had come to regard me as a secret friend who cares about her and reappears every ten years to check up on her, who remembers her as she was and would always hold a particular truth about her life. And this matches my own experience of how they seem to have experienced me. In this last contact, some were expecting me, others had rather forgotten about me, but could bring the memory back. I can't fully know what effect I may have had on them. Some spoke of thinking of me at times of major life decisions, imagining telling me about themselves as having gotten divorced, for example, and trying on how that would feel. I became for some a kind of biographer, an imaginary mirror in which they could assume different guises. Most, I think, felt pleased to have someone so deeply interested in them over so long a time. I hold an imprint of their past and their growth. Some I know better than others.

At each phase, I interviewed them for many hours,[7] sometimes asking them to make tapes or respond to questions in written form, sometimes through phone contact, but mainly in lengthy face-to-face conversation.[8] I tried to stay with each one until I felt I understood where she experienced herself in her life at that point. I was amazed at their openness. Many said they told me things they had never divulged to anyone. In that sense, I am for them a kind of private diary. Others remarked that the interview was like therapy, where "I say things out loud that I've never said before." Some told me that our conversations have often been painful, especially when they reawakened buried loss, anger, or confusion. But there is something about our interaction that led these women to strive for naked truthfulness, and that has felt liberating—for both of us. Graciously, they gave me permission to share their life stories and have trusted me to disguise them in a way that they could not be recognized by anyone but themselves.[9]

Over these years, these women have also taken on profound meaning for me. Having to confront their complexity and diversity has ensured me a sense of humility and kept me from being seduced by any too-facile formulation of women. I am immune, thanks to them, from any of the paradigms and traditions of my formal training. I cannot think in any framework that cannot contain these women I have come to know so well. I am often astonished and moved by their insight, by what they discover about life and about themselves.

Because I want to record these women's experiences of themselves and their lives, I give priority to their own perspective and their own interpretations. I think that each of these women has told me her truths as she knows them. Nevertheless, my presentation of their lives is my construction, *my* reading of the text of their interviews, and often I search for meanings they may not be aware of. Biography, and most especially, psychobiography, is always interpretive and constructed out of the concerns of the biographer as well as the subject of the narrative.

My aim in this work is to try to understand the routes and courses of the various identity pathways rather than evaluate the success of these women's lives. Who, after all, can say that one life is "better" than another? Inevitably, however, we will all have our reactions and opinions about each of these lives. And when I do have a strong opinion—if, for example, it seems clear that one woman is putting together a way of being that works for her while another is at war with herself or stepping on her own feet—I say so outright rather than letting my biases creep in under the guise of "objectivity."

I expect that people will be surprised by how these women's lives have played out. Real people tend to explode stereotypes; these women have complex and varied lives.

In addition, any effort to draw a life in linear language inevitably distorts it. Life is lived multidimensionally and involves both continuity and change that cannot be told simultaneously.[10] And I am selecting from hours of material what is important to tell. Each of these lives alone could be a book—and that still wouldn't capture a woman in her entirety. I hope here to trace the major routes of identity and see where they lead, recognizing that any such accounting is inevitably only a part of the truth.

Every reader will read the stories I am about to tell with her or his own consciousness, life experience, and values, and may disagree with the way I have characterized some of these women. But that's all right—I am writing this book to invite dialogue, rather than to have the last word.

For my own part, I can find an aspect of myself—a piece of my own experience—in each of the identity states I am writing about. When I graduated from college, I was, like the Guardians we will soon meet, bent on pursuing all my mother's dreams for me. I didn't have a serious period of searching until my mid-twenties and I explored intensely through a rocky time. Then I chose a course on my own terms, and spent a number of halcyon years clear on my goals and realizing them. After my path exploded in my early thirties, I felt all was lost, and I then drifted for many years. Now I am more organized and settled once again, but the potential to reconsider and redo my life is ever present. I write, then, from the capacity to take the point of view of the women in all the groups that I write about. I hope I succeed in honoring them all.

Meanwhile the indefiniteness remains, and the limits of variation are really much wider than any one would imagine from the sameness of women's coiffure and the favourite love-stories in prose and verse.

George Eliot, Middlemarch

2 CAST OF CHARACTERS
The Women of the Study

The women of this study were born at midcentury. They entered college just as the social debate about roles for women was nearing its height. Raised in "traditional" homes and set free in a world of possibility, coming of age in a society that was rapidly restructuring its ideas of what it meant to be a woman, they were pioneers. They grew up as the culture was waking up to its restrictiveness toward women. They would not be imprisoned in doll's houses. Instead, their struggle was with emerging freedom, what to do and be in the presence of choice, in full recognition that that choice was bounded by their experience of their own histories.

I chose the women I have studied at random. When they were seniors in college, back in 1972, I went to four different colleges and universities and drew every fiftieth or every hundredth name from the roster of students and invited them to participate, offering them a few dollars for their trouble. I wanted a group who would represent the range of women who were then in college. Because I wasn't trying to target the most highly motivated women or those who would be most likely to succeed, I did not search the elite colleges. I chose both private and public institutions that spanned the middle range. Nor was I in pursuit of deviants or women who came to professional attention because of psychological problems. I was actually wondering about what more "ordinary" educated women might be making of their lives, how the world might look to those who had not been identified as special in any particular way.[1]

I was in search of diversity, and diversity I found. Some of the women who became part of this group were raised on farms or in small towns. Others grew up in large cities or suburbs. Many came from families in which they were the first to attend college; others had privileged backgrounds and highly educated parents. Some were from families that emphasized a strong ethnic identity—Iranian or Italian or Jewish. Others felt themselves less differentiated, more blended into an "American" mainstream. Some were devoutly religious; others not at all.

The college world these women entered comprised these disparate origins. Although the women of my study never met one another, they represented the social differences each encountered on campus. Learning from one another, comparing backgrounds and basic assumptions, was often more lasting in its effects than what took place in their courses. Together they would explore possibility. Individually, each would make the decisions that would sculpt her own future.

My own earliest memories of college were about encountering people who were so different from me that I hadn't imagined that such people existed. Inevitably, I took this as an invitation to reconsider my own characteristics. The girls (and in those days it was still acceptable to say "girls") on my dorm floor thought I had a funny accent. I never knew I *had* an accent, but I promptly learned to get rid of it. People thought differently from how it had seemed to me that "most people" thought. All the things I had learned were "right" and "acceptable" were now open to question. And this sense of eyes opening is the experience I heard reflected in most of the college women I interviewed. As Debbie put it when she was 21, "The summer before I came to college, I hung around this corner all summer. This was life to me. What did I know? Then I came to college, and there were all these people who came from all different places; and there were really rich people and smart people and freaky people and people who didn't believe in God, and there were so many things—drugs, sex, hippies. It was all very confusing."

The group of women I followed includes people raised as Catholics, Protestants, Jews, and some with no religious affiliation.[2] All grew up in intact families, except for two whose fathers died when they were teenagers. Only one had a mother who had graduated from college. None of their mothers worked while they were young. All had mothers who had assumed that their own lives would be spent as housewives and mothers, although some eventually sought employment after their children were grown or because of economic necessity. These were daughters of the "traditional" fifties. Most were raised in large families, with at least two siblings. Many had four or five brothers and sisters, one as many as ten.

Only a third of these women had fathers who had attended college. Most were raised in middle-class families where their fathers were barbers, electricians, service station managers, or businessmen—blue-collar or lower-level white-collar workers. Several had professional fathers, fathers who were lawyers or high school teachers or ran successful businesses, and these grew up in upper-middle-class affluent homes. More than half of these women attended state universities and many were either paying their own way or significantly contributing to their support while in college. A few women at the private and hence, more expensive, college had scholarships. Economically, this was a "mainstream" group, middle-class on average, with a few women representing the extremes of privilege and financial struggle.

Three were daughters of immigrants and many more had immigrant grandparents. Most had parents who were mainly interested in having them marry well and expected that college would aid in this goal. Several had parents who thought it advisable for women to have marketable skills "just in case." Few had parents with specific occupational hopes for their daughters as they might have had for their sons.

Some of these women came to college because they wanted a career, even if they phrased this hope only as a wish to "do something" of consequence. Most of those who had well-defined goals were seeking careers in teaching, a job familiar to and customary for bright women. The others were less certain about a career vision, hopeful of something interesting capturing their imagination. Many came because going to college had become the norm for academically successful girls in the communities where they were raised. Others were in college to fulfill their parents' dream of having at least one child finish college. Two came to college despite having parents who believed that education was wasted on a girl and refused to support them. As a group, these women entered their college years with very different expectations and goals—some eager, some reluctant, some merely curious, some because they didn't know what else to do.

Graduating from college in 1972, they had lived their adolescence in the turbulent "cultural sixties" (which lasted until 1973). The availability of drugs and sex marked the distinctiveness of their generation from the ones before and raised a wall of incomprehension between them and their parents. In the year they graduated, the media were revolutionizing how people regarded their world through such groundbreaking films as *A Clockwork Orange* and *Sunday Bloody Sunday*.

"Make love, not war" was a banner slogan and *Oh! Calcutta* was on Broadway, but most of these women had been raised to value virginity until marriage. The availability of "the pill" had engendered a revolution in sexual standards, but, as they took their diplomas, *Roe v. Wade* was still a year away. The music of the times spoke to them of states of euphoria—drug-induced and sexual. College students listened to John Denver and Jefferson Airplane while their parents still bought records by Perry Como and Henry Mancini. Everyone, it seems, watched *All in the Family* on television.

The late sixties and early seventies were, above all, anti-authoritarian times. All authority was being questioned—the authority of the government to wage an increasingly unpopular war in Vietnam, the authority of the university to regulate student lives *in loco parentis* or impose requirements of study, the authority of the Catholic Church to decide about birth control—just about any kind of authority that had been respected when these women were children. This was a heady generation whose vocal leaders were arrogantly bent on remaking the world. And these were the days when college students talked about not trusting anyone over 30.

But none of the women I interviewed were leaders in campus politics. They were in college more quietly and less visibly. What filtered down to them in the social climate was an attitude of questioning the past and idealizing the future. Talk was utopian—all things seemed possible. It was the Age of Aquarius; the spirit was one of renewal. The mood was a restless impulse to improve on the injustice and rigidities of the past.

The civil rights movement had blossomed into a strong anti-racist sentiment on college campuses and spearheaded a general critique of society. Fraternities and sororities were held in contempt for their exclusiveness and class-consciousness and were rapidly disappearing from college life. Values of inclusion and nondiscrimination made a profound, liberalizing impression. Often, these young women came home from their college world filled with anti-war and anti-racist sentiments that clashed with the patriotic and prejudiced values of their families. Many told me of arguments with their parents, who increasingly appeared to them to be bigoted or hopelessly conservative in their values. They were quick to unlearn and resist the tendency of their families to "stereotype" or degrade black people, Jews, or other minorities. Some dated men of groups their parents despised, in part as a way of asserting their more inclusive values. Social pressure on the campus was to respect everyone. Their ideologies were largely interpersonal, concerned with how people ought to be treated.

Despite the ferment of those years, most were not politically involved (which was true of the majority of students at that time). Although they were all aware of the anti-war demonstrations, student strikes, sit-ins, and marches, few took part. They were more focused on their studies, on their relationships, on their immediate concerns. Overall, the women I interviewed were a rather conventional group. Many felt daring just to be choosing among fairly prosaic alternatives, but the idea of a woman plotting her own life was itself a kind of coup. Only a few seemed to be "hippies." Their parents may have regarded them as rebellious because of the way they looked. The changed standards of "beauty" put them at odds with their mothers, who couldn't understand why they preferred jeans to nice dresses or wore their hair long and straight and refused makeup.

By the time these women graduated, it seemed to be common wisdom that a woman could not find fulfillment in the traditional female role, but no one could really imagine what the family of the future might look like. A *New York Times* article at the beginning of 1972 presented an interview with sociologist William Goode who was speaking for the social necessity of more women in high management. The tone of the interlocutor's questions was one of puzzlement—Who was going to manage the family? How could women do both?

The women of my study came of age in a time of ferment and were bridging two worlds. Most remained clearly products of their families, but had become more liberal in their attitudes and identifiably a part of their generation in the way they looked. In going to college, nearly all had taken a step away from their mothers' paths. When I interviewed them as college seniors, all imagined that they would find a way to combine some sort of career with having a family. Their wish to work was less from ideology than from a desire to use their abilities and not be bored. "I don't want to just sit at home," many told me. Most thought that they would probably marry shortly after college, work for a time, stop work to have children, and then return to work after their children were of school age. This seemed the generic fantasy that their generation fashioned. At age 21, however, most thought of having children as something they would definitely do, but far in the future, too far to really think about. They hadn't yet given any concrete thought to how they would combine being mothers and career women and, in general, neither had the larger society. The phrase "quality time" had not yet been coined. It all felt vague. They hadn't really questioned their assumption that of course they would marry and have children "eventually"—this seemed to them part of the natural stream of life. They were thinking about what they would like to "do," meaning work, being on their own for a time, financially independent and free of the pressures of school. Their dreams were to get their own apartments, a nice car, and perhaps travel. Only five had plans to go to graduate school immediately after college, although some thought they might seek further schooling later. Their goals were largely for the short term—what they would do for the years immediately after college, leaving the rest to be decided down the road. Envisioning the "rest of their lives," they imagined that their future would play out much like their mothers except that they would also work, at least for some significant part of their lives.

Few of the women in my study were actively involved in the women's movement, although they were all aware of it and had heard the themes of feminist ideology. For them, discussion of the issues raised by feminists of the time emerged in questions about who should pay for dates, whether men should hold doors open for women, and whether or not they ought to do "wifely" things for their boyfriends. Ideas about full equality for women were just emerging. Many of these women resisted, for example, the idea of seeing a woman doctor for fear they were somehow not "as good" as male doctors, but at the same time this thought made them uncomfortable. They were just beginning to question some of the gendered attitudes so deeply ingrained in them. And the crux of the debate at that time still centered around whether or not women were inferior to men. (One could, for example, in those years say with impunity that a woman could not do this or that job because "What if she had her period?") Many still worried about surpassing a boyfriend for fear of "hurting his ego," but most were working their way around to feeling that that was something "he'd have to deal with," taking their chances on being rejected.

These women, then, were feeling their way through changing times and were most aware of the waves of social and political transformation when these currents directly affected their daily doings. If there was one political idea that united them, it was the idea of choice—that people, especially women, should have the right to choose, that no one should be kept from doing what one wished and was able to do because of race, class, or gender. Personally, they balked at whatever seemed to limit them. Conformity was "out" and individuality was "in." The "human potential" movement had its effects in a prevailing ideology of self-realization. Many kept on the walls of their rooms the Fritz Perls poster that decorated the times—a poster proclaiming, "I am not in this world to live up to your expectations. And you are not here to live up to mine. I am I and you are you and if we find each other it's beautiful."

None of these women were crusaders. None had a cause or were out personally to remake the world, although many were highly critical of the world they found themselves in. They struggled to articulate themselves with the people around them. They wanted to have friends who were loyal and compatible, and most did. They agonized over their relationships with men, wanting a partner and worrying over the details of real relationships—how they wanted to be treated, how they wished to be loved. As college ended, several were engaged and one was married. And many were eagerly looking for the "right person" to be a partner, hoping to marry as soon as such a person could be found. Others regarded marriage as something they would likely do later in their twenties, after they had more experience.

Overall, these women were optimistic about their future, although few could imagine even the faintest outline of how their lives might look ten years later. Most had a dim vision of themselves married and working and perhaps having children, but the image was shrouded in mist. At the threshold of their adulthood, they were building flexibility into their identities by leaving some options at least partially open, preparing themselves for what might come. They varied, one from another, in how they anticipated using their freedom to choose—and the differences in how they chose or didn't choose are what I will explore in this book.

TWELVE YEARS LATER: IN THEIR THIRTIES IN THE 1980S

When I found these women again in 1983, they were 33 years old,[3] and they were an even more diverse group, now living in fourteen different states, Maine to California, and one foreign country. All but one were working in paid jobs at least part-time. While all had thought as college seniors that they would be married in ten years, only slightly more than half were. Most who married by age 33 did so in the first three years after college. A few had divorced and remarried.[4] Although all had thought they would most likely have children by their early thirties, only eight were mothers. Half of these had two children already; the others had one and were planning another. If we were to speak of a pattern common to them at age 33, it would be that they were working in some occupation and either thinking about getting married or thinking about having children. But identifying a common pattern is somewhat misleading because these women were already a highly varied group who were creating very different lives. They had been offered choice by their social world and they were availing themselves of it.

In part because of the times—the Reagan era—and in part because of their own life stage, these women were in an acquisitive phase of their development. In the larger culture, "hippies" had been replaced by "yuppies," a new word of the early eighties. The radical voices of the sixties had been stilled in the rush for material success. In 1983, *In Search of Excellence* was the bestselling book and *The Big Chill* was already waxing nostalgic for the idealism of these women's adolescence. People had turned inward. The women I had known as college seniors were now focused on buying, maintaining, restoring, or upgrading their housing. Concerned about "lifestyle," a popular word of that age, they desired the material things that would give them a good life. The health consciousness of the times led them to spend more of their energy being concerned about diet and more time on exercise. Some still smoked, drank, and occasionally got high on pot. All had found some avocation—gardening, tennis, needlepoint. Many had traveled abroad.

By 1983, when I met them again, the image of Superwoman was firmly established in the public mind. These women were aware that newly wrought ideals of success for educated women expected them to "do it all." No longer a matter of breaking through barriers and proving that women *could* balance all the roles, "having it all" began to seem the mode. Consequently, these women had to articulate their personal life designs in this highly altered context.

Those who were not married were in search of partners yet simultaneously preparing themselves mentally for the possibility of single life. Those who didn't have children were struggling with the sense that time was beginning to run out; they would soon have to decide to conceive or, if they were having difficulty conceiving, adopt. (At that time, 35 was considered "old" for motherhood. The widespread phenomena of 40-year-old first-time mothers hadn't yet occurred.) Most still imagined that children would be somewhere in their future. Although two said they had decided not to have children, they did this with full awareness that it was a highly reversible decision.

Nearly a third had gone on for further education and received post-baccalaureate degrees and were working in law, medicine, business, or education.[5] The rest had found employment with their bachelor's degrees—as teachers, nurses, physical therapists, or systems analysts. Many were in the business world in various levels of administration or management. Few had plans for further education at this point in their lives, although many had taken specialized courses for certificates or credit related to their jobs. While all these women were relatively settled in their jobs, most felt their lives still very much in the process of being made. But few had higher career aspirations. Most had set limits on how much they wanted to invest in career success. As a group, these women were struggling with how to fit it all in—work, family, partner, friends, exercise, hobbies, reading.

By age 33, most of these women had moved away from the religion of their childhood. They had joined the more secular cast of the larger society. Politically, they remained uninvolved and uncommitted. Many spoke of feeling that they had grown more conservative. Economics, more than anything, had linked them to the political world. As working adults, they were aware of what they were paying in taxes and wondered where it was going. Eschewing the idealism of their younger days, they said they had become more opposed to spending for social welfare and had come to generally dislike government. Although most of these women felt themselves more allied to the philosophy of the Democrats if they could define any political conviction at all, they were more in sympathy with Republican individualist values. Some women, through their work, had become concerned about a specific political issue—educational policy, for example. Or they had come to understand where the funding for their programs came from and recognized that this was an aspect of political decision-making. Asked to name a political issue they felt strongly about, they most commonly mentioned their support for abortion rights, but few had taken an active stand. In general, these women were focused on their immediate concerns and were, if anything, even less politically interested than they had been in college.

Being out in the work world for twelve years, these women were much more attuned to issues regarding women than they had been in college. Most were aware of discrimination against women and many had direct experiences of being paid less than a man doing identical work or being given less responsibility or less acknowledgment for their skills. For them, women's issues felt real rather than theoretical, but they had found no venue or organization for complaint. Many protested on an individual level if they could; many more suffered silently.

For most, college felt emotionally very far away. Few thought that their college experience had any lasting effect on their lives and only a few retained friends from their college years. Their feeling was that college had been a life stage, an episode, a time in which they had gained some emotional and physical independence from their parents; in their developing narratives of their lives, real life had begun after that.

At this point, these women had grown more distinctive from each other. Where ten years before, I could discriminate them mainly in terms of their backgrounds and their aspirations, in their thirties, they distinguished themselves more in terms of what they were each creating in their lives. Andrea, for example, was a doctor, married, probably not going to have children. Natalie was working as a technical writer for a corporation, hoping to find a man to marry, intrigued by a parrot she enjoyed caring for. Helen had two children but continued her teaching career. And so on for each one. These were women who had fashioned identities for themselves, but all were still very much works in process, with important decisions waiting ahead. All had built a life structure by this age, more or less tentatively. Those with children were the most settled and certain; the others by and large felt they could revise as they wished. And most had a clearer idea of what their lives might be ten years later than they had had in college.

TWENTY-TWO YEARS LATER: IN THEIR FORTIES IN THE 1990S

In the next ten years, fate played more of a role than it had before. Illnesses of those they loved, infertility, economic vagaries, personnel reorganizations in their workplaces, special needs of children—these were elements many women had to integrate into their evolving identities. At this point, my group of women was more settled, more recognizably people who knew who they were. They had grown firmer, and they felt less likely to change. The contrast between who they were outwardly at age 21 and age 33 was much greater than the shift between age 33 and 43. Changes from 33 to 43 were more subtle and internal, and my participants were more likely to emphasize the continuity despite the changes. Interestingly, most of these women remembered our interview at age 33 but had no memory of the one that took place in college. Again, I had the strong sense that, for them, life began in earnest only after graduation.

This group, in 1993, were now living in seventeen states, mostly in suburbs or small towns. Few had the highly urbanized lives that the media so often depict.

At age 43, all but three were in marriages or committed relationships, including one who had "come out" as a lesbian and was living with a long-term partner.[6] More of them had children in the intervening ten years. By now, half were mothers.[7] Even though so many were raised in large families, the majority had two children and no one had more than three. Of the heterosexual nonmothers married or living with long-term partners, half of these had made clear decisions not to have children. The others remain uncertain or confused over this issue, still thinking "it might happen" or "we might adopt."

All but three women are employed outside their homes and one of these is in graduate school. Only two, at midlife, are full-time homemaker/mothers, and these women have a variety of volunteer activities. Some women have had outstanding professional success; others have merely "worked." Some at midlife are anticipating retirement; others are still casting about trying to find a career direction that suits them.

These women have lived through a psychologizing age. They have come to view themselves through the popular clichés of our times—women as victim, dysfunctional families, the inner child. Two of them in their age 43 interview told me about having been sexually abused as children, something they could not have spoken about before. Many had been physically abused as children, but had only recently come to regard it in that way—they had previously thought of themselves as having been spanked—wasn't everyone?

The culture itself was leading women to rethink their early histories and how it may have affected them. Women of this age (both developmental age and cultural age) were also much more attuned to issues of sexual harassment in their workplaces, with several now mentioning it as a problem they were taking seriously. A few identified themselves with the women's movement. Most had not considered themselves feminists at any time in their lives, although nearly all remain passionately committed to the idea of equality and choice for women.

By this age, most had acquired the things of life they felt they needed and the majority said that they were financially secure. Material concerns seemed to claim less of their interest than they had at age 33. Worry about diet continued: many were dissatisfied with their weight. All were engaged in regular sport or exercise, or felt guilty that they weren't. Drugs were gone from this group, and most drank no more than an occasional social glass of wine. All who had been smokers had quit. Most were living fairly circumscribed lives of routine and habit. A third had traveled abroad by this time, expanding their sense of the world. Most of these women continued to enjoy reading, although many bemoaned their lack of time for it. Overall, these women were busy, their lives were full. Their identities had encompassed a variety of interests and investments, and they continued to regard the future with optimism and hope. All of them counted themselves as happy, despite their individual and specific discontents.

The majority of these women, at age 43, feel the anguish of deciding an identity now behind them. They are following a life path and expect to stay, with some modifications, pretty much as they are. Having composed a life, they are living what they created in relative contentment. But they differ enormously, one from the other, and the rest of this book will explore those differences.

What continues to unite these women as a group is their common belief in choice. They bristle at the idea of coercion of any sort—people, they believe, especially women, ought to be free to choose their own way on their own terms. They eschew categorical statements, staunch in their refusal to impose their values on anyone else. These women live lives they chose, taking advantage of the new freedoms to have a career or not, to marry or not, to have children or not. They made their own decisions about what it means to be a woman in this world. This book examines how they came to the choices they made and how they revised them along the way.

But before exploring the different pathways these women took as they created an identity, I want to reconsider the question of who they may "represent." I couldn't, of course, foresee or control who would end up in this group I have been following. These were women I chose quite at random. Many familiar life configurations *are* represented here—married women with careers and children predominate, followed by married women with careers and no children. There are no single mothers—this is a category very much present among this age group in the larger society but not accounted for here. There are also no artists, no media people, no financiers, and no women who have started their own retail businesses—among other absences.

Each woman in our society has her own unique story to tell and "my group" is only a sampling from the pool of possible stories. Although there is no racial diversity, there is a wide range of social class origins. If there is any bias in the sampling that I know about, it would be in the direction of ethnicity—I have studied more women of strong ethnic background (i.e., they identify their families of origin as Italian or Irish or Greek) than might have been expected by chance. This is a result of women moving around and changing their names when they marry. Originally, I began with sixty women; I have been able to stay in contact with thirty. When I lost them over the years, I had to hunt them by their maiden names in the cities and towns where they grew up. Those with unusual last names were easier to find. The "Smiths" and "Johnsons" vanished into the crowd.

I think that these women, as a group, portray the dilemmas of women of this age—daughters of tradition, the first women of choice, pioneers or stalwarts in a time when new identities were possibile for women. I find a bit of myself in each one of them. I hope my readers will have a similar experience.

Strange that some of us, with quick alternative vision, see beyond our infatuations, and even while we rave on the heights, behold the wide plain where our persistent self pauses and awaits us.

George Eliot, Middlemarch

3 IDENTITY

Identity is the ultimate act of creativity—it is what we make of ourselves. In forming and sustaining our identity, we build a bridge between who we feel ourselves to be internally and who we are recognized as being by our social world. When we have a secure sense of our identity, we take ourselves for granted as being who we are. We feel at home in ourselves and in our world, and have an inner experience of coherence and purpose.

The psychologist Erik Erikson brought this central aspect of our existence to our attention, and his ideas about the "identity crisis" have resonated deeply in Western culture.[1] Identity represents knowing who we are in the context of all that we might be. The sense of crisis is the experience of questioning what we have taken as a given: "I have always been like this, but perhaps I could still be otherwise. I could make and live out different choices."

Most people would become confused and confounded if asked what their identity is. Identity emerges; it is greater than the sum of its parts—much like a cake is the product of its ingredients and not a simple compound. Although composed of discrete, conscious elements, identity is bound and organized internally and unconsciously and cannot be easily contained in words. In forming a core of who we "are," identity weaves together all the aspects of ourselves and our various locations of ourselves with others and with the larger society. What we connect ourselves to feels part of ourselves; the world is imbued with self: *my* project, *my* husband, *my* cause. Identity also excludes all the things we are not (and often it is easier to identify ourselves by naming what we are not). Usually, we include in our identity an economic function in society, a set of meanings we have for others, a place in a sequence of generations, and a set of beliefs and values. We may also have an unusual genetic makeup, an atypical early history or family background, an eccentric temperament or psychological structure, or we may have special abilities or disabilities. Any of these may channel our lives in one way and not another.

The *experience* of identity is one of meaningful continuity over time and place. We recognize more and more what it means to be who we are, rather than someone else. "To be adult," Erikson said, "means among other things to see one's own life in continuous perspective, both in retrospect and in prospect."[2] Identity, then, proclaims our sameness-as-ourselves in containing our life story, but identity also evolves and changes over time as we grow. It is, therefore, our continuity in the process of revision.

People, of course, grow within a culture. Identity is what we make of ourselves within a society that is making something of us. Identity "makes sense" only within the context of a particular social and historical time.

Societies limit what is possible for the individual. We might question why things are the way they are, but there are boundaries imposed by our society on the desires and ambitions we might realize and on the choices we might make. The more open the society, the more choices possible.

In modern Western society, there is much latitude in how we might earn our living, how we construct our relationships with others, what we may believe spiritually and politically, how we spend discretionary time, and how we care for our physical well-being. We differ from one another in how we arrange these elements of our lives, to what we give priority, and how we interpret what we have created. Some people do all this without giving it much thought, experiencing their identities as "natural," as givens, as lives unfolding according to inevitability, a plan constructed elsewhere. Others are self-conscious about who they are, analyzing their choices, carefully considering a plethora of possibilities, envisioning alternate selves.

Crisis in identity can be spurred either by inner change or social dislocation. We might arrive at periods in our lives where our past ways of being feel no longer gratifying, and we may then cast about for means of transformation. Or social change may lead us to have to rearticulate ourselves in the social world—we can no longer maintain our customary position in relation to others by being just as we have always been. What is acceptable and valued in one place and time may be scorned in another.

When we move about our world harmoniously, taking ourselves and our meaning to others for granted, identity functions as a silent gatekeeper. We are who we are and occupy ourselves with being rather than with creating ourselves. Erikson has said that we are most aware of our identity when we are just about to make its acquaintance. Living our identities is much like breathing. We don't have to ask ourselves each morning who we are. We simply are. As life progresses, we may add new elements and find room for them in the mixture. We may discard others through disuse. Identity is never fixed; it continually evolves. But something in it stays constant; even when we change, we are recognizably who we have always been. Identity links the past, the present, and the social world into a narrative that makes sense. It embodies both change and continuity.

As I track the identities of the women I have followed for twenty years, I am impressed by how the woman of 43 is unmistakably like the young woman of 21, yet very different. If I were to scramble the tapes and remove all identifying information, a thoughtful listener would still be able to match them up. It is also true, however, that some women have changed more than others.

"WHO ARE YOU?" SAID THE CATERPILLAR

When we feel we are "getting to know" someone, we are in the process of becoming aware of another's identity. What matters to you? What goals do you pursue? How do you want others to think of you? What do you believe in? What guides your actions? Whom do you love? What values do you hold dear? Where do you expend your passion? What causes you pain? These are the central questions of knowing another and knowing ourselves—the questions of identity.

We know ourselves both through our shared identities and our distinctiveness from others. We identify ourselves with others who share our goals or values and thereby feel affirmed in who we are. But we also know ourselves through contrasting ourselves with others, feeling the edges of our individuality in noting what so uniquely belongs to us.

Each of us confronts a different challenge in fashioning our identity. We begin with different pieces, different experiences and realities. Natural talents, physical attractiveness, social privilege, temperament, social ease, physical limitations, and traumatic early experiences—all these are building blocks that we must fit into the design. Each of us has been offered different puzzle pieces with which we must assemble a complete picture. We must each make something of ourselves. If we don't, our society will provide us an identity from the bag of deviant labels it has for people who don't create it for themselves.

Identity, however, is complex and cannot be stated simply. We are not the same in all regions of our lives, and how we make meaning may change across situations or over time. Identity is what integrates our own diversity, gives meaning to the disparate parts of ourselves, and relates them to one another. Identity is how we interpret our own existence and understand who we are in our world. I am a woman, but my identity as a woman is my unique way of being a woman in the culture in which I live. And so on with other aspects of my (or your) identity.

IDENTITY AND SOCIETY

Society, in making certain ways of being possible and others impossible or very difficult, is a powerful agent in shaping identity. "Cultures," say Shotter and Gergen (1989), "lay out an array of enabling potentials and also establish a set of constraining boundaries beyond which selves cannot be easily made" (p. ix). On the other hand, we, as a society, create these enabling potentials and boundaries and thereby shape the individuals who will compose our social world. We create them and we can change them. We have a vested interest in what kinds of identity we make possible. When we worry together about social influence, we are concerned with what sort of individuals our social conditions are likely to foster. We ask, for example, what it means to have so much violence on TV? What kinds of people will this make in the future? Or we wonder about changes in family structure. What will individual identities look like if family attachment erodes as a keystone of social life? What we create together as a society forms the framework for identity for the next generation.

Although modern Western industrial society embraces individualistic values, upholding the ideals of individual self-determination and the right to self-definition, we must have something in common with one another, some shared beliefs, goals, and attitudes in order to have a society at all. We cannot escape being affected by what each of us chooses. We are bound together, and the identities of each individual both limit and empower the identities of others.

While the context of identity is, in part, the larger culture, for each particular person, identity is understood, evaluated, and transmuted by the people around her—family, friends, colleagues, neighbors, and so on. Social influence occurs in thousands of ways, some at a general level, such as the media, but others closer to home, through people and experiences in one's immediate world. A chance conversation with an old friend can have profound impact on identity. Recognizing that someone else—someone we know and accept—is taking a risk or living a dream that we desire for ourselves can give us permission to do what we had been afraid to do. These local, personal influences are largely responsible for the rapid shift in our society's ideas about how women might live in our society. Identity, then, is not just a private, individual matter. Instead, it is a complex negotiation between the person and a society.

IDENTITY AND WOMEN

Nowhere in the modern age has the issue of identity been more vexing than in our society's confusion over the roles it is willing to allot to women. Women born after World War II spent their girlhoods in a world where women's possibilities were sharply defined and clearly delimited and seemed to have been that way since history began. A woman's mission was to marry and raise children, though she might also be a teacher or a nurse before having children or after her children were grown. Her social place and value were defined by her husband, and young girls dreamed of one day becoming "Mrs. Someone." The idea of a woman retaining her name, symbolically maintaining her own selfhood, was not to emerge until women of this (my) generation were in their late adolescence in the late 1960s. Erikson, in 1968, mindful of the social limits imposed on women, said, "I think that much of a young woman's identity is already defined in her kind of attractiveness and in the selective nature of her search for the man (or men) by whom she wishes to be sought."[3]

That identity for women derives from marriage was a theme pervading the literature of the times—and of previous times as well. In most novels, the path to marriage is the only real drama in a woman's life, the only realm of decision, of possibility, of surprise. The cultural narrative of women's lives, told in literature, was a story of growth, events, and choices leading to marriage. Carolyn Heilbrun, in her book, *Writing a Woman's Life,* discusses the way in which the courtship plot has dominated literary portrayal of women: "The woman must entrap the man to ensure herself a center for her life. The rest is aging and regret."[4]

But women of the postwar generation could extend this plot, could create lives beyond marriage, aging, and regret. These women came of age in a time of social rearrangement about what was expected of or permissible for women. They came of age in a society that was in the throes of beginning to take women seriously, as productive workers, voters with independent minds, forces within the social order, as people with a right to self-fulfillment. The society began to wonder whether women might be equivalent to men, with similar needs and deserving of equal rewards and recognition. Instead of having to resign themselves to constricted, narrow options, the women of this generation, led by the rising chorus of feminism, were prepared to demand that locked doors be opened to them.

PSYCHOLOGY AND WOMAN

Psychology, the intellectual discipline that explores—and shapes—our understanding of human life, also had to come to terms with a revolution in how it might regard women. Most psychological studies before 1970 merely disregarded women altogether or, with a wave of the hand, assumed that women were probably pretty much like men in terms of universal psychological principles. At least, the "laws" of human behavior that psychology adduced were derived from studies of men and applied to "people."

But women have always constructed their identities in different phrasing from men and, except for Erikson's comment that women readied themselves for the men they wished to be sought by, on this topic psychology was largely silent. The early efforts of psychologists to investigate identity in women, which began in the 1970s, tended to try to find "male" patterns in women or at least to discover women who were sufficiently "masculine" in their orientation that they would behave on psychological tests much like men did. Only in the 1980s did psychology begin to embrace the fact that women have a definable identity, but that they construct this identity in relational terms, different from men, but not simply as selves defined by husbands or children. Women construct themselves in the voice of care and of connection, to use psychologist Carol Gilligan's words. This led to the quest for a new vocabulary for women's identity, an effort to find ways of thinking about women that were beyond the "marriage plot," but did not merely translate women into the familiar lexicon of the male sense of self.

Identity expresses both our separateness from others (who we are within our individuality) and our ways of connecting ourselves to others (who and how we are with other people). In women, identity tends to be phrased more in relational, pattern-building terms than in the language of separateness.[5] A woman forms her sense of herself through connections with others—at home, at work, and in her values and beliefs. Identity in women is more rooted in "being" than in "doing," and a woman's life story is often ·centered on how she experiences herself, or wishes to experience herself, with others. Love is a way of delineating the self, not of losing the self, as many have wrongly concluded.

· How a woman comes to define her identity is a process of articulating herself with others, bridging what feels inner and necessary with what opportunities she has for expressing herself in interaction. With the wider social choices available to women after 1970, a woman had the task of finding her place in a more complex way than ever before. She could marry, but how she defined her marriage was open to vast possibility. She could work in the field of her choice, in domains that had been closed just years before, and she was challenged to take up these roles in her own voice. She could have children or not and, if she had children, she had to mother in a way quite different from the way in which her mother had. She could continue her professional ambitions and still raise a family. Spirituality and religion became matters of choice rather than acceptance of authority, and the defining of ideology became both more pressing and more diffuse than it had ever been. In all these spheres, a woman had the opportunity to locate herself, to define herself in ways newly available, often with no models to guide her.

WOMEN AND CHOICE

Some women embraced this opportunity for choice and tried to expand the framework in which they were raised in order to allow for greater self-expression. Others tended to take things pretty much as they found them, hoping only to "fit in." Still others tried to burst through whatever structure had contained them as girls, to experiment with themselves and try to create new selves or new worlds. Some women became heroines of their own lives, to paraphrase Dickens; others allowed circumstance or other people to fill that station.

⋅ *How* identity is formed determines its nature as much or more than the particular roles or values we may include. Rita and Jean, for example, may both be 40-year-old working mothers, and if this is all we are to know about them, we may regard them as similar. But if we also know that Rita went through a long process of choice and change before deciding to become an actress and delayed having children until she was professionally established, we understand that she is quite different from Jean who became a nurse without really thinking about it and had her children within a year of her marriage after college. These differences in the *process* of choosing an identity have been at the center of my study. How does a woman come to be who she is—with what consideration, what anguish, what commitment, and with what regret? What does she leave aside and relinquish and how does she decide to do this? How does a woman gather the reins of her life?

PATHWAYS TO IDENTITY

"I didn't have my adolescence until my late twenties," said Grace, one of the women I have been interviewing, "not until after my divorce. After that, I became a whole different person." Grace is reflecting on how she has changed, the way in which her identity has evolved, and she is noting that her progression to identity seems to her different from what she assumes has been true for most people. People differ in whether and how they experiment with and organize their sense of identity—and this itself changes with time and development.

· Initially, identity is ascribed to each of us. Babies are "identified" immediately—"she looks like your family"; "she has a bad temper just like my mother"; and so on. We are born to a certain family in a given social time, to a social class, a race and, of course, to a gender. In our families we learn what it is acceptable to do or to believe, we are given a religious framework and a set of values that form our way of viewing the world. This is the identity we carry through childhood into adolescence.

Modern industrialized societies that make available a variety of adult roles also allow young people a period in which they are granted permission to rework the identities ascribed to them through childhood. Erikson called this period a "moratorium," a time out for an "identity crisis" in which the young person is encouraged to become aware that familiar childhood ways of being and believing are not the only ones possible. With this sense of "I could be different," the young person tries out new possibilities, does some things she (or he) might never have imagined doing before, and, in general, explores a range of possible selves. But this phase has a limit, and, at a certain point, the society indicates its readiness to "identify" a person, to take her seriously as being who she has chosen to be. The individual is then expected to declare herself by adopting particular ways of being and believing—in short, to commit herself to an identity.

The young person envisions, considers, explores, and then chooses. Identity commitments are sometimes made consciously with a lot of thought; at other times, they seem to "creep up" on the person who comes to take seriously aspects of herself that she thought she was just playing at. Who she chooses as friends, what interests she pursues, how hard she studies, whether she takes drugs or plays the flute or wins at tennis—all these might become significant elements of her identity.

But there are pitfalls and byways in this process. Some people are afraid to relinquish their childhood certainty about things; they strive to stay as much as possible the same as they have always been. Others are awash in choice, and no matter how much significant people in their life pressure them, they cannot commit themselves to a way of being.

I build on the work of psychologist James Marcia who found a way to study Erikson's theory of identity formation as a process that different people undertake in different ways. He reasoned that we could determine how far late adolescents have come in the course of their identity development by investigating whether or not they have experienced a period of exploration and whether or not they have made firm identity commitments. By interviewing late adolescents about their decision-making with regard to occupational choice, religious and political beliefs, and concerns about relationships, psychologists who followed his method could divide people into four distinct groups that placed them in one track or another along the path to identity formation:

Exploration

		Yes	No
Commitment	Yes	Pathmakers	Guardians
	No	Searchers	Drifters

Guardians have made identity commitments without a sense of choice, carrying forward the plans for their life mapped out in childhood or designed by their parents. They are likely to feel, "This is how I am because it's how I was raised or how I've always been."

Pathmakers are people who have experienced a period of exploration or crisis and then made identity commitments on their own terms. Their orientation to their identity is, "I've tried out some things, and this is what makes most sense for me."

Searchers are still in an active period of struggle or exploration, trying to make choices but not yet having done so. They feel, "I'm not sure about who I am or want to be, but I'm trying to figure it out."

Drifters are without commitments and not struggling to make them, either feeling lost or following impulses of the moment. These people are likely to say, "I don't know what I will do or believe, but it doesn't matter too much right now."

Nearly thirty years of research and hundreds of studies have been conducted on college students using these four groups.[6] They have been found to be groups who can be reliably assessed and groups that share predictable personality characteristics and ways of behaving.

I interviewed the women I have been studying when they were college seniors,[7] a time when the future loomed ahead unwritten, no longer structured by their parents or the academic calendar. This was a time, as Erikson suggests, when the society was exacting choice from them, drawing the curtain on the era of preparation. What will I do next? was a pressing, urgent question. I used Jim Marcia's interview method to determine where they were in forming their identities by asking them about four areas—occupation, religion, politics, and sexual standards—in which they might be deciding, areas central to identity. I evaluated whether they had had a period of exploration in deciding on their goals and values, and whether they had yet made clear choices.[8] Had they considered options and experimented with possibilities for themselves, or had they stayed within the molds cast for them by their families? And, if they had explored, had they made some commitment, choices that would guide their next steps? Or, alternatively, were they leaving their future open to fate, avoiding choice, waiting to see where the currents might take them?

The differences among the four groups—those with and without exploration, those with and without commitment—reflect different ways of dealing with the challenges of adolescence.[9] The four groups represent types or stances, different positions on the path to identity. And women who were following each of these paths had commonalities. Aspects of their personality structure, the deeper regions of their emotional makeup rooted in their early histories, in part determined the pathway they had followed to this point.[10] But the style in which they were approaching identity dilemmas was not fixed forever. I interviewed and classified them at the end of college at an important moment, but I expected that they would continue to change, that their choices were only relatively firm rather than solid and unchangeable. But I didn't know and couldn't predict how they would change as their adulthood unfolded.

The end of college marks the close of the period that our society grants young people to experiment, to play with identity. After that, as Erikson says, society takes the person seriously—and young people feel the pressure of declaring themselves as in pursuit of certain ways of being while relinquishing others. Some of these women felt more ready to take a place than others—and this readiness was in part what distinguished these four groups.[11]

THE FOUR PATHWAYS TO IDENTITY

The *Guardians* knew where they were going without having considered alternatives. Fern, for example, at the end of college, was sure of her goals and beliefs and answered all questions about her plans and her values by referring to how she had been raised. "My parents instilled these ideas in me," or "It's what I've *always* wanted to be when I grew up" were typical Guardian phrases. The Guardians had, as little girls, absorbed the values and attitudes of their families and still held fast to them or, as adolescents, found someone else to cling to who would define what was right for them. Many had childhood occupational dreams; all had strong moral or religious guideposts. Little or none of any of this was ever questioned; the crisis of exploration was avoided. These women leapfrogged over the challenges of adolescence, clutching what was safe and familiar. Moralistic and value-dominated, most of them held to an unassailable sense of what was right and wrong. They regarded the options of the times as threatening to their sense of certainty; they never rebelled or challenged. Reluctant to "leave home" emotionally, they wanted their adult lives, as much as possible, to be a continuation of the warmth and comfort of childhood in their families.

The *Pathmakers,* by contrast, were women who had followed Erikson's progression from exploration into commitment. After making the discovery, during college, that her parents' values and assumptions "were not necessarily the only way to be," Andrea set out to investigate other ways of situating herself in life and found herself wanting to become a kind of woman—a professional woman, a nonreligious woman—that neither she nor her family had ever encountered. Some of the Pathmakers had had intense identity crises; some had only mild, but psychologically significant ones. All, however, had considered some options, tried out alternate ways of being or believing, and then made choices that they intended to be the basis for their adult sense of themselves. They were women who had taken some risks and tried out new ways of experiencing themselves that led them to integrate a stable sense of personal independence and make choices on their own terms. These choices were often formed in the context of important new relationships, but the choices felt self-authored—what I want for myself, what I have designed. These women charted their own course. They had enough inner strength to tolerate crisis and uncertainty and to design their lives to suit themselves. They stood on the threshold of adulthood with a plan, with a template of how they wanted to realize the identity they had sculpted. But, having relinquished childhood certainty, they were often anxious, worried that their plans might not work out, afraid sometimes of their own capacity for change. They had made compromises to achieve closure, but wondered if they hadn't perhaps given away more than was necessary.

Those women who were *Searchers* at the end of college were in the midst of crisis. Uncertain, sometimes intensely confused, they were struggling among possibilities, and were finding it hard to decide which road to take. These are women who fought their families and left their churches to march in anti-war protests, experimented with mind-altering drugs, had sex—and felt guilty about it all. They were critical of society and the obvious roles available to them and wanted something different for themselves—but what? The choices seemed overwhelming. How could they know what was Right? Highly perceptive, lively, and engaging, these women daydreamed of experiencing many things and finding a way of being that felt authentic. Other times, rent by ambivalence, they felt great anxiety about the future. No choice or value seemed completely comfortable, but they were wrestling to make choices nonetheless. Millie, for example, felt herself on a bumpy road and described her experience of searching like this: "It starts when you're little. You think your parents are gods. Then you find out they're only human, but you still believe what they say because they're your parents. I really don't want to hurt my parents, but I've got to live my own life. The more I learn, the more middle of the road I become. I learn that there are two sides of every story and it's hard that way because I like to have the Answers. But it seems like that's the way it's going—that you just can't say that this is right and this is wrong. It's hard to make decisions about things because there are so many avenues to go down."

Many Searchers felt guilty about having forsaken the values of their childhood and fearful that they weren't quite sure what they were doing with themselves. At the end of college, they were still wrestling with choice in the areas of their lives most significant to them. As graduation approached, however, the Searchers were still unable to choose.

The women I classified as *Drifters* were women who were neither in crisis nor had they made commitments. They were like leaves blown by the wind, living each day, sometimes happily, sometimes despairingly, but they tried to ignore the approach of the future. There were many different kinds of women in this group—no one person exemplifies it—but what they had in common was that they avoided decision-making. The daily choices they made were choices of the moment, and they didn't require themselves to be consistent or to make sense. Asked about her future, Debbie said offhandedly with a shrug, "When the time comes, I'll do something." Many had occupational dreams that lasted for a short time only to disappear until another might take its place; their relationships seemed equally unpredictable. Their values or standards shifted with each situation. They seemed to feel they would "go with the flow" wherever the flow might take them. When I got to know the Drifters better as college seniors, I found that many of these women had early inner conflicts that made it difficult to grapple with the developmentally more advanced issues of identity. While a few were simply "free spirits" who were exploring intensely and refusing to tie themselves to any post, others were preoccupied with unresolved emotional problems that showed themselves in impulsivity, depression, or personality fragmentation.[12] As a group, the Drifters were swept along, sometimes enjoying themselves, sometimes in great pain, but they thought of the future as something that would organize itself when the time came.

No categorizing system, of course, can contain everyone. People always more or less fit into any grouping. These four groups represented an effort to sort people based on their ability to tolerate uncertainty and change, their readiness to imagine possibilities for themselves, their ability to use what they gained from their families without being enslaved to it, and their capacity for commitment at the end of college. When other colleagues listened to the tapes, we were able to agree about where each woman best fit, so this seemed to be a reliable as well as a meaningful form of classification.[13]

These categories were designed to be descriptive rather than evaluative. Each style has both its advantages and its costs. The *Guardians,* for example, in their steadfastness can be regarded as either loyal or rigid, the *Pathmakers* as independent or prematurely certain of themselves. The *Searchers,* depending on one's point of view, can seem flexible and philosophical or anxious and indecisive. Similarly, one might respond to the *Drifters* as creative and free-spirited or irresponsible and disaffected. I mean only to name their characteristics and to explore what awaits the women who follow each path. I am not suggesting that one path is necessarily better or worse than another.

IDENTITY AND REVISION

These four groups represent gateways to adulthood. Where a woman was on the path to identity determined how she would enter her adult life and this, in turn, would influence how the next chapters of her life might be written. The pathway she was following at the end of college served as a portal to the future, a way of entering adulthood, with conviction and direction, with openness and flexibility, or with confusion and tentativeness.

Although Erikson showed that identity is the central task of late adolescence, he did not suggest that identity, once formed, is inscribed in stone or, if not formed in adolescence, never will be. Identity continues to be modified throughout adult life; it builds on and incorporates earlier choices. Identity · is always both product and process; it embodies continuity and change.[14]

Never again in life is identity as malleable as it is in adolescence. As we progress through life, our own decisions limit what we may decide later. If I have spent ten years as a psychologist, it is much more difficult for me to decide to become an art historian than if I had set out on that road in the beginning. Similarly, getting married or having children bonds one to relationships that may limit mobility or time. Nevertheless, we continue to make changes, to better understand ourselves, to better know the social world in which we live. The woman of 40 knows herself, experiences herself, and expresses herself differently from the woman of 21.

And, as the life course progresses, the social world is itself changing: choices become available that may not have been there before. Ideas that have been around for some time may not be taken up as a part of someone's personal biography until years after others have incorporated them. People of the same social and historical period derive different meanings from the same events that occur in the larger society—adopting change, resisting it, or remaining indifferent to it.[15] What is least to be expected is that, over twenty years, people will remain the same.

These four groups greeted their adulthood in different ways. About to graduate from college, these women entered their future from one of these four doors—some with a clear sense of themselves that came of experimentation with their own possibility, some with a sense of self rooted in the authority of the past, some uncertain of how or what they wished to become, and some avoiding the question altogether. These were important gateways in that they opened out onto avenues that phrased the questions of life in different ways.[16] The next stages would have to unfold distinctively. What became of the women who backed into grown-up life holding fast to the past? And what of those who were living only the present, hoping to stave off the future? And what would happen to those who still, at the end of college, felt unable to choose? How would they ultimately decide and what would their openness gain them—or cost them?

These groups, then, represent starting points rather than lifelong categories. I have followed these women for twenty-two years. All of them, by age 43, have carved a more or less reliable sense of identity, or circumstance has provided them one. In the intervening years, they have continued to revise themselves. At age 43, some are in the midst of midlife questioning and reworking; others are content with who they have become and feel themselves to be pretty much who they expect to be for the rest of their lives. There is continuity and change—both within the groups and over time. In order to tell their stories, I continue to group them in terms of the exit door they took from their adolescence. As the complexity of life increases after college, so do the differences among them, and they divide less neatly into well-marked groups. (To reorder them at each ten-year interval would become too confusing and, in any case, we lack the psychological instruments to categorize the identity process in adulthood.) I therefore use the group names to refer to where these women were at the end of college but not to label their adult identities.

I am interested in exploring the ways in which these women's lives unfold. Thinking of the four groups as different starting points, representing different personalities and orientations to life, is a useful conceptual vantage point for identifying the different courses that women follow as they continue to grow. At the outset, we cannot know if one or the other path may be the more direct or certain route to adult fulfillment and satisfaction. Or whether each path may lead to a unique form of adult life experience. I wanted to discover what became of women who took each of these different identity routes. I hoped to learn about how these differences play out as women encounter and respond to the challenges of living.

Above all, I hoped to discover what the differences among these women could teach me about identity in women. What are its components and what are its crucial determinants? How can we name and appreciate both the commonalities and the differences among women as they construct their identities and, in doing so, weave their lives?

In the next part, I introduce the women in the four groups, one group at a time, and explore the way in which they have pursued their lives. I highlight the way in which the identity pathway taken at the end of college affected the course of their adulthood. In this part, I look for communalities within each group and point out the differences I find between them. I also look at the ways in which people, in making and remaking their identities, carry elements of their beginnings while taking on new attributes—intermingling continuity and change.

Part Two

OUT OF
THE GATE
AND BEYOND

THE WOMEN

Guardians	Pathmakers	Searchers	Drifters
Emily	Alice	Laura	Debbie
Fern	Andrea	Leslie	Donna
Grace	Betty	Millie	Erica
Gwen	Brenda	Marlene	Evelyn
Helen	Clara	Natalie	Jennifer
Harriet	Maria	Norma	Vicky
	Nancy	Regina	Yvonne
		Sandra	
		Theresa	

There was one woman not classified into these groups.

Thrice happy she that is so well assured
Unto herself, and settled so in heart
That neither will for better be allured
Ne fears to worse with any chance to start,
But like a steddy ship doth strongly part
The raging waves, and keeps her course aright.

Spenser, Sonnet LIX

4 THE GUARDIANS

Like sailors caught below deck in a storm, the Guardians as young women were holding fast to a post, oblivious to the waves of change crashing around them. Surrounded by the pulse of newness that greeted them on arrival at college, they clung even tighter to the familiar, wanting to retain the emotional comforts of their childhood at all costs. They were Guardians of their heritage, foreclosing on the possibility of forming an independent identity by seeking to preserve ways of thinking, responding, and valuing that had always been. Preoccupied with security, they chose what felt safe. Although they may have heard the call of liberalizing sexual attitudes, of possibilities for experimenting with other ways of believing and being, they felt morally superior to those who partook of impulse and risk. They flourished in the stability that came of moving along the tracks of others' expectations of them. They had learned, growing up, to silence inner wishes that did not meet others' approval, orienting themselves to please, to be "good," but they remained, at the end of college, quite unconscious of having done this. Only much later, sometimes as late as midlife, could they look back and see how they had been fettered.

Mired as they were in tradition and obedience, these were quite person-ally rigid college women.[1] Many had been introverted or socially isolated as teenagers and had exempted themselves from the confusions and distractions of adolescence. They told themselves that they didn't *want* to be part of teenage waywardness; that wasn't for them. A deep longing for security and safety kept them from ventures that might imperil the inner certainty they had. If impulses of any sort might emerge—to consider being sexually active, question their religious beliefs, take part in a demonstration—they were firmly clamped down. These women lived their moral sense: right and wrong were givens, unquestionable, and provided them the backbone to stand their ground. Erotic and moral freedom were out of bounds, but academic achievement or wishes for career success could, given certain family values, fit well into their basic orientation to life. These young women had always been "good girls," and their self-esteem had all their lives rested on submis-sion to exacting regulation. The liberalizing of attitudes that usually takes place during these years was a process they dogmatically resisted.

Psychologist Roger Gould points out that the tranformation from child-hood to adulthood is marked by giving up certain childhood beliefs—among them, that (1) "I'll always belong to my parents and believe in their world," (2) "Doing it their way, with willpower and perseverance, will bring results. But when I become too frustrated, confused or tired or am simply unable to cope, they will step in and show me the right way," and (3) "Life is simple and controllable. There are no significant coexisting contradictory forces within me." (Gould, 1978, p. 40) But the Guardians had given up none of these beliefs. They clung to the security of their parents' world and their belief that life is controllable and responsive to their efforts.

Years of research on college women in this identity group have shown that they tend to have overly involved parents who discourage dealing with unacceptable thoughts and feelings. As a result, these people become author-itarian, approval-seeking, but sure of themselves. They are attuned to what they "should" do, think, and feel and they follow along.

The bulwark of security to which the Guardians clung was the authority of a parent (or a long-term boyfriend) who structured life and set standards for them to reach toward. They merged their own sense of identity with this idealized other person who seemed to know best. All goals, striving, and sense of self were phrased in terms of earning and maintaining that person's love or approval. And from this blessing, the Guardians derived profound strength. They felt secure and certain of themselves, safe against dangers that might arise both from within and without.

The Guardians idealized their families and experienced them as warm havens, places filled with love and appreciation of their goodness. Their self-esteem was high and their anxiety low. Secure in knowing what was right and certain of their family's approval of them, they could press forward on their path, undistracted by temptation or inner crisis. They worked hard, studied hard, did what they were "supposed to." Whether earning high grades, going to church regularly, respecting their teachers—whatever they did they did because they experienced it as "right" rather than springing from inner desire. Or, perhaps more precisely, their effort was to make their inner desires identical to their sense of right. These were idealistic and perfectionistic women. They had a clear vision of the mold into which they intended to pour their life. They were conscientious planners; they pledged not to leave anything to chance.

Being a Guardian did not mean having been raised to exclusively traditional female roles. These bright young women were often the hopes of their families—the ones groomed to achieve, to make something of themselves as well as to carry on the family heritage. Usually, their achievement dreams were rooted in childhood and not subject to the doubt and rethinking of adolescence. Feeling a sense of destiny, their occupational choice had long been a part of them and not open to question. Fern as a child had been the only one in the neighborhood willing to play with a little girl who had cerebral palsy. Right then, she decided that her life work would be to help such children and she had only to learn of the profession of physical therapy to make a firm and unwavering choice. Harriet, Helen, and Gwen all regarded their grade school teachers with adoration and decided that there was no more wonderful role to take than being where their teachers stood. Both Grace and Emily had fathers who were fascinated by law, and their childhoods were marked by feeling close to and special to their fathers through sharing these interests. Their choice to enter the legal profession was, in part, a way of maintaining this unique bond. All of these women in college knew exactly where they were headed—for their childhood professional dreams, for marriage, for children, and for recreating the family harmony and closeness that they had felt as children and wanted to keep forever.

On matters of religion, these young women were similarly unquestioning. Their beliefs were the same as their parents'. For the Catholic and Protestant women in this group, this was a matter of holding firm to ritual and dogma. For the Jewish women, family traditional observances and ethnic solidarity formed the core of religious identity. All these women expected themselves to carry forward the heritage they had inherited.

Sexuality posed the more stubborn quandary. Here is where the line between childhood and adulthood is most dramatically crossed. The little girl now becomes a woman, and this is the place where the Guardians were most likely to apply the brakes. To be sexual meant to be without their mothers, for they knew their mothers could not approve—or, if they did approve, at least, they could not go with them. So the Guardians held back, cited morals as a reason for remaining virginal. "My mother thinks the world of me," said Helen, "I couldn't break her heart."

What the Guardians were most trying to sustain was their childhood selves. They had an identity—one ascribed to them or that they had taken up early on—that made them feel secure and certain. Internally, they were directed by a sense of right and wrong that they internalized from childhood. They vaulted over the developmental phase in which the harsh tone of conscience is tempered and in which ideals are reshaped in line with reality.

The push to experiment that occupied the Pathmakers and the Searchers was squelched, if they experienced it at all. They already felt firm in their commitments. This certainty gave the Guardians a somewhat dogmatic air. When I interviewed them in college, I had the feeling very often that they were instructing me in how life *ought* to be rather than telling me about their own individual choices. They were strong women, that was clear, but I wondered if they were also brittle, if their intense need for security and certainty wouldn't perhaps lead them to be less resilient in life, less able to bend and adapt to the inevitable twists and boulders awaiting them on their paths.

Psychologically, the Guardians were unwilling to notice and mourn the end of childhood. Either they grew up in families where they felt insecure and clung tightly so as not to lose their moorings or they were raised in intensely close and comfortable homes that were so gratifying they had no wish to move on. The dominant motif of the Guardians as college seniors was fear of change and a wish to retain control at all costs.

When I spoke about this group of women at psychological meetings, I found that psychologists were more critical of the Guardians than of all the other groups. Doing what they were "supposed to" do all the time, they were not working at what psychologists thought they were "supposed to"—that is, trying to rework their childhood selves and achieve adult autonomy. They were getting older, my colleagues would point out, but they didn't seem to be developing. They seemed to be undertaking the impossible project of remaining little girls. Perhaps they would put on adult clothes and impersonate adult roles, but that is not the same as the inner restructuring that goes with real adolescence. Surely they would someday face a crisis and would have to endure the torments necessary for growth.

When I reported on these women when they were in their mid-thirties and found them still rooted in the same basic psychological structure, my colleagues knowingly said, just wait ten more years. By then they'll have changed—they can't stay the same forever.

In fact, this group of women does change. They explore and open themselves to experience, but later in life and in more circumscribed ways than women in the other groups. They become more insightful, more self-aware. As they approach middle age, they become less in thrall to security and learn to recognize another kind of strength in themselves. But, in the end, or at least this far in life, they aren't brittle. None of them has fallen apart. To the contrary, some have become among the most interesting and lively of the women I have followed.[2]

FERN

—At the End of College   Fern had always seemed to me the epitome of a Guardian, almost out of the Victorian age. When I first met her as a college senior, she was wrapped tightly in her Catholic faith and sense of family mission. She was filled with resolve and purpose, and couldn't comprehend the commotion that her agemates were making around her. "I don't understand people getting high on drugs," she said, "I can get high on life." In many ways, at age 21, Fern seemed to be already "middle-aged," full of scorn for those who were still trying to get a handle on how to live.

Fern's father had been sick throughout her life and died when she was 11. In many ways, life had not indulged Fern the luxury of an adolescence. Her childhood had been organized around caring for her father; his health limitations kept the family from venturing far from the neighborhood. Her mother's Catholic faith provided solace and structure and her mother's greatest wish was to have Fern's father convert to Catholicism before he died. She enlisted her daughters in this enterprise and Fern joined her mother in fervent prayer, fearing that without her father's conversion, they could not all be reunited in heaven.

After her father's death, her mother sought work for the first time in her life and house chores and care of her younger sister fell to Fern. Her family was relatively isolated. There were no cousins or aunts to cushion some of the tension. And Fern was not very successful in making friends. When some of the Protestant neighborhood children taunted her as a Catholic, she fled home in tears. Her mother counseled her that there were mean people in the world and she would best stay at home. "I became aware of what kinds of things exist," Fern said in her college interview, justifying her retreat from what had the potential to hurt her. She idealized her parents: "I don't think I could pick parents who have given more to their children than my parents did to me." They expected a lot of her and she was proud that she could always succeed in school. But she was jealous of her younger sister who was "manipulative" and always managed to get clothes and privileges that Fern wouldn't dare even ask for. As a teenager, after her father's death, Fern developed a fantasy relationship with a patron saint who she believed protected her; she turned to her faith when she felt fearful and found security there.

In high school, a teacher noticed her shyness and her loneliness and invited her to join the drama club. With his patient guidance, she began to come out of herself a bit, to join the other kids and gain some feeling of connection. And she adored this teacher; she imagined him as a kind of substitute father. She remained wary of others, however, even through college, and was sensitive to what people said and easily offended. She was very attentive to "creating an impression" on others and felt unable to be spontaneous or playful.

Fern chose to attend a state university near her home. It was all she could afford, but she expressed no wish to go elsewhere. She was already set on becoming a physical therapist and the local university had a good program. Through college, she continued to live at home and avoided much of student life. She had "several acquaintances, but no real friends." She was often a "shoulder" for others' problems, and tried to engage with others by taking care of them when she saw the need. She was still oversensitive to criticism or rejection and easily shocked by others' actions. One woman whom she liked and had begun to develop a friendship with started cutting classes. Fern was confused and judged her friend harshly; she tried to persuade her not to do this. But when she didn't change her ways, Fern found that she couldn't tolerate her friend's "dishonesty" and distanced herself. She began to date for the first time in her junior year, but the relationship broke off because the young man thought she was "too critical." She knew she lacked confidence in her femininity but worried more that she would not be able to find a man who would live up to her standards. "I'm not willing to change. Someone will have to like me as I am—respect my standards and beliefs." She feared that she might become a spinster.

At the end of college, Fern was very clear on what was right and wrong, on doing good and being good. "I'd never question authority," she asserted proudly. She wanted to be as close to an earthbound saint as she could. In this, she looked to her mother as a model, rhapsodizing about her good sense, her devotion to her family. Fern wanted a life of giving to others. The world seemed to be one of sorrow and malevolence and she wanted to make it better.

While I admired Fern's tenacity and fortitude and recognized the trauma she had suffered in the loss of her father, I worried for her personality constriction. So much of life seemed to be ruled out for her, and she appeared to be imprisoning herself. I thought that if she wasn't depressed at this time, surely she would be someday.

—*Age 33*   I met Fern again when she was 33 and found her, as a person, quite unchanged. Still, she seemed relaxed and confident, sure of herself, in control. In her life, she was fulfilling her wish to "serve others" as a physical therapist and her dedication had led her to a position as department chair in a large university hospital. She carried enormous responsibility and was enthusiastic about her work.

In her first job, Fern had met a man who seemed "compatible" and they married a year later. Like her father, he was not Catholic and Fern was intrigued with the idea of converting him. She appreciated his understanding of her "need to help" and he was willing to allow her freedom to engage in her professional commitments as well as a number of charitable organizations at which she volunteered. They had two children and he was willing to be equally involved and helpful. But Fern was disappointed in her marriage in some ways. "Fred is not as affectionate as I would like and his morals aren't as high as mine." Separation, of course, was not a consideration and she sought help through prayer. "This must be life," she said, "and with all the happy times, sad times, and hard times, I wouldn't change it because through everything we have always had each other." At the very least, Fern had established a new base of security.

Fern took delight in her children, although she had had a hard time with them when they were toddlers. They were "daring, defiant and mischievous"—qualities Fern had never been able to experience in herself. With them, however, she was able to express and receive the open loving she missed with Fred. She worried about not always being there when her children needed her, but her dedication to her career—and the good she felt she could do for others—was unwavering.

Fern was deeply invested in her work. Again she had found some "fatherly" men willing to teach and challenge her. One helped her expand her abilities as a therapist. Another showed her the art of managing. She felt herself in a period of intense professional growth, gaining deeper and broader skills.

In the twelve years since college, Fern had also made some women friends, people from work she could confide in and share with. She also described herself as having "become more accepting of superficial friendships." In general, Fern seemed to have become a bit less demanding of others. She remained close to her mother who, after retiring, came to live with Fern and Fred for several months a year.

At this age, Fern was fulfilling her dream of serving others and was certainly not depressed. She had dealt with some disappointment in her marriage, but there was much else in her life that was developing as she had hoped. Reflecting on her own history, Fern was recognizing that she had never had the opportunity to be an adolescent. "I missed a lot," she said wistfully. "I was a mini-adult." She could see, from the vantage point of age 33, that she had been racked by inferiority and insecurity in her teens, and seemed to wish that she had been able to experience more fun.

—*Age 43*   Not until she turned 40 did Fern have her first real "identity crisis," when a job upheaval led her to risks she could never have dreamed of undertaking. The management at her hospital changed and, under pressure of tight economic circumstances, services were reorganized and her department was allotted far fewer resources. Fern labored under the changed guidelines for several months, then began to realize that, given these new limitations, there was no way to provide the quality of service to which she had devoted herself. She framed this as a moral question, and decided that continuing in her position would be unethical. "I couldn't compromise myself any more," she said. It was simply wrong to hold herself out as a physical therapist when she was not able, as a therapist or department chair, to provide what she considered adequate service. So she resigned. Her new dream was to establish a private service that would function independently and be able to serve disadvantaged clients who were being turned away under the hospital's system. With her husband's agreement, she emptied their savings, procured a new mortgage on the house, and invested everything in setting this up. Fern was frightened: she was putting her family's welfare in the service of her scruples, giving up a secure paycheck that had been the majority of the family's income. (Fred was working in a low-paying government job.)

Fern prayed. But the reality was more turbulent than what she had ever imagined. Business partners reneged on their commitments. People she shared an office with left without paying their rent. For the first time, Fern had to be careful about what food she put in her grocery cart. "But it was not just the pressure of not having the income, but knowing that if that business failed, I would have lost everything of the family's." Fern describes these as "the insane years, the unsettled years, the radical years—what most people go through in college." She weathered it by relying on the strength in her family and appreciating that. They supported her, didn't bemoan their changed lifestyle, and endured deprivation without complaint.

In three years, Fern has organized her business to a point where it is afloat, although not yet thriving. She is feeling a bit less terrified, but wishes she could worry less about the income. She had hoped to be able to work fewer hours, but actually is working many more. Her gratification is that she is doing it her way. "I really felt I was going to be in a better position to provide for families—not cranking out numbers and bringing in dollars. I didn't realize then that it would really be much more like missionary work. . . . Our practice goes beyond providing the concrete physical and occupational therapy modes. We end up being counselors of a sort, dealing with family issues and financial issues and school issues for their children. Knowing that the holidays are not good for them because they don't have money. We put together food baskets at Thanksgiving, organize clothing drives. . . . We work with a population that no one else wants to work with in a place where no one else wants to go. . . . You have a responsibility to provide." What drives her to this? "Knowing that I have two healthy children and a commitment to knowing that I'm supposed to give back and to do it in a way that I am gifted to do it." And here Fern got tearful, and her thoughts turned to her father.

Her commitment to serve was consistent with how Fern had seen herself all along, but the venturesomeness was new—and much else as well. Fern had, in her thirties and into her forties, evolved into an extraordinarily open and insightful woman. Where her life had been dominated by "shoulds" and formulas, she had, in midlife, discovered feelings and psychological complexity. She was struggling to make sense of this fluid sensibility and had, in the process, learned to regard herself with a sense of humor.

Part of what initiated her revision of herself was her success in bringing about her husband's conversion to Catholicism. They had renewed their marriage vows and embarked on a series of "marriage encounters" through their church. "I hoped it would change him. *I* didn't have any need to change. I was the perfect wife," she said in a tone of self-mockery. "So it was a revelation to find that there were things I needed to change as well." She learned a lot about feelings and about communication, things she had missed in her relative isolation while growing up and in her supercilious contempt for others in college. "There is no education for becoming a couple—no education that prepares you to make a relationship with someone you are going to spend the rest of your life with. How can you be responsible to each other? For a lot of us who grew up in families where it didn't happen or was much more mechanical or superficial, [we had to learn about] having that depth and really being able to communicate things and being able to look at each other and know what is there."

Fern began to understand for the first time the way in which she substituted caretaking activities for relating to people. She began to gain some emotional distance from herself as a caretaker and recognize the way it kept her from deeper engagement with others. Coming to see herself as "a caretaker" in the self-deprecatory form of that word, she began to understand that it was more important to empower her patients than to take care of them. She realized that she had been being "a caretaker" in her marriage and eagerly took up new modes of communication. Her marriage has felt much improved in the past several years, despite all the stress and distress with work. For the first time, she is able to allow herself to be emotionally vulnerable. "Sometimes I have periods where there is no energy and I feel discouraged. Sometimes I have significant mood swings where I can be very quiet and introspective. And Fred instinctively knows that its not a good time and he can sort of cheer me up. I think we offer each other a good balance."

Even more rethinking of herself followed after her mother's death seven years ago. Although deeply saddened, Fern reviewed her past and found herself writing a whole new life history. No longer viewing her mother through a glorifying lens, she began to be able to tolerate an awareness of some of the more negative aspects of her upbringing, something she could not do at all in college or in her early thirties. Now she could see the unfairness of the caretaker role she was thrust in. She realized that throughout her adolescence she had been the parent and her mother the child, but she had been too dutiful to allow herself to know this. She hadn't been permitted an independent self, hadn't been granted the right to her own feelings. "Feelings weren't discussed in my household. It was neat and orderly—the Ozzie and Harriet family—so feelings didn't enter into it. If your parents said jump, you said how high? So I don't think I had the independent ability to evaluate my own self-esteem. But looking back on it now, knowing what self-esteem is, I know now I didn't have it. Because I was too preoccupied with being too much to other people to have had an independent life myself."

Fern wasn't dwelling on her anger about this, but trying to be vigilant and change those parts of herself she felt were damaged. What she most resented was the way in which her mother always made her feel not good enough. "I think it was her way of trying to push me to be as good as I could be, but I always felt I was held up to be like somebody else or as good as somebody else. Report cards came home and she would ask, well, what did 'Susie' get? Then if I didn't do well, it was 'I don't care what they got, what did you get?' I felt terrible because it was never good enough. I think that's part of what drives me to be as intense as I am—it's always are you good enough? And I don't have to prove it to anyone but its still a part of me. I'm not really sure who I am proving it to. And I worry about that with my children." Jim, her older son, now 16, often does less well than she thinks he can. "I know he is not producing to his fullest potential, that he's just being lazy about that stuff but I am terrified of speaking those words, of saying Well, what did X get on his report card? and holding up to him what was held up to me. And I really am terrified that I will become my mother, that part of her that always made me feel that my best wasn't good enough." She recognized that she got her strength from trying so hard to be good for her mother, but was now becoming aware of the price she had paid. In some ways, Fern said she was relieved her mother had died before the crisis in her work. "I'm glad she never had to see how hard we struggled. Knowing me as the person who could do it all, I think it would have killed her."

Fern is in a neverending battle with herself to keep her perfectionism modulated. And the fight to be less critical and demanding than her mother is an arduous one, requiring an ongoing capacity to observe and understand herself. Last year, Jim's school class was taking a trip to Rome that Fern, despite their financial difficulties, didn't want him to miss. Her need to feel like a good provider to her children led her to juggle expenses to pull together the money. "So he went on that trip to Rome and I was so angry at him because he came home and the main thing he wanted to talk about was leaning out the hotel windows and hollering up to the girls above and talking about other experiences that I could have arranged in the seedier parts of town here for much less money. He wasn't talking about seeing the Vatican. His first recounts were of adolescent experiences and I was furious . . . I wanted to say, 'I didn't work for the last six months for you to come home and talk about this stuff.' So I just didn't say anything. I know my expectations were different than his, but I still have a hard time letting go of mine. Because that was my dream too that went and what came back was not the dream that I sent." And here, with the poignancy of that statement, she laughed. I, however, was touched by her insight, admiring how far she had come to be able to have that awareness.

Dealing with the adolescent challenges of her children when she had avoided these experiences herself presents continual puzzles. Again, Fern responds not with the rigidity of her college-age personality but with an effort to remain open, to respect her sons' selfhood. Sex has been a difficult issue to talk with her sons about since it had never really been discussed in her family. "But his father isn't doing it and he has to hear it from one of us. We've talked more about AIDS than the mechanical things but then you go up and find a wasted condom under the mattress and *Playboys*. I sort of die. So its been an awkward thing for me. I wish I had had girls, I think it would have been easier. And we've talked about *Playboy* and how that's not what a relationship with a woman is about and that's not what sex means." She still has her religious scruples but wants her sons to decide for themselves. "I think I have evolved to allow them to be what they want to be and do what they want to do instead of just feeling that it has to be my way."

Coming into awareness of her own emotional life has led Fern to be more respectful of others' feelings, less demanding that they live up to her principles. Fred had always kept his feelings to himself, sometimes not talking for days. Their new "tools" for communication, however, opened the floodgates of feeling, both loving and angry ones. And Jim, in Fern's perception, is much like Fred. "I am not a confrontational person, but I am more so than I used to be. I used to be a peace-at-any-price person. You never saw anything that wasn't nice." (Here Fern is referring to her former self, how things were at home and accurately describing how she appeared to me at the time of the college-age interview.) "I come home from work and I might tell how my day was. I think its important that they see that adults have feelings. I don't want to burden them, but they can see what I feel." Often, she must manage— rather than squelch—the feelings that erupt among the other members of her family as well. "Jim stores things and then something stupid sets him off and he starts screaming at the top of his lungs and then he and my husband will start screaming at each other and I will have to verbally separate them and make them cool off. I don't like that, I don't like to have to be the one to get in the middle of that. I don't like the fact that they don't deal with their anger in a more appropriate way. Is it all right for them to have it? Of course. Because I'd rather have it come out than have it come out in some other way. Do I like that stuff? No thank you." But she can bear it. She can allow others as well as herself to feel what they feel. With John, her younger son, the issues are somewhat different. John says what he thinks and feels "and my husband doesn't like that. John has modeled [himself] after me and has learned that sometimes its all right to stand up for what you believe. So he will talk back and sometimes my husband doesn't know how to deal with it. But I tell John that I admire his courage, and just because you're yelled at, don't stop doing it."

Fern has also developed more openness and comfort about her sexuality. This, too, has improved with time. If anything, she is sometimes rueful about having missed out on some of that, too. When asked the interview question about experiences of sexual harassment, Fern laughed and said, "I wish I had the body that someone would want to harass." (Fern is quite overweight and not very attentive to her physical appearance.) She wished she were sexier, and fantasies along these lines came easily to her. In contrast to the fear and moralism of her twenties, Fern at 43 was vibrant.

Fern's faith is still what sustains her. If anything, Fern said, she has become more prayerful and her faith is deeper. "The quality of it has changed," as she feels she now understands her faith in a deeper way. Part of this is related to her concept of service, of giving to others, of being called. Some of it she cannot articulate. "I don't know how people manage to exist without some form of faith. . . . At least I am too vulnerable not to have something to fall back on. As an individual, I can fall back on Fred or the kids or friends, but there are things about myself that I need to fall back on something that is larger than them."

Fern at 43 has designed her own path. She has rethought herself, revised herself, reclaimed the parts of herself that were locked away or disowned, and she has shaped a more complete sense of herself. She continues to live her vision of moral purpose, but in an enlightened way. This woman who would never question authority in her twenties has found a way in her forties to reach and understand her own authority and be more empathic of others as well.

Like Fern, all the Guardians carried their preoccupation with being good and succeeding into their career planning. All except Fern have advanced degrees and all have enjoyed professional acclaim. Two of the six women I classified in this group became lawyers and both eventually rose to become the first female judges in their states. The Guardian capacity to doggedly stick to a path and work hard served all of them well. For some of them, career success became a new base that allowed them enough security to explore and be daring in other aspects of their lives. Only after being professionally established did some of them reconsider themselves and begin to chart courses based more on their own wishes than on their need to please others.

EMILY

—At the End of College   Unlike Fern, Emily was beginning to explore during college. She was leaning over the edge a bit, seemingly making a transition to a period of testing. But her central identity was rooted in her closeness to and identification with her father, and she answered most questions with reference to his opinions and wishes. For this reason I classified her a Guardian. Emily's father, who had run a successful business, had entered law school just as Emily was finishing high school. She joined him intensely in his new project and avidly listened to all that he was learning. For Emily, this represented a shift in her own personality organization, but she seemed to have moved from intense involvement with her mother to a similar kind of involvement, though about different issues, with her father.

Raised in a well-off, liberal Jewish home, Emily had no religious strictures to govern her behavior. Until she left for college, she had been very close to her homemaker mother, who was concerned that she have "the right clothes, the right friends, be in the right crowd and be a cheerleader." And Emily did all of this. But when she got to college, it all seemed so silly in retrospect and she grew closer to the more serious pursuits of her father. He led her to an interest in politics, but her opinions were just like his. She found that she could derive the same sense of approval and well-being that she had gotten from her mother by intellectual involvement with her father. She intended to go to law school and perhaps even join him in his practice.

Like the other Guardians, Emily idealized all aspects of her family and growing up. With four siblings, they were a close unit; they traveled together and played sports together. Emily felt she had a secure place that she was reluctant to leave. She imagined she would have a life much like her mother's, presiding over a warm, close-knit large family, but with a place in her father's profession as well.

—Age 33   After college, Emily did go to law school, put all other considerations aside, and buckled down to study. When I interviewed her in her early thirties, she had become the first woman state's attorney in Missouri, where she was raised, and had what she described as a "Camelot" job. Once settled in her career, however, Emily began to experiment with herself in earnest. She started to consider more who she was in relationships and what she wanted from them. She let loose and allowed herself to have some "wild times." She had become comfortable with her sexuality and examined how she felt about sex with love and without it. Her first serious involvement ended when she realized that she could not abide being with a man who was less ambitious than she. Feeling "no doubt about my attractiveness to men," Emily intended to select the right one. In her late twenties, she lived with a prominent attorney whom she loved but left when it became clear that he didn't want to marry. At the time of the interview, Emily was in love with a man living in New York whom she was hoping to make a life with. She was prepared to give up the job she found so perfect to follow him once they decided to marry. She would simply begin again in New York. She had confidence in her professional skills, and felt she could transport them wherever she went. Her main concern was to get on with the project of marriage and family.

At this time in her life, Emily retained her closeness to her father. He "was tremendously supportive of my career and he remains an inspiration to me. He has always been encouraging and helpful to me and has been a wonderful adviser whenever I have to make important professional decisions." She also stayed in close touch with her mother, who worried with her about the ups and downs of her romantic involvements. Emily had, at this point, attained a part of her dream, the professional side, but the more personal vision was harder to settle and realize.

—Age 43   I learned when I met Emily again in her mid-forties that her planning had eluded her control. The man she had hoped to marry balked at a final commitment. Crushed, she entered therapy to better understand what she was doing in her relationships with men. Meanwhile, she had been appointed to a judgeship, again as the first woman to hold such a position

in her state. Just after taking office, when she was 35, she drew closer to a man who had been a friend and began to think of him as a romantic partner. When he asked her to marry him, she accepted. And they created what she described at age 43 as a "fantastic" relationship, filled with sharing and travel and mutual support. But, being fifteen years older, her husband did not want to have children—which meant that Emily had to revise the dream she had always carried. She hadn't quite known how adamant he was about this. "We didn't really discuss it. I just thought that we would. But if he had told me, I would have married him anyway," she said. Emily described having gone through a process like grieving, giving up the family she always thought she would have. "It's a life experience you don't have and I'm one of those people who wants to try everything. It sort of makes me feel left out at times, it distinguishes me from my friends who do have children, you have less in common. But I can't say I've been devastated by it." She has "adopted" her brother's two children as substitutes, and enjoys indulging them and taking them on trips.

In midlife, Emily has set about building a life for which she has no clear models. When she was in her late thirties, her parents divorced and in the bitterness of their struggle Emily became estranged from her father. They haven't spoken to one another in five years. Her mother later remarried and moved to Florida, where two of her siblings live. This left Emily in a prominent position in her hometown, but with none of her family there. Emily was by then on her own feet, making a life out of her marriage to "an incredibly special guy" and her career success. She missed her family and was thinking about moving to Florida in several years when her husband was ready to retire. She wants to be with them for warmth and closeness, but security she has found now on her own.

GRACE

—At the End of College   Grace shares some elements of both Fern's and Emily's stories. Like Fern, her father died when she was 11 and, like Emily, she became interested in law through him.

Grace adored her father who adored her. He was a Greek immigrant, full of humor and "incredibly smart" with a passion for politics. "He was a really fantastic individual. He and my Mom existed for us kids. He used to take us on vacations, had high expectations for us. I think I was his favorite. We both read constantly and I was sort of a tomboy. We used to talk politics and I would impress the kids at school with what he thought. He took a lot of time with me." He was a barber, but, if he had had the chance, he would have been a lawyer. So Grace's aspiration was to fulfill his dream and keep him alive in that way. After he died, her mother became withdrawn and bitter. But Grace, in her college interview venerated her "determination and strength of character. She doesn't give up." Grace began to work at age 14 to help out with family finances and was paying her own way through college.

Through high school, Grace had felt different from the other kids at school. The necessity to work kept her from teenage activities and she felt more mature, less interested than they were in pranks and mischief. She studied hard, but questioned nothing that felt part of her unshakable bond to her father, still the source of her sense of security. Grace had a boyfriend whom she described as "really nice, not very attractive, but intelligent and nice." She felt comfortable with him because he "lets me do what I want and doesn't try to dominate me." She wasn't interested in marriage before she had established a career. Horrified at the thought that she might get pregnant, she was also deferring sexual behavior. She wouldn't take birth control pills because her mother might find them. "She really thinks I'm something and I wouldn't want to do that to her." She felt at this point that sex just wasn't an important part of her life and that "my boyfriend doesn't feel deprived or anything." Her sexual reticence suggested that she was trying to stay her father's smart, political, favorite tomboy. But Grace was clear on the path she wanted to follow.

—*Age 33*   Grace stayed in this Guardian position until her early thirties when a crisis in her marriage led her to reconsider what she had put together in her life and how she might rearrange the pieces. This became an acute period of searching from which she emerged with a very different sense of her identity. In recounting her life story at age 33, Grace told of how she had finished law school passionate about finding ways to have a positive impact on the world. After she graduated, she married her college boyfriend and followed him to Rhode Island where he had wanted to do graduate work in architecture. She won a highly competed-for job as a state's attorney, and was intent on trying to be helpful to the disadvantaged. While focusing primarily on refining her professional goals, she had, along the way, settled into marriage, given up her Catholic religious beliefs and practices out of deference to her husband, and decided to delay having children until her husband had gotten his own professional life underway.

In retrospect, Grace could see that she had not given marriage much thought. "We were like a couple of old shoes," she said. They had been together for eight years—getting married seemed a natural next step. "I didn't feel passionate about him, but I didn't think that was important at the time for a successful marriage. I was very comfortable with him." But the marriage didn't work out. As she became more successful, he became more childlike. He refused to help with house chores, didn't work consistently, spent most of his time playing golf. Worse, he offered her no emotional support, wasn't interested in her experiences at work, and very likely was threatened by her mounting success. (Grace was often in the newspaper.) They began to be "at each other's throats" constantly. Being dogged about what she wanted, and having been raised with Catholic values opposed to divorce, Grace wished to continue trying to make things work, but eventually he decided to leave the marriage. Grace found herself on her own for the first time since early in her freshman year of college. "I was very upset," she said, understating her pain. Far from her home, she had developed few friends and, taking stock of herself, she sensed she had lost a lot of her spontaneity and gregariousness during the marriage. She felt lonely again, as she had through high school. Her husband, old shoe that he was, had been her bulwark, the pillar to which she had clung to make much of her achievement possible. She sought psychotherapy, which, she said, "helped me to face forward and get on with my life."

"The divorce," Grace said, "is what made me develop. It forced me to get out again, to make some friends, get involved in social activities, even rethink how I looked." Her dark hair had been long and straight, emulating Joan Baez, and Grace, in remaking herself, emerged with short curly hair and learned to use makeup. For the first time, she began to think of herself as "okay-looking, maybe even pretty." She hadn't ever really dated, so this was a whole new avenue of learning. She bought a house and set about decorating it. She took a vacation alone. When I interviewed her when she was 33, she doubted that she would remarry. She regretted giving up the hope of having a family, but thought that "the question of children for me is pretty much an outside shot." Divorced two years at the time of this interview, Grace said, "I found, through my divorce, that its nicer to be happy by yourself than miserable with another person. I'm happy to think that I'm the type of woman who does not need a man, however unappealing he may be, rather than be by myself." She had just ended a yearlong relationship with a man who tried to dominate her; he found it hard to accept any signs of her independence. "I couldn't tolerate his jealousies and recriminations. He couldn't talk about feelings at all." At age 33, Grace was occupied with making a life alone and with friends. Her mother and sisters, though five states away, were the people she felt closest to, so there was still a core of attachment and old connection to fall back on. She was rethinking her assumptions and understanding about marriage, but putting most of her energy into her work, which served to "compensate." Grace was forced to forge a path that had not been charted for her.

Having remained internally close to her roots, Grace could draw strength from the part of herself that had preserved her family's heritage. Rethinking her family, she could see in herself and her brothers and sisters a kind of "oddness—none of us would blend into the mainstream. None of us are big on conformity." Her siblings had become artists and musicians. She had distinguished herself by her education and achievement. The ethnic Greek in them still felt very strong. "We love each other very hard, scream at each other very hard, and protect each other very hard." Far from home, she had the least responsibility for looking after their mother. This was a relief to her since she realized that she had become the family leader after her father died—the "strong one emotionally, the one who fixed things." She still had the role of being the arbitrator who resolved disputes, but she was called on to do this less and less. Her sense of family remained a bedrock of continuity in the midst of all the change. Thoughts of her father, for whom she had set her course, had faded from her consciousness, however. Her goals now felt like her own.

—*Age 43*   Between her early thirties and early forties, transition and revision in Grace's life burgeoned. Grace in her mid-forties is married with three children and became, like Emily, the first woman judge in her state. During her election campaign, she fell in love with the lawyer who managed her campaign finances and they married shortly after she won the election. With age 40 approaching, Grace set about having babies. This was an intensely busy and stressful time, assuming the new duties of a judgeship and motherhood at once. And after her third child was born, she developed a massive infection and was so ill she had been given Last Rites. When she recovered, with the acute vision emanating from her near-death experience, she took stock of what she was doing. She hugged her children to her with reawakened intensity, cut back her work hours to have more time with them—and painfully allowed herself to acknowledge that her husband is alcoholic. At age 43, Grace seriously fears for the future of her family as she regretfully contemplates the possibility of another divorce.

Professionally, Grace's goals are sharper, more defined. Working in a court of general jurisdiction, she hears cases that range from murder to small claims. The work load is immense, the intellectual demands formidable. She has just triumphed in her election to a second judicial term. Vociferous about women's rights, she has become a leader in the women's movement. Her life is full, rich, challenging—and of her own devising.

But Grace longs to spend more time with her children. They have given her "a dimension of joy" that surprised her. She wishes that she and her husband could attain the economic security that would allow her to resign and work part-time. This had been their plan until she had recently begun to worry about whether they would stay together.

Hopeful and confident when her marriage was new, Grace had appreciated the intellectual and emotional companionship she and Garrett had. She also found the first really fulfilling sexual relationship of her life. And this time she thought about marriage scrupulously, trying to learn from her first mistake. They lived together for a while and Grace found that "you are able to be a lot more flexible after you have been through one marriage where maybe you expected too much." She decided to take the risk and share her life a second time. They had fallen into "the yuppie pattern of a bottle of wine with dinner and then maybe a drink or two after." But she gave up alcohol when she got pregnant. After their third child was born, she began to resent the emotional distance and increasing verbal abuse that came from her husband's drinking. Having children strained their marriage. "Children add stress to the family—it gives Garrett more things to become short-tempered about." He agreed to get psychological help. "I love Garrett and I feel very committed to him. So I will be flexible to a certain degree, to be understanding and encourage him in his efforts to gain control. But I'm certainly not going to put up with it for any great length of time."

Being flexible is an ongoing struggle for Grace, who has always wanted things the way she wanted them. But the limits of flexibility are what she has had to revise continually. In her mid-forties, it is her children that light her life. "I could listen to them all day long," she said. As they grow older, she enjoys their maturity and their ability to articulate themselves. "They're wonderful kids, creative, smart, funny." As she has gotten older, Grace feels her goals have become more personal, less directed at saving the world. "After being so sick, my focus changed 180 degrees. My personal life has been so enriched. And being a mom has also made me a more compassionate judge."

Pulling again on her roots, Grace also returned to the spiritual side of her life and decided to raise her children in the Catholic church. "I want to raise them the way I was raised. I think that if the children are going to grow up as moral and responsible adults, then a spiritual home life is only going to contribute positively to that. So in that respect, I'm like my mother. But I don't think I'm as structured as she was. My mom was a widow raising six children by herself. So she was pretty frantic and she could be tremendously emotionally abusive to us. I see that now looking back on it. And I think it was because she was isolated and frustrated and alone. She used to threaten to put us in orphanages and what did she do to deserve such mean rotten kids. And I don't let a day go by without telling my children how much I love them, how good they are, how smart they are. In that respect, I'm different. But I don't want to paint a grim picture of my mom. She really overall was a good parent and there's a lot about her that I would like to achieve in my parenting skills. But I want my environment to be an A+ loving environment. . . . I think I am a good mom but I think I make a lot of mistakes. I yell at them and I shouldn't do that and I try not to."

Like most other Guardians who began their journeys with such unquestioning certainty about the perfection of their families of origin, by midlife, Grace no longer idealizes her childhood or her parents. This leaves her free to take from her early life what is useful and serves her, but to revise other aspects of herself and chart her own course. She has learned to live with less control over things, and is poised to adapt to the future, shaping what she can, but is more humble, more philosophical about forces beyond her.

HARRIET

Other Guardians have not traveled as far from their psychological homes. Harriet has spent most of her life tied to her mother; only at midlife has she been able to clearly perceive herself as shackled by that bond and to make an effort to loosen it.

—At the End of College   The only daughter of middle-class Jewish parents, Harriet had always wanted to be a teacher. Her parents thought she could aspire to more than being a classroom teacher and encouraged her to try special education. Her mother had started working as a nursery-school teacher after Harriet and her brothers were all in school, and this seemed an excellent model for her own life. When she was in college, her dreams for the future were to have a life exactly like the one she had known in her family.

Harriet had been a happy, popular child, but it seemed to her that when she entered high school, everyone else changed. She found herself unable to "connect with the other girls who were preoccupied by themselves and not willing to open up to others." They seemed only to want to show off. They got involved with smoking and drinking, and Harriet balked at such behavior. She retreated to her mother's support, trying not to care about her increasing loneliness. "I used to go home and cry every night, I was so unhappy. But I still felt I was right."

College was better. She began to date and had more success in finding friends. She found that she could open up to others. At school in Chicago, she still called her mother in Detroit each day to talk over events. At the time of her college interview, Harriet, although highly articulate, could not describe her parents as people separate from her with their own lives and inclinations. She missed them, but could only depict them to me in terms of who she took which kind of problem to. She wished at this time to have more confidence in herself, and tried to put herself in situations where she was forced to cope. But Harriet was hesitant, afraid to venture far. Even in her senior year, she was often homesick and looked forward to returning to the comforts of her family.

—*Age 33*   After college, Harriet returned to the Detroit suburb where she was raised and began studying for a master's degree in learning disabilities. She wasn't yet sure enough of herself to start working. Her success in her graduate program gave her the boost of self-confidence she needed, and she began her career at a school she considered excellent. Surrounded by children all the time, Harriet noted that "you almost forget what its like to be an adult." And, at age 25, Harriet was still deeply unsure of whether she wanted to be in the adult world. At age 33, she thought she wouldn't feel fully adult until she was married with children.

Throughout her twenties and early thirties, Harriet had been eagerly in search of marriage. But, looking back at age 33, she realized how "naive" she had been about men, sex, and relationships, especially through college. She had been frightened about sex, which was rarely discussed in her home, and had internalized her mother's moralistic stance against sexual experience before marriage. "I grew up not knowing much of anything and, bit by bit, I've learned a lot more, relaxed a lot more, and feel much more comfortable in the area."

But "more comfortable" to Harriet at this point was still not very. She had spent seven years with a man who had serious sexual problems and remained a virgin. "I felt very insecure about my functioning as a woman," she said. She clung to the hope that, if they married, the problems would resolve themselves. This, at least, was her mother's opinion. He was, in both Harriet and her mother's view, "perfect" in other respects. Harriet spent most of her twenties struggling with this relationship, unwilling to give up the feeling of "having" someone. More than anything, she needed to feel not alone, bonded in the intense twosome she had felt with her mother. "I need to know that I'm needed by another person and that I can need another person. I don't mean dependency. I just mean to know that if I needed another person, there would be a person there for me. I'm a strong person and used to having others depend on me and I need the security of knowing that I too could fall to pieces and have someone there." Her greatest fear was being alone. "If something happens to me, who is going to be the person that really cares? I used to make Marvin swear that if there was some sort of nuclear attack, he would come look for me. I had to know that there was one person whose main goal would be to look for me and to take care of me if I were in a time of need." When she was 26 and in a period of estrangement from Marvin, she had a serious appendicitis attack and her parents canceled their vacation to take care of her. "Thank God I had my parents," she said. "Who else would have been there?"

By the time she was 30, it became clear that Marvin was not going to marry her and Harriet broke off the relationship. Her mother thought she should have given it more time. "The few times I stood up to my mother were in regard to him. But I was always afraid of doing something she would not approve of, and what I finally came to realize was that I will always hope to have her support, but I will not always have her approval. I was a long time getting to that point," Harriet said at age 33. But the end of that relationship drove her back to the comfort of her mother and she still had to wrestle for her independence. "When my engagement with Marvin broke off, she was there when I needed to depend on her, and when the time came for me to pull myself back together, we had gotten into this pattern and she was taking charge of a lot of things and I was afraid to break away from that for fear of hurting her. Its only been in the last two years that I've been able to stand up to her."

Shortly before I interviewed her when she was 33, Harriet had become engaged to Len, a man she had met eight months before. She was delighted by their growing love for each other. "He fulfills a lot of the ideals that I have been looking for. He makes me feel so good and wonderful and secure. And it's a really passionate relationship." But when I asked her to list the people she felt closest to at that time, she couldn't decide between Len and her mother for the top of the list. She hoped that once they married, Len would be the clear first choice.

The hope and security she derived from her engagement to Len led Harriet to rethink her life from this vantage point. "I have a regret that I grew up to be such a goody-goody. A lot of my life has been geared to pleasing my mother. And I probably didn't even know that until the past five or six years. I remember, as a child, if my mother and I would have a disagreement about what I'd wear somewhere, she'd say one thing and I'd say another and she'd say to me, OK, do whatever you want and I would always wear what she said."

Harriet's dream at age 33 was much the same dream she had had since childhood. "I look at other families and see a close-knit family and I *long* for something like that—where families get together for the joy of it. It does give them some direction." She wanted to have children as soon as possible and was ready to abandon her teaching career with no regrets.

—*Age 43*   Finally getting the home and family she had always wanted is what prompted real growth and revision in Harriet by age 43. As fantasy evaporated into reality, Harriet found her own voice and began to make her path more her own. When I asked her then what had been most significant in her life over the past ten years, she said, "Marriage was a wonderful change, but having children was most significant and not the storybook image I expected. I remember thinking, 'Is this what I've been waiting for all my life?' It hasn't been easy. I'm a working mother. I took two years off after our daughter was born. But I was very isolated, exhausted, and tense most of the time. I didn't know how fatiguing it could be." She was relieved to go back to work and, in any case, it was a necessity if they were to be able to afford the comfortable suburban home that Harriet also desired. She amazed herself that the decision to have a second child "wasn't automatic." But she wanted her daughter to have a brother or sister (not to be alone—the old fear). With their second child, Harriet took off six months, then Len took a leave from work for the next six months. Harriet was on her way to effecting new definitions of family. Life has become child-focused, and Harriet is rethinking how she wants things to be. Their first child was born a year after they married and she regrets that she and Len didn't have more time alone together, more time to be spontaneous and have fun. She misses the passion and romance they didn't—and don't—have time for, but tries to content herself with his being her best friend.

Recently, Harriet has begun making more time for her women friends, something she had treasured but was crowded out of her life by having children. She has one very close friend she can discuss everything with and she finds that just saying things out loud helps reduce her stress. But she is also part of a group of friends, all teachers, who go out together to have fun and talk. They connect her to feminist issues and she wishes she had more time to pursue this new interest.

Harriet didn't begin taking charge of her life in a more considered way until after she had battled her way out of the disillusionment and disappointment she felt after her first child was born. Her sense of "Is this all there is?" punctured the idealized balloon and she had to make a dream of her own. At age 43, she was still in the same teaching job, still family-centered, and outwardly her life looked much the same as her mother's had been. Inwardly, however, she was thinking in her own terms about how she wanted to construct her life. She has recently thought about changing careers, often feeling "burned out" by teaching, but, assessing herself, she feels she is "not a go-getter," and doesn't have the energy right now to give up the sense of competence she has in her work to undertake something else. Her mother was still ever-present, but Harriet also has a new view of this relationship. She has gained a perspective on her mother's intrusiveness, and makes choices about when to speak up and what to let go by in order to preserve harmony. She has asked her mother, in a kind way, not to come into their house and change the curtains, for example, but she lets her mother give advice without getting angry at her. She still sees her mother nearly every day, but feels that is for her mother's benefit, not her own.

This deep, emotional mother-daughter knot seems to be passing to the next generation. Harriet has a hard time with her younger daughter, age 5, who is stubborn and oppositional. She finds herself losing patience and yelling at her. Her daughter will not be controlled. But Harriet does not connect her experience as a mother with how she had felt as a daughter—that is an insight that yet awaits her. And she is still, in her own daughterhood, grappling with how a loving relationship between a mother and a daughter can also have boundaries. "My mother created me," she said. "But she brought me up not able to say how I feel." Harriet still couldn't confront her mother very much, but she was now able to know what she feels. "There are a lot of positive feelings and the resentments I push aside." Accepting the limits in her relationship with her mother has paralleled Harriet's accepting other struggles in her life—with her children, with balancing work and family, with accepting that she can't do it all and having Len take over the cooking. "It isn't a TV family. It isn't ideal." And, for Harriet, accepting that it is not ideal was an enormous stride toward maturity.

THE OTHER GUARDIANS

The other women classified as Guardians while they were in college have life histories much like Harriet's. They built their lives as they had imagined them, but then later had some regrets about not having explored or experienced more when they had had the chance. Helen, for example, completed her undergraduate studies in three years, in a hurry to marry her boyfriend, put him through medical school, and start a family. But her husband changed his plans and did not go to medical school, Helen had fertility problems, and it took a long time to get pregnant, so Helen ended up taking her teaching career more seriously. Now, at age 43, with three children and a semi-invalid husband, Helen wonders why she had been in such a rush. She still has choices, she realizes, but so much of their life is restricted by her husband's illness. With regret, she thinks back to those carefree years she never allowed herself.

Gwen, raised on a farm, also became a teacher and married the man on whom her life had been centered since high school. But the marriage was a difficult one, with Gwen continuing to feel that if only she did things better, her husband would be more attentive and less critical and nasty. Not until her husband left her did she enter a period of deep mourning from which she emerged "a new person." From the vantage point of many years, she came to realize how much she had subsumed herself into her husband since her teenage years. "I learned who I was through that divorce and my healing time." Now engaged to a man "for the right reasons," Gwen looks forward to remaking her life, to picking up some of the parts she had ignored because of her husband's jealousy and possessiveness. She plans to retire soon from teaching and do something different. "I feel I have some artistic talent, [I feel] like there are lots of things I can do and do well, but I haven't put my finger on it yet." Gwen, in midlife, has entered a period of searching.

THE GUARDIANS AS A GROUP

The Guardians, in personality style, remain still more rigid and moralistic, more suspicious of change, than the other women I have been learning about, but this rigidity is also their personal strength. They remain perfectionistic, although this quality has been tempered by their maturity. Their lives continue to be founded in family, heritage, and duty instead of pleasure or self-examination. They insist on their wishes by framing them as ethical concerns; this frequently leads to clashes with those they love and with whom they work. Being judges and teachers suits them well (although they could well be found in other occupations); these are roles that embody tradition in society and maintain order. The Guardians rework their proclivity to control themselves into an effort to effect social control. But they have to stretch for flexibility as parents and spouses; compromise and sharing the moral high ground are less habitual responses. Harriet, for example, reports that the only thing that she and Len argue about are morals since he was raised so differently. Recently, on a family outing, their older daughter found a bracelet in a museum. Len's impulse was to keep it; Harriet insisted on returning it to the museum office. Harriet saw this as a matter of the values they were teaching their children. Len regarded it as a lost bracelet. They, of course, returned it. Still, this was upsetting enough for Harriet to tell me about it.

Into their marriages, the Guardians carry their adolescent sense of certainty and conviction and are unlikely to be the partner who gives in. Some have found men who are relieved to have a wife to structure their lives—or, at least, men who don't resist too much. In this arrangement, these women are the dominant force, the more ambitious, often the larger wage-earners. As mothers, as we have seen, they struggle about control. They want their children to be well disciplined and do what they tell them. These women are still fundamentally authoritarian, but this is something they more or less perceive in themselves and more or less combat.

Some who began as Guardians were likely to look to men to structure their lives for them, and they held onto unsatisfactory relationships in the romantic hope that, if they did everything right, there would be a happy ending. Half the Guardians reported histories of staying for long times with men who they ultimately had to recognize were unsatisfactory partners. For them, working their way out of these relationships was a primary trigger for reworking their own identities.

Revision for these women who began their adult lives as Guardians has been wrenching, but relatively invisible to the casual eye. The external markers of their identities have changed less than the internal frame of reference they operate from. They have come to take some distance from themselves and see themselves as individuals with a history rather than ones who evolved just as they "should." As they grow, they come to make their own acquaintance, to discover emotional experience they never knew they had, to own their sexuality, and to begin to acknowledge the imperfection in both themselves and their families of origin. This awareness allows them a new freedom to choose, to try to become what they are, rather than fit themselves into an idealized mold outlined by others.

College was an experience that barely touched most of the Guardians. They got their degrees as entrees to professional fields, but did little reworking of their inner sense of themselves. Only later, usually after some aspect of their life planning went awry, did they begin to grow internally. Some reached this place of self-searching only after they had achieved some new security in their lives—either professional success or a comfortable marriage. Leaning on this secure base, they could look into themselves and see that they were more than they thought they were. That moment arrived for the Guardians much later than for the Pathmakers—not until their early or mid-thirties or even later. From that vantage point, they assessed themselves and found inner aspects they had long ago buried. What was silenced was given voice as they learned to live on their own authority. What had appeared to be rigidity in their earlier years served them well later as a source of strength and a core for revision. The strong convictions of their youth, opened to question only much later in life than for many other women, paved the way for more independent decision-making in midlife.

Afoot and light-hearted I take to the open road,

Healthy, free, the world before me,

The long brown path before me leading wherever I choose.

                    Walt Whitman, Song of the Open Road

5 THE PATHMAKERS

On graduating from college, Betty was quite certain she wanted a career as a physical therapist. Growing up in an athletic family in northern California, herself a championship skier, she was interested in the body and how it functioned. She briefly considered a career in medicine, but was impatient to get on with things and didn't want to spend so much time in school. She was happy about her choice, looked forward to being able to help others return to good physical functioning, and had completed a demanding training program. She described herself as a person of many interests and worried only that she might eventually get bored in any one profession. Yet she felt confident that she could always find something else interesting to do.

Through a period of sexual experimentation, Betty had staked out her independence from her parents and gave up the Catholicism of her family. She had been much influenced by a charismatic professor who challenged everyone's beliefs, outrageously questioning many of the values Betty had always taken as universal truths. Intellectually, she felt windows opening in her mind. At the end of the process of arguing with him—both in class and in her mind—Betty stoically gave up her belief in God and attempted to define her life in terms of feeling responsible for herself. It was wrenching to no longer pray to God for help but to come to feel in charge of her own fate. She also began to experiment sexually, which felt to her like "a tremendous breakthrough." For a time, she slept with anyone toward whom she felt "a magnetic pull," rationalizing that "it's part of life, so why pass it up?" But when she met Dennis early in her senior year of college, she devised yet another perspective on her behavior. She began to worry that she had been promiscuous, and was besieged by guilt. As she and Dennis came to care deeply about each other, Betty reworked her understanding of her college years. Perhaps, she thought, what she had been seeking all along, without realizing it, was a committed relationship. Maybe sexual freedom wasn't so valuable or, at least, wasn't valuable for her. Sex with caring, she decided, suited her better.

By the end of college, Betty was standing firmly on her own ground as she looked at her self-chosen path. She was planning a life with Dennis in which they both would have careers but would center their lives in their shared enjoyment of sports and the outdoors. Eventually, she hoped, they would raise a family.

Like other Pathmakers, Betty had authored an identity on her own terms. Unlike the Guardians, the Pathmakers did not claim the authority of the past or the counsel of their parents as the underpinning of their choice. They had done the psychological work of independence and crafted an identity out of what they felt they were and wished to be. They had taken the step of belonging to themselves. As they approached adulthood at the end of college, the Pathmakers seemed to be like hikers who were blazing a trail through uncharted territory. They carried with them the ties and talents of their past, but they faced forward, surveying the terrain and picking a path. At each step, they paused to consider. What are the choices here, where would I like to go? What is possible? If the underbrush is too thick there, I may not be able to go that way, but here I may be able to carve my route. And I must think about what I am carrying with me. Perhaps I could lighten my load, but there are some things I don't want to be without. In this manner, they made their way. Their path is not necessarily a revolutionary path, or even, often, a highly original one, but it is clearly their own.

Within psychological theory, the Pathmaker identity style in late adolescence has been considered the most developmentally advanced: these are people who are "on time" according to the developmental clock. But we have known little about what happens to such people later in life. What characterized the Pathmakers at the end of college was their capacity to integrate aspects of themselves with their growing understanding of their world as they were both finding and creating it. This was an often silent cartography, deeply internal, and partly unconscious.

Despite their differences in personality and the divergence in their life choices, women who were Pathmakers as college seniors developed into adulthood along similar psychological paths. Entering adulthood, identity for these women continued to be an act of charting and balancing, stepping up to new challenges, backing off from what was too daunting. What they added at each turning determined what might be possible in the next step, one road leading to the next, leaving the other roads behind. Having made a path for themselves, they widen and extend it and plant aspects of themselves within it. For a time they invest most of their energy in one part of it (while tending the other parts), and later move to focus on another region, all the while aware of what may lay beyond, of how they might enlarge what they are creating. Sometimes they stood still for a time, the better to know where they were. Yet they continued to look ahead, following an internal compass, picking their way with great care.

These are women who were confident and clear as college seniors—they scored at the high end of psychological tests of autonomy and self-esteem. But they were not very internally focused, and elected to work toward a goal rather than examine their feelings. Self-analysis in itself was not very appealing—they were more oriented to action or choice.[1] Many were rather uncomfortable with their emotional experience and did not linger long with it, preferring to present to themselves and the world a rational front, a sense of self in control of matters. Unlike the Guardians, they experienced anxiety and guilt—the emotional runoff of taking their lives in their own hands—but had a variety of means to defend against these feelings, to keep these feelings from overwhelming them or inhibiting their capacity to act. They made changes in increments, taking on as much as they could bear. Theirs are odysseys of slow and progressive change, rather than lives of turmoil or wrenching inner drama.

Over the years, I found that most have grown into centered and capable women at midlife, women who continue to find solutions to conflict rather than fan the flames. They have become busy women, engaged in their lives, leaving only occasional moments for introspection or rumination. They were buffeted by the elements while they moved along their paths—most have been rocked by fairly strong winds—yet most of them held to their course, integrating the wind along with everything else. They made compromises along the way, but most ended up feeling that, in the end, they arrived where they had intended to go.

THE JOURNEY TO THE PATHMAKER GATE

The Pathmakers were women who had, by the end of college, done some exploration before making identity commitments. Unlike the Guardians, they had taken some important step beyond their childhood selves. For some, wide vistas of occupational possibility opened avenues toward self-realization. But for many of them, a more immediate—and therefore more important and present—focus of experimentation and self-definition apart from their parents was in sexual experience.

In college in the late 1960s, sexuality was the realm where the world as they found it was most at odds with the teachings of their parents and their childhood milieu. Raised in homes where virginity at marriage was sacrosanct, entering a world where sexual license was a sign of modernity and maturity, these young women often chose sexual experience not so much for its pleasure as for its meaning as a sign of independent thought and decision-making. One way of phrasing the change went something like: "My parents have *their* way of thinking and they aren't going to change. But for me, if I feel strongly about someone and we love each other and hope for a long-term relationship, I think that sex is not only permissible but desirable. Of course, I could never tell my parents. They would have a heart attack—or disown me." Internally, this stance signified a shift to thinking on their own and making their own choices. It necessitated being able to bear guilt and anxiety. Knowing that her parents wouldn't approve, the young woman took a step toward living by her own values, without parental support. In choosing to be in charge of what she did with her body, she chose to be in charge of herself.

Pathmakers did this in a value-dominated rather than an impulsive way. They agonized about whether this was right for them; they struggled with how this might square with their parents' views. Their decision-making was thoughtful, circumspect. Here are the possibilities—what is right for me? Their ties to their parents and their parents' approval were thereby modified. In doing this, they had to internally renounce the old sense of being a "good girl." They could no longer be the ideal daughter, but had to rely on their own ability to approve of themselves, to set standards for themselves to live by. As a result, they gave up the certainty and freedom from inner conflict that the Guardians clung to. They felt anxiety (maybe this really isn't right?) and guilt (maybe I'm not really a good person if I do this?). But an inner push for autonomy gave them the permission to be the one who chose—despite their anxiety, despite their guilt.

This shift—deciding to be in charge of themselves (rather than the fact of sexual experience itself)—reverberated in other areas of their lives. They didn't disattach from their parents or disengage from their families, but they took over the reins. They no longer felt they "belonged" only to their parents and their parents' world or that their parents could always keep them safe. In all areas—choice of friends, choice of career, choice of religion and political beliefs—they came more and more to experience their own decisiveness, with all its accompanying distress. After all, they wondered, were they really qualified to be in charge of something as important as the rest of their lives?

This was not an easy matter, to find inner ways of choosing when all their lives the "right" course had been charted for them. Many looked back wistfully at the end of their adolescence, yearning a bit for the comfort they had felt earlier when things were so much more certain. Following their parents' blueprints, they could feel that wiser people were guiding them in matters of significance. Having charted their own course, they were now free but vulnerable, feeling the risk inherent in doing it their way. The process of exploration was filled with fear—How can I know? What if I make the wrong choice? I recall one of my patients, in the midst of such a crisis, expressing this distress poignantly. "Human beings ought to come with owner's manuals," she said. In claiming themselves and their right to choose, the Pathmakers disclaimed the owner's manuals that their parents had provided and, with full awareness of the gravity of their task, set out to "own" themselves.

Very often, they chose to preserve much of what had always been part of their lives. The Pathmakers did not abandon their prior selves. More often, these women sifted through what they had been, thinking about each piece, deciding to keep most of what was already there, modifying or adding new pieces. Yet—and this was most important—deciding on their own terms. Little was taken simply as a given. Having explored, trying out some options, learning about themselves in different circumstances, with different people, doing things they had never before done, these women also had the capacity to choose. They explored a small region of experience at a time—as much as they could take on at once—then chose a way of being in that realm and moved on to another. When I first met them as college seniors, the Pathmakers were set on a course. They had a story of experimentation behind them, they now knew which wilderness they wanted to head for, had their equipment, and were ready to forge ahead with the choices they had made.

Although the Pathmakers were the most likely of the four groups to rely on themselves, they were also the most likely to have deep and cherished connections to others. They were self-reliant, but within this independence were strong, intimate ties to others with whom they could share and on whom they could rely for support. Andrea, in her senior year of college, told me about a childhood daydream that typifies the inner psychological world of the Pathmakers: "I used to daydream about a castle out in the woods with dungeons. It was spooky, but exciting, with things there trying to attack me. But I was looking for the treasure. I was with a friend, and *as long as someone is with me, I don't get scared.*" This blending of a longing for adventure in a context of connection is the hallmark of the emotional structure of the Pathmakers.[2]

Each Pathmaker began with different pieces to shape into an identity. And the needs of her life partner have often been an important aspect of determining the way in which she could put those pieces together. As other important people have been joined to her inner circle, their needs, too, have been added to the plan, revising its details. So the Pathmakers' story is not only one of amalgamating aspects of who she was with who she will be, but also a story of putting together who she is and will be with the others who are important to her and what they need.

I classified seven women in this group while they were in college. Now, as women in their forties, they still continue to live by their own lights, following paths of their own crafting, except for Nancy who got blown off course in her late thirties and, when I met her at 43, was still struggling. Of the six who have stayed at the helm of their lives, all have undertaken new periods of exploration where they once again sifted through options and then chose anew. In them, we witness the continual process of identity revision. They remain committed to the essentials of their path in life, although it may have undergone many turnings since they started out. At present, all these women work full-time in professions or as managers (except Betty, who works part-time). They vary in how close their careers are to the center of their lives. All are married except for Brenda, who is living with a long-term partner. Four have children; three do not. Among them, they have created lives quite different from one another, but alike in that each in her own way has mapped a life in a creative form, a life course that is uniquely hers.

BETTY

—Age 33   We left Betty several pages back, clear on her plans at the end of college to marry Dennis and begin a career in physical therapy. When I saw her at age 33, I learned that they had indeed married shortly after Betty graduated. I remembered that, in college, Betty had told me how she valued Dennis for his support; they were good at lifting each other's spirits. Dennis was younger and, during her last year in college, she sometimes saw him as juvenile and enjoyed mothering him. But she was attracted to his bravado and zest for living. She insisted that he finish college, even though he was often chafing to get on with what he felt was real life.

Betty worked in physical therapy to support them for two years, after which they decided to begin a whole new life together in Vermont, a state both of them loved because of its rugged wilderness. Betty found it difficult to find work that she liked there—there was not much demand for physical therapists. While waiting for an opportunity to open up, she worked in various jobs related to her skiing expertise. Although it took several years for her to find employment as a physical therapist, she eagerly grasped the first opportunity. Dennis, meanwhile, set out to make his fortune in real estate—which he did in a short time. So short, in fact, that he was ready to retire when he was 30. He envisioned a life they had always daydreamed about, a life of travel and adventure, not tied to the routine of job schedules. But Betty had believed this was only a daydream—she didn't think it would ever come true.

The change in Dennis' fortunes quite literally meant that Betty had to drastically revise her vision of her life. Dennis didn't want her to hold a job that would restrict them, but she wanted to use her professional training—she loved her work. On the other hand, she also loved to travel, which they wanted to do for half of each year. Dennis suggested that Betty find a way to do her work "on call," substituting for others who were on leave, a solution that allowed her to have both her work and their travel. They built their house (which they designed) not too far from a university medical center where Betty could find "on-call" work opportunities and the basic shape of her life was set. Half the year, they spent in Vermont while Betty worked as a physical therapist. The other half, they explored the world. Their son was born when Betty was 32 and they still continued to travel.

When I interviewed her at age 33, Betty's main challenge seemed to be maintaining a sense of her own identity in the face of Dennis' exceptional competence. She admired him for being able to make wonderful decisions—about what stocks to buy, what airlines to fly, how to build their house. "He certainly makes a major contribution to the decision-making process," she said. Their relationship had shifted from their college days when Betty felt like the older, wiser one to Dennis now having that role. Betty was trying to hold onto her professional aspirations as a way of delineating her own competence. It was a struggle not to feel overshadowed.

—*Age 43*　　But fate generated more hurdles in Betty's path. Several years later, they discovered that their son was seriously disabled by speech and learning problems, a syndrome no experts could precisely diagnose. Betty had to become his champion, understanding him when no one else could, finding schooling for him, being his companion since he was quite unable to relate to peers. His difficulty has been, as she describes it today, at age 43, "all-consuming" for her, and she had to develop a whole new kind of expertise. And still they traveled, even after their second child, a daughter, was born five years later.

Betty's path at midlife is far from anything she imagined as she graduated. But her determination to choose for herself, to shape her own life, remains. Betty's life is intricate and interwoven, focused on myriad relationships in her family and her effort to make peace among often warring family members, to find a place for everyone. Thinking back over what she feels have been the main turning points of her adulthood, Betty describes moments in which defining herself in relation to others have been paramount.

One such moment came in the process of mediating between Dennis and William, their son. Dennis was disappointed not to have the son he had fantasized, and Betty was absorbed by trying to help him overcome his sense of loss and learn to love and accept William as he is. But Dennis persisted in thinking that punishment would at least help control some of William's more destructive behavior. And so he would spank him, much as he had been spanked as a child. Betty found this intolerable. "I had to stand up in a very strong way. I had to physically intervene and say that this type of treatment of this child makes me so sick and I will not participate and I will not allow you to participate and I will remove the children from this. My intent was to make him wake up and see that this is just not the way to go. I'm not saying that he physically abused them on a regular basis, but his attitude toward discipline was spank and they'll straighten out, and when that doesn't work as a technique, one shouldn't continue to pursue it. So I had to be strong for a number of years on that issue. I think it was very important for all of us and it has changed. He's kept his hand at bay, realizing that it never solved the problem. So I see that as a turning point. Because I'm a strong person, but not in an adversary situation. As soon as there is adversary [conflict], I'll sit back because I don't like confrontation. But it was really important to do."

Growth for Betty has also involved standing up to Dennis in other ways. Several years ago, he found an island off the coast of Maine for sale that he very much wanted to buy and live on. "It would have meant an absolute total life change. We would have turned all our money over to that property. I couldn't decide where I fit into this. The land was absolutely gorgeous. You get on this island and you can't think of anything other than living there. It was like being in paradise. Finally, I said no, I couldn't do it. It took absolutely everything I had—because it was so awesome and so overwhelming to be there. I'd get there and I'd feel I couldn't even think about anything else. And I'd get away and I'd think what about the difficulty of getting out, what about not being able to get medical service for my son. . . . What about living so far away from my family? . . . We were about to change everything and I finally got the strength to say no, I couldn't do it. My husband was in love with this property and I was too. And I realized that this was just the wrong decision—for me."

Betty, like the other women who began as Pathmakers, has continued through her adulthood to find and to feel her place—in the context of others' needs and interests, but not on anyone else's authority but her own. These women have attained the capacity to approach their life by asking "What is the right decision—for me—in relation to all that I am and all who I care about?" Betty holds to her work identity, she says no to her husband, she finds resources for her son when none are apparent.

At midlife, Betty is aware of how influential her husband has been in shaping her life—both his needs and his financial means. Yet she continues to try to define her own realms of competence and decision-making. She figures out and implements the home schooling of the children when they are on one of their long journeys. She maintains her work involvement even when abroad by keeping up with professional literature. She takes charge of their charity work and contributions, and is engaged in a number of volunteer activities centered around environmental issues. She takes care of her invalid mother-in-law. Her parents have retired to a place in Vermont not far away and she maintains a close relationship with her mother and sisters. And, in each domain, one can hear her defining her stance based on her own needs and those of others, putting them together, not losing but interweaving herself. She asks: Where do I fit into this? Betty is clear that when she looks at their life, she can see her stamp on it.

For half of the women who entered adulthood as Pathmakers, the challenge has rested on how to have a self, a marriage, and raise children at the same time, and how to find a balance between these realms that is comfortable and satisfying. Generally, this has involved a great deal of creative life architecture.

MARIA

Maria built her early adult identity around her determination to both have a career *and* raise a family. While this was not an unusual wish in the early 1970s, it seemed like heresy to her traditional Italian family, who held strongly that a woman's place was with her children.

—At the End of College   Maria's parents had never put much stock in a career for a woman and never encouraged her in any particular direction. In college, Maria majored in psychology, hoping to work with retarded children, but she was impatient with her studies and, like Betty, was eager to get into the world and begin her life.

By the end of college, Maria had already had some years of making her own choices. Her move to thinking on her own came during high school when she began dating an African-American boy, much to the dismay of her family. She did not (at least, consciously) see this as an aspect of rebellion.

She had taken seriously all the church teachings about loving one's neighbor and expected her family and friends to accept him. Reflecting on this relationship when I interviewed her in college, she said, "That was a decision I had to make. With religion talking about love thy neighbor and all men are equal, and it was all right until he asked me out. Now, after six years, my family has accepted it." She intended to marry this man. "It's a decision I've thought about for a long time and it still bothers me. But when I think about it, I know its going to be my life and I can't go against my own ideas for my parents."

Standing up for herself against her parents on this was at the cost of much emotional pain. Maria, while in college, spoke with great warmth about her family; it was an intensely close one with many family traditions, expectations, and "rock-solid support." Her father had been strict with discipline and she battled with him about rules, sometimes sneaking out of the house. Maria thought of her mother as "very giving . . . she'd give anything to her family." She regarded her family as "almost ideal," except that her mother seemed too submissive to her father. She hoped to create a similar family, but to be less submissive—which she seemed well on the way to doing.

Growing up in her larger extended family, with grandmothers, aunts, and cousins just around the corner, Maria felt as if she had "ten mothers." She was popular in high school and served on the student council. Maria's adolescence was happy and secure, but a part of her was reaching even then for her own definitions—through her relationship with someone her family would never have expected her to choose.

Reflecting on her college years as she was about to graduate, Maria stressed that what she had mainly learned concerned the limits in helping relationships. "Experience has taught me not to be so idealistic. When I went into the treatment center for retarded children [during an internship], I thought that if I just cared enough, it would change things. That a lot of these people just never had anyone that really cared, and I did really care; and in a lot of cases things didn't work out, and I didn't become callous, but it taught me that there are a lot of limitations working within certain structures. You want to do so much, yet you can't." Fortunately, Maria had a supportive supervisor who "showed me the realities of various situations and encouraged me to go to graduate school." With his help, Maria was able to maintain her goals and learn to bear the frustration.

As she approached the end of college, Maria had charted her course and faced the future with optimism. She planned to find work, marry her boyfriend (and fight the prejudice), eventually have children, then resume work after her children were of school age. She remained fiercely loving of her family. Her sense of individuality did not undo her ties to them.

—Age 33   When I met Maria again when she was 33, I found her less vivacious than she had been in college. She began the interview by commenting that of course I wouldn't recognize her since she had gained fifty pounds since college. Even more startling was that this Maria seemed weary. Gone was the sparkle, the idealism, even the determination. Her life had gone through many revisions in the intervening years, with burdens greater than she had expected. I met her in her office—she had become a nurse and advanced to Director of Nursing, but her life was centered on motherhood.

After she graduated, Maria's relationship with her boyfriend began to unravel. He had become more involved in the drug culture, dropped out of school, and Maria slowly and painfully realized that he would not make a good life partner. What she came to know about herself was that what she wanted most was to be with a man who would be a good father to her children and a reliable husband to her. More and more, she began to recognize that, while she loved her boyfriend, he would not offer these things. Reluctantly, she ended the relationship and set out to "see what else was out there." She became closer to George, a colleague and long-time friend in the Center for Retarded Children where she worked. Although she never "fell in love" with him in an intense way, she knew George to be "sensitive, caring, handsome, somewhat shy, and responsible." He loved children and had the same values, and she felt that they "fit together" well. Maria reasoned that he was the partner she really needed and they married within a few months.

Rethinking her goals at that time, Maria came to feel that having a family was most important. Her work in the state-run children's center was becoming increasingly frustrating and disappointing, laden with paperwork and bureaucracy. Again, Maria stopped to think and investigate. She began to consider switching into nursing because it offered flexibility for working mothers. Not about to give up her wish to work and feel productive, Maria thought she was now sculpting a life structure that would allow her to realize her goals: to have a good partner for the family she wanted to create and to have work that would be meaningful and possible to integrate with her family life.

Maria's daughter was born two years after she and George married. Maria quit her job to pursue evening courses in nursing. When her son was born two years later, she began part-time work out of financial necessity, but she and George were able to arrange their schedules so that one of them was always with the children. And Maria was most proud of that. She had done it—managed to have both, despite the skepticism and disapproval of her family. "I feel like a big group is watching me, asking in subtle, indirect ways if I am sure I am doing the right thing." Not long before, she had overheard her mother telling someone, "Maria is married and working and her kids are okay." At that moment, she felt she had triumphed—on her own path.

At age 33, her children were the center of her life. "I believe they need quantity and quality time with both parents." She was pleased that George was so child-centered, but regretted that physical problems kept her from having more children. Sometimes she wished that she wasn't working, and could have more time for herself, for crafts and exercise. But she loved the people she was working with. "We're a small, close-knit team."

The anchors of Maria's identity at age 33 were not that different from the fundamental values she had been raised with, but she experienced her choices as her own. It took Maria some time to find out what was centrally important to her, finally deciding that what she most wanted was "to be of help to others." With more time, she came to see that she could do this most meaningfully within her own family. Unlike the Guardians, she could ask herself what she wanted, rather than automatically do what was expected. Although wearied by all that she had taken on, Maria was content with her life. She managed her stress by overeating, resigning herself to weighing more than she wished.

—*Age 43*   By age 43, however, Maria seemed even more beleaguered by life—and with good reason. Maria had been feeling that her life structure and ways of coping were running smoothly until, three years ago, George, at age 46, developed a brain tumor. Although he survived a very risky surgery, he was left with multiple disabilities and spent over a year in the hospital. Just before his tumor was discovered, they had lost six close family members: both of George's parents, three of her aunts, and one of George's uncles. "All this trauma . . . does make you reevaluate some things in your life and what's important—your friendships, your relationships with people are more firmly cemented by these events or you realize some relationships weren't as strong as you thought. You see who is really there for you and who isn't. I look at things a little differently. My family has always been very important for me. It's even more important to me now . . . everything else really falls by the wayside and that becomes the real core of your existence and when you are faced with that kind of thing, nothing is more important—not your job or your financial situation. I think someone's health—its such a basic, basic thing. I had more aspirations professionally. Now I'm not so sure I want to keep climbing that ladder. That maybe I should be content pretty much where I am and not always try to move ahead and take on more. Personally, I'd like to develop more personal interests and take more time for myself than I did in those first ten years. George's mother's death was particularly difficult for all of us because it was very sudden. She was young and healthy and just dropped dead one day of a heart attack. She didn't have the time to enjoy her life that she really deserved."

Maria continued, "The last ten years have been an extended period of trauma. And trying to keep your kids together and keep your job because now you're the only breadwinner. And I was in my last semester of graduate school at that point. But people were very good to me, understanding. My boss was good to me in terms of time. So there are people who stand out as being there for me."

Maria's professional life offered her something of a respite from her personal trauma and an arena for a sense of success. She is in the same job as Director of Nursing. Of the last ten years, she says, "Professionally, I've grown. I've been in the same position I've been in for fourteen years as a manager. But I did go to graduate school—that was positive. I was nominated as Nurse of the Year one year. My program got an award from the AMA as one of the outstanding programs. I've done a lot of community work with this program and I'm well known in the community. So professionally I feel that I've done well and I've been recognized for it. I feel secure in that. There's been times I've thought it would be nice to keep moving up the ladder administratively. The hospital here has gone through many administrative changes in the past few years and I jokingly say that if you climb that ladder you can fall off. That top layer changes frequently, yet the people who are department heads and are closer to the patients and do the nitty-gritty work have stayed more stable. So I've kind of reevaluated—how far do you want to go? Do you really want to move on? Sometimes I think I should try something different and I may some day but its not—it won't be—because I want to become president of a hospital. It would be because I want to expand my horizons."

Maria is aware of the irony that although her mother and aunts had regarded her work as self-indulgent and dispensable, it has now become a necessity. Even though she takes pride in having been able to become the breadwinner, she also lives within the constraints of that responsibility. When she toys with the idea of applying for a higher position, she fears losing her livelihood, which is no longer a matter of discretion. The massive administrative changes in the hospital make her worry in a new way. "I have to decide whether I want to stay at this job or move on to something else. There have been times when I've really struggled with that and continually chosen to stay where I am, although I have sometimes been very tempted to try something different. I [now] have some fears about losing my job because they have tended to let go managers here who have a lot of seniority. A lot of people say that's an economic decision because you are at the higher end of the salary scale and people who I worked with here as long as I've been here have been fired. And I don't know how I am going to fare. I think before my husband's surgery, I would have been. . . . Now I say if it happens to me, it happens to me, I'll find another job. We're not going to starve to death. I may not like it as well, but it may turn out well. I can't stay up nights worrying about it. Maybe having been through what I've been through, it gives me perspective. I don't know who they can find within the organization who has the experience or community contacts that I have, but you never know. Sometimes that gives me maybe a false sense of security. I was offered another job at a considerably higher salary and I really struggled for about three days but I knew that the responsibility was going to be enormous, the place was a mess, and I knew that it would take a long time to build everything up. I weighed where I was and the comfort level there and I said, no, I don't need to do that now. If I was out of a job, I would have jumped at it. My husband saw the more money and he said go for it, but. . . . The other thing would have been leaving the people here who mean an awful lot to me and I just kept weighing back and forth and this place won out. I've thought about moving up to a vice-president level. I think if they post it, I'll have to sit there and make a decision. Sometimes I think that from that position I might have the ability to make more positive changes. But the other side is about job security—is this a group of people I can work with? I don't know."

Again, we see Maria continuing to plan, to weigh options, to make her choices, within the constraints of her life, in considered fashion. Decision-making for Pathmakers is never obvious; nor does it feel as if it is determined by outside forces ("the only thing I *could* do" or "the *right* thing"). They realize that they could just as well have made another choice. Having chosen, Maria maintains her confidence that, come what may, she will find a way. Losing her job would be terrible, she thinks, but may also lead to new possibilities. At the same time, she is not ready to leap at just any other job, even one that offers more money and status. She thinks through in quite pragmatic terms how she would experience herself in a different role.

It was not just George's illness that fueled Maria's professional identity. She had always been the more ambitious one of the couple. Even before his illness, it bothered Maria that George showed no interest in progressing beyond the work he was doing at the Center for Retarded Children where they first met. On the other hand, Maria had valued other qualities in him—his devotion to the children, for example, and his willingness to be a full partner in their family life.

Maria admires her husband for the recovery he has made. "He had major determination that I'm not sure I would have had in that situation. He has had a lot of fight from the beginning and has exceeded anyone's expectations in terms of his recovery. I just don't think that I have personally that kind of determination and fight. But I also don't think that you know until it hits you. You know I've seen so many patients—that human spirit kicks in and you don't want to die. But I've also seen the work he put in and the struggle. I don't know if I ever would have had that stamina. I'm a more laid-back individual, more introspective. My husband is very concerned about his appearance, always had been. For him not to be able to talk and have a paralyzed body—that body-image stuff for him. Whereas I may have been more accepting of it. . . . I have such respect for him—how he would never accept the limitations that others kept putting on him. And I think he also saw a strength in me. I held things together. I worked. I took care of the kids, visited him in the hospital every day. It brought us closer. We found each other. We care about each other. We care a lot about our kids. We are committed to each other. We've been through some rough times together and I can see where this could drive people apart."

Maria's children are now teenagers, which has changed the issues surrounding their care. She still wants to spend as much time as possible with them, but they have their own lives, which leaves her alone with George much of the time. There are stresses being with him because of his remaining cognitive disabilities and preoccupations with his capabilities. "He just wants to keep reliving what happened to him." He has become increasingly isolated from people, and Maria feels that she is his only friend. As a result, she feels guilty leaving him and wishes she could find a way to make time for herself to be with her friends or pursue activities apart from him.

Reflecting on her marriage, Maria feels that it has turned out much as she expected. "It's kind of what I envisioned. I wanted someone who is very family-oriented and that's what I got. I wanted a husband who was around—I compare him to other people I know and I think this is really what I wanted. I didn't want a part-time husband or a part-time father for my kids. There were times I wished we had more financial security. Now I don't care as much. Financially we've had some major struggles. I'd look at people who are more affluent with some envy. I've thought what it would be like to take golf lessons or belong to a gardening club and not have to work as much as I do. There are times in terms of my children that I've regretted having to work as much as I do. . . . There are always some things you miss—not going on field trips. But I do make an attempt to do things with them in their school, even if I have to take time out to do it."

The strongest bond between Maria and George has always been their children, but now the children are less willing to be a focus. Maria was, however, most passionate in the interview when discussing her daughter, Linda, now 17. "I'm having a tough time dealing with her. She has been dating a boy for over a year, which I am having a real hard time with. And what's funny is that I was involved with this guy before I got married for seven years and I was at my cousin's for Easter and we were talking about our daughters and I said I wish she'd broaden her horizons and I don't know why she'd want to stick to one guy and my cousin turned to me and said, 'Sounds just like her mother.' And I thought, my God, you're right. And the more I try and discuss it with her, the more she digs her heels in. She's always had a stubborn streak, but we've always had a good relationship and this is the first thing that we've hit that we just don't see eye to eye on at all. And I'm not particularly fond of him. He's not a bad kid, but I think he has some real problems and I think she sees herself as a helper. I never drank as a teen and neither does she, but she went to a party the other night and all the guys gave her their keys to hold and it was like looking in the mirror. I was called the "Mother" at my high school. And I see Linda—she is the dependable one—and I look at her and I think, She is me. Yet it's making me angry to see her in this long-term relationship at this young age. She won't even let me open my mouth about it. I've used all the skills I have to talk to her about it. And my colleagues, who are therapists, are telling me that this is her separation issue and lighten up about it, so I try, but I find this is the first big struggle I'm having with her. She's a very bright girl, does well in school, has never been in any trouble. She's a child most parents would die for. Talking to her about college is a real struggle—she could care less. She's got so much potential but she is so caught up in this relationship."

I wondered why it would make Maria so angry to see her daughter repeating her own pattern. "Because I look back and know why I rebelled. Because my parents were so strict. But I've let her do almost everything. I feel like I've done just the opposite of my parents in bringing her up and here she's doing the same thing. I didn't expect it from her. I expected her to be a little more worldly and not to get caught up intensely in a relationship. She's seen her mother be very independent and work. I've supported the family for three years; I've always worked outside the home. The different awards I've gotten. She's come to the dinners, so she's seen her mother. So I always felt she didn't have the same role model as I did—you know, a mother for whom marriage was almost arranged and was very subservient. She saw a very different relationship than I did with my parents. I just don't understand why she's had that need to get so involved in such a monogamous relationship at such a young age. And this is really her first real relationship. She says to me, don't worry, I'm not going to marry him. And I say, then why are you doing this? They spend almost every waking moment together and I've tried to limit the time but she just gets more angry so I kind of let up. She does what she's supposed to do, but that's been a major struggle."

So although Maria does not complain about her life or her choices, she has in mind quite a different narrative for her daughter. And this suggests that somewhere deep within her is buried another vision of herself, a self that is less of a "Mother," more ambitious perhaps, more self-oriented, a self she couldn't find room for that she now hopes to express through her daughter. Perhaps this might foreshadow further revision in her own life, a revision still in embryonic form, that may or may not be born.

As I listen to Maria, I hear the unspoken pain behind her words and behind her quiet, modulated, enduring voice. I find myself missing the feisty young woman she was twenty years ago, the woman ready to take on the world's racism. But I see also that taking on what she has taken on has required the same kind of courage. Like many other women who began as Pathmakers, Maria does not give voice to her discontent. Instead, the forces for change gather in the wings, preparing to push for action at the opportune moment. These women tend to live somewhat stoically, finding value in what they have created: "As I look back on my life, what stands out and what gives me most value is my children. I've never had a lot of trouble with them— they do well, they have friends. . . . To me, I'll sacrifice anything for my children—time, money—they just mean everything to me. A lot of people say to me, 'Think about yourself' and I'd say this is not my time to be selfish.'" I asked Maria if having children diminished her life in any way and she emphatically said, "No! I've enjoyed every moment of it. If anything, I regret that it's gone so quickly."

While Maria's strong sense of family commitment feels derived from her family of origin, she believes that in every other way, she has been a different kind of parent. This is another way in which she feels she has authored her own identity. "I'm a lot more liberal than my parents certainly. My parents have a very strong religious and spiritual sense that I don't. They wouldn't let me date and I was sneaking around a lot and I very much said to my children that I wanted them to be honest with me and I would be honest with them. They are more open about coming to me with issues that I would never talk to my parents about. My daughter tells me who is sleeping with whom. There is no way I could imagine ever saying that to my mother. We have a more open relationship, and can talk to each other. But our commitment to family and to each other—that's the same. That being paramount. My mother was there for me more than anyone was when my husband was sick. She was there for them. My kids saw that. She just moved in for three months. Which was great for me and for my kids. Having someone take care of them while I was out in twenty different directions. My kids see what I do for them. My kids see what I do for my parents or how I respect my parents and am still in close contact with them."

Looking back at her life, Maria is proud of herself—for her children and who they are, but also for her own life planning. "When a crisis came I was able to handle it. I've had so many women say to me, my God if that happened to me, we would have lost our house. I feel a certain amount of satisfaction that I could pull it off, that I could handle it. And I wonder Is this how men feel all the time? That they are the ones in charge and in control and have to provide for everyone else and have that burden? And sometimes I've felt it as a burden but I've also been happy that I could do it. And for that, I'm proud of myself. That I got an education, that I have the skills that I have, that I do the job at my job that I do, that I make a decent salary so that, tough as it was, I could hold it together. I feel like no one's ever provided for me since I left home and for me, there's a certain amount of satisfaction that you can do that for yourself."

Maria's complex life, as we meet her in her mid-forties, reflects both change and continuity, adaptation to trauma and expression of strength and capacity. She had wanted to realize both her strong sense of family commitment and her professional ambition and has worked out a way of doing both, integrating the changing needs of her husband, the increased pressure on her to provide for the family, and the ever-changing relationship with her children. And although Maria regrets that the most intense mothering years are behind her, she is nevertheless beginning to eye the possibilities of professional advancement, surveying the territory, thinking about new paths that might be available. And she looks forward "to not being as torn between all of the commitments. I can see that happening a little bit. I feel like my life is still too frenzied. I get up, go to work, come home, cook dinner, run the kids here and there. I'd like more time to myself." And she plans to take that time for herself: to garden, to play golf, to exercise and lose weight, to read, and be with friends. The main highway of Maria's life is the commitment to her family, but there are many branching roads as well.

Both Betty and Maria's lives have been profoundly affected by the changed circumstances of their husbands, which has made a framework bounding their freedom of action. But they have relied on the resilience that characterizes the women who were in the Pathmaker group. For them, decision-making has involved finding solutions that suit both "their needs *and* my needs."

ANDREA

Andrea has struggled quite consciously with balancing her needs with others', sometimes finding it impossible to find such an inclusive solution. Among the Pathmakers, she has been most clearly the architect of her own destiny. Andrea exemplifies the hallmark Pathmaker characteristics: she sets her own goals and pursues them; she is independent; and she has the capacity to integrate parts of herself into a reasonably well-functioning whole.

—At the End of College   Andrea was difficult to get to know in college. She was shy and reserved, and wasn't very willing to talk about herself. Reflecting on herself or wondering about herself seemed foreign to her way of thinking. Andrea thought only about her activities and her goals. She laughed nervously throughout the interview, and her blandness made it hard for me to warm to her.

Andrea planned to go to medical school and that was at the center of the identity she was constructing. Her father had shared her interest in science and she found that she enjoyed things that were difficult and a challenge. She had made decisions about all the main issues that defined the identity categories, but had done this rather quietly, without overt crisis and rebellion.[3] She was raised a Catholic, but while at college, she joined a much more liberal wing of the church. She had strong political opinions and had come to her own ideas about standards for sexual behavior; one could sense the strength at the core of Andrea's purposefulness. She was clearly a young woman who thought on her own.

Although Andrea portrayed her family as having been close and overprotective, she seemed to have moved away from their control gradually but firmly. She spoke of her father with great warmth, and the hours they spent discussing ideas, particularly about science. With her mother she struggled more—about how late she could come in at night, whether she could have friends her mother didn't know, and other issues of freedom.

Throughout high school, Andrea had been seen by others as "the studious one" and had only a few close friends. Despite her being at the top of her class, her parents thought college was wasted on a girl. They planned to send her brother to college, assuming that she would work as a secretary until she married.

Without rupture or fight, though recognizing its unfairness, Andrea accepted their decision and quietly made plans to put herself through college. She chose an inexpensive public university and found part-time office work where she could earn enough to support herself while living at home. What was striking was that Andrea expressed no resentment at her parents for this. She spoke in a somewhat flat way about their viewpoint, emphasizing with a verbal shrug that she was doing what she wanted to do, so what was the problem?

Working so much and studying in a difficult and competitive pre-med program left Andrea little leisure time. But she was enough a part of the student community to begin to recognize that the bedrock assumptions of her family and religion were "not necessarily the only way to be." This led Andrea to more battles with her mother over freedom to choose friends and ideas. Her mother still didn't like Andrea going out with people she didn't know.

But Andrea was gaining more and more certainty about defining things on her own: her career goals, her friendships, and, increasingly, her more radical political beliefs.

In her sophomore year, Andrea met Arnold, who seemed to her much like herself but more self-assured. He cheered her ambitions and encouraged her to pursue her goals; he gave her a pep talk when the road ahead seemed too much. In other ways, Arnold opened new horizons for her. "He made me more sure of myself, more willing to try new things. He helped me to grow up." They planned to marry just after graduation and support themselves, somehow, through medical school.

—*Age 33*   By the next time I saw Andrea, when she was 33, she had developed into a much more lively and engaging person. In her late twenties, she had done more thinking about herself and was more open, more interested in reflecting on her own development.

Andrea had finished medical school, obtained a Ph.D. in biochemistry, and was shaping a career that involved part-time research and part-time clinical medicine. She settled on this plan when she became interested in hormonal disorders during her residency and wanted to be on the forefront of advances in this field. As planned, she did marry Arnold, but they were struggling with the problems of coordinating their careers. Andrea had just received a prestigious job offer in Philadelphia, but Arnold did not want to leave Chicago, where he had started his practice. They had discussed the possibilities of a commuter marriage, but neither really believed it could work. Andrea was disappointed to turn down such a wonderful offer, but felt this was the best decision. It wasn't that she didn't like her current job; in fact, she was finding enormous satisfaction both in working with patients and in her research.

Andrea's life at this age was almost completely absorbed by her work and by Arnold, whom she still very much enjoyed being with. Over the years, his support of her career had become somewhat less wholehearted since he was the one to suffer from the long hours she put in at the hospital and the laboratory. When she chose to pursue her additional graduate degree program, he was furious at the idea of more years of nights and weekends without her, but ended up resigning himself to what seemed to be the priority she was giving to her intellectual interests. Andrea regarded Arnold as less career-oriented and also as less able to find other companionship. She saw him as the needier partner, waiting at home wondering when she would arrive. But she said, "We have deep feeling and a long history together." And, although Andrea felt that they had a very successful twelve-year marriage, she found that she also needed other men in her life. While involved in an intense affair with a colleague, Andrea realized that she needed both—the marriage and the affair. She was forthright about this with Arnold. After exploring all the ramifications, Arnold resigned himself to this, too, recognizing that Andrea needed independence and not to feel restricted. "I don't feel it's immoral to have extramarital sex," Andrea said, "as long as its not hurting my partner. If there is an understanding between you, then it is not wrong to have other relationships." Over the years, Andrea has had two other strong relationships with other men, but neither interfered with her commitment to her marriage.

In both work and love, Andrea was cultivating the ground in her own way. She not only went to medical school, but got another advanced degree to be able to pursue a carefully phrased interest. She didn't become "a doctor," but a doctor who was balancing clinical and research interests, crossing lines in the service of her creativity. Similarly, in her marriage, Andrea was also not accepting tacit definitions. Although raised in a strict Catholic environment, she was able to speak about a need that violated social and religious conventions and work out a marriage that suited her wishes and gave her the space she craved.

She and Arnold were in agreement not to have children. "Gradually I realized that I'm not going to be able to do everything. I didn't think I could take care of children and maintain my life style and my work. I do not feel the need to procreate," Andrea said at age 33, just after having her tubes tied. There was, of course, social pressure from Andrea's family to have children, but Andrea had never paid much attention to social pressure. Andrea had set clear limits on her mother's intrusiveness and continuing efforts to control her. "I tell her what I think she won't get upset about. She realizes that, at this point, if she pushes me too much, she won't see me." Although she wasn't enjoying the time she spent with her mother, she carried out what she saw as her daughterly duties with a great deal of care and concern, particularly after her father's death, which occurred six years earlier. Even though there was little that she and her mother really shared, Andrea tried to plan activities that could bring them both pleasure.

Looking to the future at age 33, Andrea was certain there would be change, change that she would welcome because it would mean further adventure and challenge. Research funding was increasingly uncertain, and Andrea thought she probably would make some kind of career move. And she wondered if perhaps some other man might someday claim her affections, even though she then felt strong in her commitment to Arnold and had just reaffirmed it in turning down the Philadelphia job. At age 33, Andrea had won self-confidence. She was self-assured, certain that she would continue to enlarge and enliven the path she had forged.

—*Age 43*   By age 43, she had indeed continued to do just that. As the exigencies of practice changed, Andrea had to modify the structure of her professional life. The rise in malpractice insurance and the necessity to pay full-time rates even for part-time practice drove her into work for an HMO where she could practice under their insurance umbrella. A shift in research funding led her to another lab, but in both instances she was content with her situation. She had become the first woman appointed to the examining board in her specialty, an honor that she enjoyed but added to her responsibilities.

In the intervening ten years, she has divorced and remarried. The divorce was a painful time for Andrea. Although she had come to recognize that she simply wasn't happy enough with Arnold, she couldn't help feeling that she had failed. And a sense of failure was not something Andrea easily endured. More and more, she had come to sense that they were incompatible. "We bought a house, but I wasn't pleased about it. He wanted to settle in and work on the house. It was impossible to drag him away to travel or do things. He didn't want to develop new friendships, didn't want to try new things. I may have gotten tired butting my head against the wall. I didn't like having other relationships—it was a way of avoiding the problem. I suggested therapy, but he wasn't interested. I was having lunch with a friend who was getting a divorce, and I realized that that is what I wanted to do. Once I decided, things moved rapidly, but he was very angry. Once I left, it was nice to be alone and to be able to do what I wanted to do when I wanted."

After living alone for a year, Andrea became involved with Charles, a musician who had been one of her patients. He was full of life and charm. In some ways, it was exciting to be with someone not in medicine, someone who could show her a different world and introduce her to different kinds of people. Unlike Arnold, he was not dependent on her, enjoyed the spontaneity of travel, and had the resilience to deal with the unexpected. Eventually they married. "I didn't really think about it. He asked me, I said yes, and once I decide to do a thing, that's it." Andrea was still not highly self-reflective or analytical.

The challenge in their relationship has been coordinating their schedules so that they have time off together. Her new marriage has changed her, Andrea feels. "I'm more relaxed, take more vacations. We have a different range of friends, he's very social." Something emotional changed in Andrea and, at age 43, she admitted she might have considered having children with Charles. But Charles doesn't want children, and anyway she had had her tubes tied. They compromised on a puppy "as a surrogate child."

Andrea feels finished with extramarital relationships. "I always felt guilty.

And I realize now that it was all a way of avoiding the problem. I wouldn't condemn anyone else, but its not what I want for myself."

It is in their intimate relationships that some Pathmakers have been most creative, trying to find a balance with a partner they care about who suits their own needs, often taking a stand against social convention. They don't merely accept ready-made social definitions. Brenda is in a long-term relationship with a man she lives with but doesn't plan to marry. They do not want to have children, and she sees no gain in marriage except to "make my mother happy." She feels committed and bonded and, it seems to her, that is what ought to be important.

Alice, recognizing that she had married immediately after college out of fear of her own freedom, divorced several years later. Her husband was idle and abusive and she knew that the marriage was not right for her. She then took several years to choose more carefully.

Although these women, entering adulthood as Pathmakers, are women who had the capacity to anchor themselves on their own ground, their life courses are shaped inexorably by the people they choose as partners and by the exigencies of those they love. Somehow, in the way these women apprehend their decision-making, painful choices between self-interest and others' needs don't arise. They devise a creative strategy before the problem is ever phrased in either-or terms. To use Clara's words, "You have to flex and improvise and compromise."

The Pathmakers' planning is so intricate, taking so many variables into account, that they live with the awareness that their lives could well have been lived otherwise. None tried to persuade me that hers was the best way to live (although all seemed proud that it was *her* way). Parallel possibilities accompany them along their paths. Reflecting on a choice she and her husband made to move back to the States after living abroad for ten years, Clara said, "It wasn't just a conscious decision—there were so many factors. If things had happened differently, we might have made a different decision. But we've never regretted the decision to come home. There were negative things about the other choice too." Unlike the Guardians who, at the outset, try to live their lives as though it were the only right way to live, the Pathmakers recognize that many life structures might be possible, that many factors influence their choices. Their lives are the cumulative product of roads they have taken and not taken—they are not *the* path to absolute Goodness. Not striving for perfection, the Pathmakers ask only that their lives be "good enough." They live embracing their compromises, ready to assert themselves, but also ready to remain flexible.

Career decisions have been shaped by multiple forces of which ambition and talent are only a part. All the Pathmakers changed their plans from what they had envisioned as college seniors. As they got into the work world, they became more sagacious—and sometimes more cynical—about what was out there and, with greater knowledge, could better match their own needs and interests with what opportunity offered them.

All the Pathmakers have taken up responsible professional or managerial occupational roles, yet all share a sharply realistic stance in regard to the rewards available in the work world. Much of their learning and growth in the past twenty years has been about coming to terms with what they can reasonably expect to gain from their occupational lives. For most, their learning in this area has come through disillusionment or what they describe as eye-opening experiences. Work itself, they have discovered, is not always meaningful. The real joys of working come through the relationships they have with those with whom and for whom they work. Moving ahead is not always the wisest course. The workplace is not always fair or reasonable. Don't trust institutions too much. Bureaucracies are dehumanizing. These are the hard-won occupational lessons these women told me they have learned.

Andrea, assessing her occupational ambition at age 43, says, "I used to want to be a department chair somewhere. Now I think it's not worth the hassles. I'm not interested in status. It's more important that I like doing what I'm doing." Work lives are regarded like other aspects of the Pathmakers' lives—in hardheaded fashion—what is gained, what is lost. The Pathmakers are too clear-eyed to be entrapped by status and money.

Clara recognized that she had to earn a library degree in order to be taken seriously as a book conservator. She hated the graduate program, found it intensely boring, but persisted because she saw that it would take her where she wanted to go. Her job description is still not exactly what she wants to do, but she believes that she can move laterally until she gets to shape the work as she wants it to be. Hierarchy, however, does not interest her. Pathmakers do not romanticize their work—they want to enjoy, they want to feel effective. Since most are supportive of feminist causes, they would strenuously renounce the existence of glass ceilings. But they would not themselves feel impelled to try to get to the top. They fear getting to a high place where work may cease to be meaningful.

While work, partners, and, for four of these women, mothering, take up the bulk of the Pathmakers' time, some of the most meaningful moments in their adult lives have come through revised relationships with their families of origin; this, too, is a central aspect of their identities. None of the Pathmakers live in the cities or towns where they were raised, although all are within one to three hours driving distance from their parents.

Secure in the personal authority of their own identity, the Pathmakers are the most interested of all the groups in forming adult relationships with their parents through knowing their parents as people with their own histories. As they move into midlife, the Pathmakers increasingly see themselves in generational terms, as children of one generation, parents (or nurturers) of the next. Internally and emotionally, they have struggled to detach and distance themselves from their childhood anger over their parents' failings, but at the same time have learned to appreciate their parents for what they are able to offer. By midlife, they have come to know their parents better, to accept them, and to forgive them. And, in doing this, to know themselves better as well.

In college, Alice described her parents as quiet, retiring, and hard to get to know. They were solid, reliable, but "average," without characteristics or values she could define. "I always wanted to please my parents, I wanted them to be proud of me." But she felt cheated out of closeness to them. There wasn't much they would talk about: she learned the "facts of life" in school. She felt they could never understand her experiences with drugs, sex, wild parties, or political rallies. And she was shocked in college when she became aware that other girls could talk to their mothers about things. But Alice went on with her life, always having a boyfriend and a best friend to talk to, not dwelling on the emotional distance she felt from her parents.

By the time she was 33, Alice, now married, divorced, and remarried, mother of two, living in a small town three hours away, felt "much closer" to them. At least they could hug and kiss occasionally, but she still found it impossible to "discuss anything intimate with either of them." She was still disappointed, still bravely fighting off the resentment, denying her longing. Alice thought of herself as much more assertive and extroverted and was content to experience herself as attached to her family, but completely unlike them. As she entered her forties, Alice had resigned herself to her relationship with them, but began for the first time to see parts of them in herself. Through the persistence of Adam, her husband, she began to see that she, too, was often at pains to discuss her feelings and shrank from physical demonstrativeness. For the first time, she began to think of herself as having come from "a dysfunctional family" in which there was no communication. "I was talking to this friend who was going to an ACOA [Adult Children of Alcoholics] group and although I had some of the same characteristics as she, I never connected it to how I grew up. We never talked about feelings in my home. I remember one time, my brother came home and yelled at my parents and my mother's response was 'Maybe he should see a psychiatrist.'"

Although her redefinition of her family life did not change her relationship with her parents, it did provide Alice with a new version of her own history, one that made it possible for her to make some changes in herself. Now she has become more sensitive to her own "closing up." Through seeing her parents differently, she gained a new perspective on herself. "I'm learning more and more about myself all along. I've known for a long time that I had a really good denial system. For example, I never even cried about my divorce until about two years later. I've learned to depress my emotions really well. My father never expressed any emotions at all. My husband has been really good about making me open up and making me start expressing feelings more, which was not part of me in the past. And having this knowledge about myself and the family in which I grew up has made me concentrate on making sure that there is a closeness with my kids so I don't repeat that pattern. And I feel really good about what's happened so far. My 12-year-old son had a conversation with me about masturbating about a month ago, so I feel I must be doing something right."

Clara had a similar lifelong struggle with her demanding, critical mother. Only after a long therapy in college was she able to right herself and be able to go about her life without her mother's approval. At age 33, Clara was living in Italy, delighted to be far from her mother and her criticism, still feeling some pain at not having the support and love she had always craved. By age 43, however, Clara described her mother matter-of-factly as a "very difficult person" who had to be handled carefully at family functions. "She is very negative about life and I always thought that that was being negative about me. She's never felt good about herself. She rewrites history with herself being victimized or someone else being at fault. It's very complicated and very exhausting." Clara had at last forgiven her mother for being who she is and learned to work around her. When her niece died and the family was in a paroxysm of grief, her mother, true to form, said some harsh and blaming things. Clara then took up the charge of running interference for her, trying to keep her brothers from ostracizing her.

Maria, who works with disturbed young people, has had to come to the painful recognition that both she and her brother were physically abused as children. She hadn't wanted to see her "ideal" family in this way, but she has also, in midlife, arrived at a complex understanding of her father. "He'd get out of control—it was beating. But I see it more as a cultural thing. I knew it didn't come from hate or wanting to hurt a child. This is the way Italians disciplined their children. It's difficult culturally for people to find other ways to deal with their kids. I don't know if I intellectualized it, but I always knew it didn't come from hate and was just my father's way." With much shame, Maria recounted her struggle with the part of her father that was in her. "I remember slapping my daughter when she was 3 and leaving a mark. George [her husband] came home and I thought he was going to kill me. To him, you just don't hit your kids. And I grew up with this and I knew intellectually that I didn't want to bring up my kids that way and I didn't want to be physically abusive. He reacted with such horror and anger to me that that was it. I never hit her again. And I never hit my son. [My father's abusiveness] did affect me. You realize that rage is inside you, and you realize how easy it can be to lash out when you are tired or under stress. If I were married to someone who was different, I wonder how different I would be."

The Pathmakers, then, did not grow up in ideal families or have notably excellent relationships with their parents. Human development is not that simple. Most of these women had fathers who, though distant, seemed to have confidence in them or were proud of them. Many spoke of their fathers as supportive presences whom they admired and who admired them, or at least seemed to understand them. They could emotionally lean on their fathers while they fought their mothers' protectiveness, a protectiveness they deeply knew was a product of love. This knowledge made the struggle with their mothers for control of themselves a tortuous and complex one; traversing it seems to have given them strength.

Most Pathmakers feel closer to their mothers as adults than they did in college. They have won their right to their own lives, and could then rejoin their mothers in a revised relationship. Brenda says that her mother still worries about everything she does: worries that she will not be able to afford the house she built, worries that she does not have children, worries when she takes a long boat trip, but Brenda lets all this roll off her back and she and her mother genuinely enjoy spending time together.

Growing up in these families, the Pathmakers learned to experience and integrate ambivalence during their adolescence. Unlike those who took the Guardian route, they did not idealize their parents, but learned to love them and be loved by them imperfectly, aware of their parents' failings and flaws, chafing at their restriction, challenging their values, but maintaining connection.

When I interviewed them in college, most Pathmakers spoke poignantly about having wished for more love or approval from their parents. In their age-thirties interview, this pain still rankled and continued as a source of distress in their lives. But by the time these women were in their mid-forties, the wounds seem to have healed—or had been put aside. They remember their old grievances, but the pain is replaced by bemused resignation. Adulthood has offered them another chance at relationship with their parents—relationships of attachment and roots, rather than relationships defined by dependence or needs for approval or righting the wrongs of the past. They find new ways of maintaining meaningful connection to their parents.

But making adult relationships with their parents has been complicated by the fact that, having chosen lives on their own terms, women who began adulthood as Pathmakers are often living lives quite different from their parents. For many, that was the whole point. Brenda grew up on a New York City street with no trees. She built her house on fifteen rural wooded acres, a world totally foreign to her parents. But she enjoys having them visit her, and delights in their growing appreciation of the natural surroundings she loves.

Maria saw her mother's narrow life that was channeled into subservience to her husband. She has a much more equal relationship with her husband and a strong commitment to her career. This arrangement is perplexing and somewhat distressing to her mother, but Maria has learned to navigate the potholes in their conversations about life.

An important goal for all these women who became mothers has been to do a better job of it: those who felt there was silence at home focus on an effort to communicate; those who felt there had been too much distance in their own families of origin pride themselves on making families that do things together; those who felt their parents were too intrusive try to allow their children more latitude.

Differences, then, have to be tolerated—on both sides. The Pathmakers' political liberalism, their lack of religious practice, their career commitment, their philosophy of raising children—all are aspects that their parents—and often their siblings—are at pains to understand. And these women have had to accept that their families will never fully know them.

The Pathmakers have rich relational lives, and friendships are a fertile source of self-exploration as well as companionship and stimulation. Although most Pathmakers have not retained friends from college, Brenda stays close to two college friends. Despite living far away, they reunite at least three times a year and she feels she has never since been able to make friends she feels as close to. Alice has a similar experience with her best friend from college. The others have made new friends along the way, friends from different aspects of their lives, from work, from shared child-rearing. But friendship often takes a back seat to the many other aspects of their lives, especially when they have committed relationships with men—and they regret this.

Those who entered adulthood through the Pathmaker gate have continued a gradual and thoughtful process of revision as they grow toward and through midlife. Some made choices they later recognized as "bad" ones for them—Alice's first husband, Clara's first profession. Others did not decry their choices; instead, their revision consisted of enlarging their frame, expanding themselves. They had a sense of direction as they put college graduation behind them, but they kept changing—adapting themselves, adjusting their world, revising their place. Their learning has been dominated by new understandings about themselves in relationships, who they are in them and what they can effect in them—at home, at work, and in the world. Revision has encompassed opening up more, being less inhibited, expressing more of themselves to and with others. As the Pathmakers have grown, they have learned to trust others more with core parts of themselves. Their sense of growth is one of increasing inner freedom, although many speak of this as being something they must work for. Sharing themselves with others involves giving up some control.

Across the time that I have known them, the Pathmakers remain pragmatic women: they are doers. Their lives are built of multiple investments—career, partners, children, parents, siblings, friends, charity, sports, exercise, travel, reading—in various orderings, all in delicate equilibrium. They are practical and down to earth; there is a hardheaded sensibleness about these women. None of them retains religious connections, although most were raised in a strong religious tradition. They rely on themselves. "You have to be strong not to believe in God," Betty said in college. They are women who started out trying to feel in charge, in control of themselves and what happened to them. They thought, by and large, that if they could plan a life, they could realize it. All have learned to temper this sense of control, and to recognize deeply how much they can't control. Many now (in midlife) see their lives as marked more by "luck" than they ever had before. "Luck keeps disaster away," said Clara. None of them made their lives come out just the way they imagined. Necessity and circumstance refracted their lives, yet all have realized some essentials of their own desires. All feel that they have pretty much gotten to where they had intended to go. Often, however, they put aside dissatisfaction and rationalize away longing, only to have these resurface later as a positive force for change. Andrea, for example, swept away her marital unhappiness— or, rather, found ways of fulfilling herself despite it—until one day the conviction of her wish to divorce seemed to burst on her fully formed.

As they look back, the Pathmakers acknowledge how scared they were at various times—as they took on new work roles, embarked on marriages, or faced life alone after a divorce. But fear is clearer to them in retrospect. They rise to what they decide to do, quelling the anxiety. Pathmaker mothers also speak about the strain of their transition to motherhood, the doubts about having made the right choice when they were sleepless and exhausted by their infants. In their thirties, they recounted being overwhelmed by young children, longing for some time to themselves. So the Pathmakers feel life's stresses—but they are psychologically stoical. They don't allow themselves to be governed by a need to escape painful feelings. Nor do they wallow in them. None of these six "successful" Pathmakers has experienced enough psychological difficulty to seek psychotherapy (although Clara had intensive therapy during college).

Voicing the motif of the group when I asked her what she feels most proud of as she looks back over her life, Clara said, "I am pleased with myself for having put all this together." For her, as for the others, integration is the key. The Pathmakers root what they create, but they recognize that all is subject to change. They value continuity and stability as a testament to the viability of the lives they have created. For many of them, houses take on special meaning—often they have built or rebuilt them themselves or, at least, chosen them to reflect themselves—in the woods, in a special town. All of them have dogs, that great symbol of home, companionship, and responsibility.

Pathmakers are professionally ambitious, but in a tempered way. They want to do well, to see themselves as affecting others in a positive way, but fame and status do not appeal to them. "I don't expect to make the history book's pages," said Alice, "nor do I care to. I wish to be contented. I am now and expect to continue to be. That's all that really matters, isn't it?"

These women all count themselves as happy enough. In talking to them, I sensed them as settled and sure, but with rumblings of discontent percolating beneath the surface that keep them alive to possibility. Despite having made what seem to me some very weighty compromises, they have wistfully shrugged aside regret. They opt to focus instead on what they are or have accomplished. Though settled, they are not rigid. They have become firmer with age, more self-confident, less self-conscious. They have always taken themselves for granted a bit, directing their gaze most of the time beyond their inner worlds to the exigencies and intrigue of reality outside themselves. But they are poised for further change and growth. For the mothers, the aging of their children promises new challenges both in relating to them and realigning their mothering with their other activities. In Maria, the stirrings of greater professional ambition coincide with seeing the end of at-home parenting. Clara, too, is eager to get on with her profession as her last child starts school. Betty continues to find new projects that call to her, now broadening her range to an international scale, thinking about working in disadvantaged countries. Andrea, who has already achieved much professionally, wants to enlarge her personal interests, to make more time for travel and exercise. Brenda, too, has had her fill of investment in her work and wants to go around the world in their boat. Alice sees her growth taking place in greater self-expression, in knowing better the parts of herself she has kept locked away. Their stories are not finished, but their basic approach to their lives—weigh and decide, shift without losing the center, know who you are, but be ready to make changes—remains consistent.

Making one's own path requires, above all, the capacity to tolerate uncertainty, doubt, anxiety, and guilt. Most of the women who finished college as

Pathmakers had a profound sense that they were skating free, having let go of the external supports that sustained them through childhood. Relinquishing this inner certainty, they had to find validation in supportive others—husbands, friends, bosses, mentors—or in increasing recognition of their own capabilities and values. Most of these women, as I interviewed them, narrated their stories with a sense of conviction in the basic meaningfulness of their lives and choices. Self-doubt was present but not disabling—they were aware that they might have made other choices, that some of their choices had led to pain or dead ends, but these women had the capacity to rally themselves and choose again, hoping to do so with better understanding and insight.

NANCY

Nancy provides a contrast to the other Pathmakers. Although she, like the others, continued to revise through her twenties and thirties, she found herself, in her forties, dissatisfied with all aspects of her life, trying to reorient herself and find her way again. At age 43, she was in a period of searching, rethinking herself, not sure what to preserve of what she had been and what to create anew.

Like the other college-age Pathmakers, Nancy was moving steadily toward independence through college, questioning the values of her childhood, flirting with left-wing political activity, preparing herself to become a high school math teacher. She had had no deep involvements with men by the time she was a senior, but was intensely connected to a group of women friends with whom she compared herself and tried to maintain a sense of distinctiveness. It had been a challenge to learn to live with people so different and "to stand up for my own rights." Beset with fears about her adequacy that had been with her since childhood, Nancy worried a lot about her "worthiness" and wanted to be special in some way or at least to do "well enough." Above all, she deeply feared failure and humiliation. Throughout her school years, she had been at pains to leave "the security of my seat" and perform in front of others. She was very sensitive to what she experienced as pressure from others, and was looking forward to finishing college, escaping from her conflicted relationship with her demanding, critical mother and "being truly independent."

In retrospect, I could see these worries foreshadowing Nancy's first major hurdle. Despite finding a teaching job just after graduation, Nancy could never feel secure in front of her class and, after two years of struggling each day with her anxieties about teaching, decided to choose another career. She worked for a while in low-level jobs in the business world, which made her aware of the necessity of having an MBA. So she went back to school to earn this new degree and, when she finished, began work in the purchasing division of a large retail sales company. Through several promotions and carefully timed job changes, by age 33, she had become a high-level manager. Although she continued to fear competition and doubted that she was doing enough, she took on more and more responsibility. She enjoyed the challenges of her work, the problem-solving, and the sense of accomplishment she derived from it, even though it was often frustrating to be limited in her authority by rules and bureaucracies.

Nancy married early in her thirties. Her husband, a systems analyst as ambitious as she was, was a man with whom she felt a great sense of security, although there were conflicts in her marriage. "Marriage has met my needs," Nancy said at age 33, "in that I am no longer lonely, I have a full-time friend to talk to and to be around. I thought marriage would be easier than it is; it requires lots of work and time and, unfortunately, my job takes a lot of my time and energies."

Negotiating the demands of her marriage and those of her job became an ongoing source of difficulty. To meet the pressures emanating from her work, she was home little. Then her husband would, in retaliation, get overinvolved in his work and be less available to her when she wished to be with him. At age 33, she couldn't see how she could make room for children, although she did want to have them. She was putting off the decision, worrying that it would be made for her by default because she couldn't bring herself to make a "yes decision." Early in her thirties, though, Nancy still felt herself steering her own life, creating her path, having many decisions yet before her.

By age 43, however, Nancy felt that life had gotten away from her. She worried that she had become a "workaholic" and that her husband had, too. They had so little time for each other, and, when they were together, it seemed all they did was criticize and undercut each other. They had separated twice, but each time decided to try again. In the midst of the last, recent separation, Nancy lost her job because of economic cutbacks and then felt that she had nothing at all. In addition, her mother died suddenly, without her having a chance to feel they had resolved the more difficult feelings between them. At age 43, Nancy was in crisis. She had found another job, but she hated it and felt pessimistic about her job prospects in the poor economy of the time. She felt herself clinging to her husband, but not too hopeful of making it the kind of relationship she wanted.

But the "age-40 crisis," as Nancy termed it, led her to rethink her life. With the help of a therapist, she began reexamining her childhood and discovering the roots of her lifelong doubts. "I began to come to terms with my inner child." She wondered, looking back, if she and her husband had immersed themselves in work out of fear of having children. And she began to understand better how her relationship with her mother had affected her. "When she died, it was very stressful because I hadn't resolved anything. She loved me but she didn't make me feel confident and secure or have a high self-esteem. She had all these goals and expectations, but I always felt inadequate because, no matter how much I did, I never felt it was enough. I really think I married my husband because of the relationship I had with my mother. Because his love wasn't unconditional. I was always having to prove that I was doing good things, preparing good meals, on his wavelength. It was a repeat of my mother—trying to gain his favor. All those things hit—when she died." Looking back, Nancy feels that neither her marriage nor her career is anywhere close to what she had been trying to build. Although she got overinvolved at times with her work, she at the same time felt that through her twenties she hadn't really taken her career seriously enough. "I sometimes think that I never worked really hard on developing my career because I was always kind of looking for a relationship, to feel needed and to feel part of a couple and so on. Those needs have been fulfilled. But the partner I picked did not help to build my self-confidence and make me strong."

Thus, neither Nancy's work nor her primary relationship offered her the security she needs to flourish. In times of intense stress, she turns to both alcohol and overeating to soothe her, but both only contribute to her self-criticism. At age 43, she feels blocked, too paralyzed even to get herself back to psychotherapy—and anyway, she doesn't want to go if her husband doesn't for fear that it would seem like she is the one with the problems. She watches the paper for other jobs, but feels "I don't have the strength to push myself right now." She senses a need to give herself time, perhaps to persuade her husband to start all over again in another city, maybe far away.

Nancy's Pathmaker beginning was disrupted by a combination of circumstance and her inner self-doubting. At times, she seems to have been stepping on her own toes. At other times, her world offered her little support. Through her early thirties, she was much like the others who took this route out of their adolescence, but disappointments in her marriage and in her work have led Nancy to a dead end—at least for now. "We all enter into things with our eyes kind of blinded and closed," she said at age 43, reflecting on how she had come to where she was. Nancy's history, then, is an important coda to the story of the Pathmakers. Not everyone succeeds in fulfilling in reality the parts of themselves they wish to express. And this engenders the painful frustration of "I know who I wish to be, but I can't make it happen."

Nancy alternates between trying to find a way to realize the identity she has attempted to fashion and trying to remake herself around something more easily accessible. "I always feel that I'm trying to be more flexible to changes because I don't think I really am." Nancy was at a crossroads at the time of this last interview, in a renewed period of searching that may yet await other Pathmakers. We can't yet know how she will make her way from here.

Let me think: was I the same when I got up this morning? I almost think
I can remember feeling a little different. But if I'm not the same, the next
question is, Who in the world am I? Ah, that's the great puzzle!

Lewis Carroll, Alice in Wonderland

6 THE SEARCHERS

The Searchers, at the end of college, were still engrossed in the maze that the Pathmakers had found their way through. Or perhaps their mazes were—or seemed to be—more complicated. They were in an "identity crisis," filled with conflict, torn between the demands and expectations of their parents that were firmly inside of them and the wish to extricate themselves and make their own choices. They had no intention of following any well-trodden paths, but not doing so was a frightening prospect. These are the women who left their churches, protested the Vietnam War, became feminists, criticized their parents, experimented with sex—and felt guilty. These were the women who were asking the great philosophical questions—and often feeling stymied by their own perceptiveness. Emotionally attuned to options, these women knew that they could design their own lives, but were frequently awash in their own inner contradictions. They dreamt of glorious careers helping others, but were unsure if they could rally themselves to translate this into realistic occupational goals. They were tempted and intrigued by sexual experience but were not yet fully ready to give up the comforts of being virginal little girls. They both wanted to leave the world of their parents and hold on at the same time.

Unlike the Pathmakers, the Searchers could not integrate the warring sides of themselves and choose a way to live. Perhaps they were still on the road to choice, still in the midst of the struggle, still stumbling through the period of exploration that was already history for the Pathmakers. Or perhaps they were stuck, caught in ambivalence and angst, their fear growing as the end of college loomed.[1]

As I got to know these women, it seemed that they had more at stake psychologically than the Pathmakers. They were trying to restructure themselves more, to emotionally separate from their families more completely, and to feel more independent. They watched themselves closely and took self-realization seriously as a goal. They worried about whether their values and choices were truly their own, trying to analyze themselves down to some basic core. Living closer to their feelings than either the Pathmakers or the Guardians, they were reaching for a deep form of authenticity. But they experienced themselves as a gathering of inner selves in conflict, pulling in different directions. To resolve this internal warfare, they were in search of some unassailable place to stand in relation to the world, a place that they couldn't undermine with their own questions and doubts. Whatever they did, they were critical of themselves, chagrined that another way of being or believing might be just as legitimate—and possible.

In some ways, the women in the Searcher group seemed to be asking more of life than the other women—or, at least, life seemed more complicated to them. They sought unwavering answers to their relentless questions, and they were more responsive to the cacaphony of voices that surrounded them. They wanted their choices to have the feel of some larger sense of Rightness, but, unlike Guardians, they did not accept the authority of their parents as an imprimatur of goodness. And, unlike Pathmakers, they were less ready to compromise or be pragmatic. They were more idealistic and unwilling to accept less.

In part because of their questioning and self-awareness, I found the young women in this group to be enormously engaging. I was moved by their often painful self-examination and their honesty. They were the most mindful, the most animated, and the most self-reflective of all the women I interviewed. They took themselves very seriously and worried about everything. They talked on and on. Their interviews were very long: no question had a simple answer. To any query, many sides of themselves had a response. Here is what I am doing or what I believe, they would say, but here is the other side of that, here is where I am not comfortable, but I can't find another way. If I did or believed this other thing, then there would be other problems. So there is no one answer. There is no right way. There is no certainty. *In a minute there is time for decisions and revisions that a minute will reverse.* What on earth shall I do?

Erik Erikson described the way in which modern industrial societies make available a "moratorium" period for young people to explore and choose identity. At the end of this time that society allots, society then expects the young person to declare herself and the path she will follow. The Searchers were in the midst of such a period, but the time for society to call them to account had arrived. Sooner or later, this bottomless conflicted state had to end. And, as psychology has understood the process, it should eventually lead to the making of a self-determined path. But there was no telling how the Searchers might do this, or how long it would take. Would they resolve their enigmas by turning away from the conflict, by going back to be the people they had been earlier in life, or would they move forward to meld the contradictory aspects of themselves and create a life course truly theirs?

THE SEARCHERS IN COLLEGE

The search, for the women in this group, took many forms. Most were confused about what felt to them to be central dilemmas of value or belief, but they were perplexed in different areas of their lives. Although some had made tentative occupational choices or formed political stances, the larger questions of how to "be" remained. They worried about how and where they might find a place for themselves in the world, who they would connect themselves to and how, what it meant to be a woman in the world that was rapidly changing around them, and how to make a life when they spurned whatever models they saw.

Sandra made it clear to me, when I interviewed her in her last year of college, that she was just in college to please her parents. "In my house I'm expected to please my parents more than myself. I think I'm living my father's life for him. I'm going through this because my father didn't have an education and he wanted me to have an education. He wants me to be a doctor, but I know my capabilities and they are not medical school. He just won't admit I have limitations. I feel I am disappointing him." Living at home, Sandra's life was dominated by her struggle with her father. They argued about everything, but she couldn't disengage from him. To spite him, she majored in philosophy, simply because she liked it, but recognized that it would have no practical impact on her life. She longed for escape from these conflicts that permeated her life. She thought of going to Europe after graduation, perhaps working for an airline, anything that would take her away. Unlike the Guardian and Pathmaker groups, whose lives felt charted to them, Sandra was filled with conflict and uncertainty.

As Sandra constructed her life at the end of college, it seemed to her that she had to find someone on whom to pattern the new self she wanted to create. She looked to others to show her other ways to be. When she made a friend, she would find herself trying to be what that friend wanted her to be, until she resented it so much she would break off the friendship. She found herself "growing out of people" and worried about that. "I sort of bend toward people," she said, "but I have such varied friends that there is always opposition pounding at me." She was in search of someone to define her, but she fought whoever tried.

Sandra wasn't sure what in herself felt real. Having grown up as an obese child, she felt rejected, isolated, and mocked. After she lost weight in high school, people began to respond to her very differently. Men were now attracted to her and she had to learn to manage advances from her professors and her boss. But this was a complicated process. On the one hand, she enjoyed their attention and their desire for her, and often couldn't bring herself to say "no." On the other, she often felt like "just a sex object" and worried about the men who seemed to have no interest in talking to her and only seemed interested in sex. "I used to want a lot of attention and now I've got it and I'm not sure I want it." She had been in an abusive relationship with one boyfriend who treated her as "a sex slave," and, although she knew this was wrong for her, she couldn't firmly break off the relationship. Another boyfriend she rejected because he "didn't discipline me enough." Whatever she did, he accepted and this confused her. These are the sort of knots the Searchers found themselves trapped in during college.

Uncertain of their own worth, the Searchers were unsure what to seek for themselves. Many were drawn to relationships with men who seemed sure of themselves and wanted to define them as well, but often these were men who also treated them badly. Then these women would agonize over whether to stay or leave. Millie used a boyfriend to help her separate from her parents. "I used to be very sheltered and narrow-minded and never did any thinking. I used to let everyone else do my thinking for me. He changed all that. He made me a lot more open-minded. He was a freak. He was very messed up." This boyfriend led her into drugs and sexual experimentation, beat her occasionally, and abandoned her frequently. But he seemed to her the means of staging her independence from her parents. They hated him. She was obsessed with him. She didn't recognize, of course, that she had merely substituted one source of external control for another. "I was torn between my parents and him, and I couldn't condemn them for their motives because they only wanted the best for me and everything I did was wrong and everyone was always mad at me and there I was in the middle. I really don't want to hurt my parents or to make them feel they've failed as parents, but I have to live my own life."

These conflicts about the right to live one's own life were central among the Searchers. As Millie stated it so well, their fear was that living their own life involved harming their parents, disowning or discrediting them. This idea filled the Searchers with intense guilt and anxiety. But, despite the pain, they propelled themselves forward. Millie again speaks for the group: "The more I think about it, the more confused I get as to what I want to do with myself, where I think I'm going. It's scary in that sense, but it's good in the sense that I'm not living a life that's already been made for me—like I'm not just falling into a rut that I just didn't even question—that I'd just go to college, get married, live in suburbia and be a housewife, and naturally I would be a virgin until I got married."

Many of the Searchers I interviewed came from working-class homes and were the first in their families to go to college. Their parents could not really imagine what they were experiencing in this phase of their life, and many were threatened by it and responded by pulling on the reins. The Searchers wanted something else beyond what they had seen at home, but did they have a right to it, were they good enough to deserve it, and what was "it" anyway? They had an intense sense that there were many possible ways to live a life, but weren't sure how to choose.

All the Searchers had deeply questioned their religious beliefs, disdaining what they felt was the hypocrisy of organized religion, but they gave up their religious practice with a lot of guilt. "These things are ingrained in me," one of them said, so they were haunted by the rituals they had disavowed.

Many had been somewhat politically involved during the late 1960s—the marches, the student strikes—but this, too, led to disillusion. Millie again: "I was believing what people were saying—that you can give up your grades for people who were over in Vietnam dying. You can make a sacrifice for them and I felt 'Yeah, that's what I'm going to do.' But there's no correlation between me not going to class [during the student strike] and them dying over there. It's not doing them any good. And I got really screwed. And nothing ever came of it. The summer came and everyone went home and that was it. And I had three incompletes. I'm apathetic now. I really did get involved. And all I could see is I was getting screwed and nothing was coming of it. And I really believe my emotionalism duped me and I was really disillusioned."

The effort to define themselves in terms of achievement and career fared no better. The Searchers kept changing their majors, losing interest in one field, hoping for better from another. Or they would define an interest and then not be able to bring themselves to do their work at a level that would get them accepted for the program of their choice. Lacking in self-confidence, they were often in search of a field that would adopt them and make them feel that here was something they were "good" at. Some handled this anxiety by putting career questions on hold, hoping to travel or explore before making a choice. "I think I'd like to be a bum," Millie said. "I'd like to start doing some traveling. I don't want to settle down in a job right now since I've been settled down in school for so long. I'd like to do something before I start." They all wished to "do something," but were finding it hard to define what that "something" might be.

Those who *had* made career plans were in conflict about how important they wanted to make their careers in their lives. Perhaps it was more important to marry and raise a family, perhaps career was just a way station until they got on with the real business of life. On the other hand, just being a wife or mother looked very unappealing. Theresa, for example, wanted to be a teacher, but her Sicilian parents thought, "What is a woman who isn't married?" Similarly, Natalie was hoping to have a career as a journalist or a writer. But, she averred, if she married someone who objected to her career, she would give it up. Theresa and Natalie, like other Searchers, weren't sure, couldn't know what would be expected of them—and they weren't yet able to think of themselves as the ones defining things.

The Searchers usually phrased their identity questions in very totalistic ways. Confronted with difference, they felt they had to make an either-or choice, to stay as they were or change completely. Theresa said, "I feel confused. I'm in the middle of two societies—a liberal one and a very, very strict one. I don't want to go into the liberal one and I don't want to go into the strict one. I don't think I can decide ever." Throughout college, Theresa continually classified herself as being similar or different from everyone she met and then pondered transforming herself to be more like those who were different. "I believe that every person you meet, you become like them in some way. In my senior year of high school, I felt more like my friends than I was like myself. Then in freshman year of college, I met a group of hippies and had a hippie boyfriend. I was in a different world. I had never before seen anyone with a beard, long hair, and without shoes. It was confusing because I wasn't sure how I fit in with them because I was so different and I found myself becoming like them. I was leaving my old life [and entering] into a new life. Before that I wouldn't go to a guy's apartment or smoke grass or go to a demonstration. I was doing these things because they were doing it." But Theresa was unsure whether these things belonged to her as well. Just like Sandra wasn't sure if she was in college for herself or her father or whether she lost weight for herself or for other people. Or Millie couldn't tell whether she was doing things for herself or her boyfriend. In college and after, Searchers strive to be clear about who is in charge of their decisions and actions, but they often feel muddled. (This is in sharp contrast to the Pathmakers who, once having formed a sense of identity based on their experience of their own initiative, simply don't raise such questions.)

The Searchers came from families that clearly defined their values and expectations of them. But unlike Guardians, the Searchers did not want to carry on family tradition or meet parental demands. In contrast to the Guardians, Searchers were more adventurous as college women and less preoccupied with security. Unlike the Pathmakers, however, they couldn't assert their right to separateness and modify themselves. They felt caught by the pulls of the very past they wanted to escape. All had parents that they found to be unsuitable models for one reason or another. Marlene was the daughter of Holocaust survivors and knew little of her parents' history except that their lives could in no way provide examples for her own. She spent her adolescence embarrassed by their age, their accents, and their foreignness. Theresa, daughter of immigrant Sicilian parents, learned English in school. Although she idealized her mother for being kind to everyone, she saw that her mother had never really found a place for herself outside the home. And, being an only child, she grew up in the shadow of her father's unmasked despair and anger that she was not a boy.

At the same time, many college-age Searchers grew up feeling exceptional, unlike others in some special way: Marlene, because of her parents' background, felt different from everyone else; Sandra and Leslie were fat; Laura had been born with a deformed foot; Theresa's mother treated her "like a princess"; Millie was especially good. Carrying this sense of specialness, they often romanticized their future. They felt that some sort of prince was on his way to them, not necessarily a man, but something out of the ordinary. Some had dreams of remarkable achievement—Millie imagined finding a cure for cancer, Natalie wanted to write a bestseller. But their goals were phrased, even if only unconsciously, as attainment of an ideal. They often set impossibly high standards for themselves. In that sense, they frequently seemed quixotic.

But at the same time that they were reaching for so much, they were also frightened and craved security. The tension raged within them: stay with what's safe—no, reach out for what might be right. They were vehemently leaving home, but feeling stranded and abandoned. Where the Pathmakers were engaged in building and modifying, the Searchers seemed to throw everything in the air at once. But they were constantly fearful about having burned the bridges that could lead them back home. They loved to argue and discuss issues, but needed a lot of reassurance and approval from someone that their views were acceptable. It often took them years to learn to hold onto safety with part of themselves while exploring and reworking other parts. And they varied in the amount of time and struggle it took to settle on a path.

After college, the Searchers pursued their exploration in quite different directions. While they resembled one another in college, they evolved into very different women. There is less commonality among them in midlife than within the other groups—as we might expect since searching is itself such an unstable state. Some had protracted searches, not really finding themselves until their thirties or even forties. Some found a path that suited them shortly after college, but experienced renewed periods of questing in midlife. Others were overwhelmed by powerful inner demons, old and tenacious conflicts from childhood, demons that they needed therapeutic help to contain before they could move ahead. Still others found the road intolerably bumpy as they left college and found a psychological return ticket back home.

PROLONGED QUESTS

The Searchers who in college had thrown their identity questions open to wide possibility jolted and bumped through the next decades. They cycled through hope and despair, revising themselves, revising their plans, testing various combinations to get the pieces to fit. Both Millie and Marlene in college were filled with stirrings and desires that neither woman could quite translate into life plans. They understood their origins but rejected them, recognized and valued their families but guiltily wanted their lives to be creations of their own. They were soaring and flapping their wings at the end of college, regarding the world with critical eyes, uncertain how to shape or organize all that was in turmoil within them.

MILLIE

For me, Millie embodied the essence of the identity crisis and therefore seemed the quintessential Searcher. I told her story again and again as I lectured on the issues of identity formation. We heard from her at the beginning of this chapter. She was delightful—because of, rather than in spite of, all the anguish she was experiencing.

—At the End of College   Millie was a perky, cherubic-looking young woman, who arrived at the interview dressed in the "hippie" garb that came to symbolize the era of the late sixties and early seventies. Millie was raised in a Philadelphia suburb, the middle of three children. Neither parent had attended college, but they wanted her to have as much education as possible. Her mother was loving and self-sacrificing, her father stern and exacting. She had always been a good girl and a good student. She remembered her home as a secure, harmonious place where she was just like her parents and all the other kids were just like her. She ventured away from home to a large,

private university in New York where she felt dazed by the lack of structure, but intrigued by all the possibilities.

Millie had expected that she would become a nurse like her mother, but, she said, "I didn't have the temperament." While in college, she had switched her major three times. After giving up on nursing, she applied for a physical therapy program, but could not get accepted because of her grades, so opted for a psychology major. "But that was making me get too much into myself and I was afraid that more psychology would screw me up," so she changed again to biology. One summer when she had worked at a hospice and had become close to a young woman who was dying of cancer, she began to consider a goal for herself. "I couldn't stand it, so I decided that what I really wanted to do was cancer research." After a few semesters of biology courses, however, Millie was becoming upset at the idea of killing frogs in her physiology class, and had come to realize that she would not have the stomach to do cancer research. She wished she had just gone into teaching, but it was too late.

When she thought about her future, she couldn't quite picture herself being married. "I don't like to think of myself as 40 years old and unmarried, but right now I can't imagine it. I can imagine loving someone or living with someone, but as soon as there is a legal bond—that this is the way it's going to be—I get scared." As for children, she said, "I don't want my life to be my children. I want my own life. I've seen too many parents—like mine—who have put their whole lives into their children and then when the children grow up, they're lost. You've got to realize from the start that eventually they're going to leave."

Raised in the strictest Catholic tradition, she had become increasingly aware of the church's "hypocrisy." When she noticed that many people were going to church only to see what other people were wearing, she stopped going. "I know my parents would like me to go to church and I'd like to do it for them, but I couldn't because I'd be a hypocrite and I'd be deceiving them into thinking I'm a good Catholic girl again when I'm not." But she wasn't sure what to believe instead. "I do want to believe," she said, "because just to believe in reality is not so nice because there are a lot things in reality that are not so nice."

On the question of premarital sex, Millie had very definite views. In her opinion, "someone who is 22 and a virgin is perverted." In formulating her own standards, she felt that "you shouldn't make love just to satisfy your animal desires." The first time she had sexual intercourse, it was with a man she loved and hoped to marry. "He changed my ideas because I used to be so inhibited. He changed my whole way of life because I used to be very super-straight and closed-minded. I got over the idea that if you have sex before you're married, you go straight to Hell." But, Millie confided, she was sure her parents would "freak out" if they knew about her sexual behavior. And she worried that men might think she was "a slut."

In all areas of her life—occupational choice, religion, politics, relationships, sexuality—Millie was in conflict. She felt close to her family but worried they didn't think she was very "normal." After all, she dressed in the fashion of the times rather than like them. And she spent so much of her time and energy with her "freaky," abusive boyfriend—she surely was not going to come home and take up a traditional middle-class life like theirs.

As she approached graduation, Millie wanted something to embrace that was unassailable. If she could find flaws in a religious belief or a political action, that meant she must reject it. She was at times exhausted by all the effort she was putting into trying to make sense of things: "I always want to run away but I never do." Millie felt pulled in many directions, but couldn't be certain what was most herself—or where she might find a place for that self in the world. When she felt most confused, it was easy to seek out someone who would tell her how and what to be—as her parents had—and then the cycle of struggle and rebellion would begin again.

I was worried about Millie as she was about to graduate. She was charming—and she could articulate the struggles of her age so well. But she seemed swept up in a vortex of confusion with no evident way of coming to rest.

—*Age 33*   Millie stayed in my mind for a long time after this first interview and I was eager to see her again and learn how she had fared. When I saw her at age 33, she was pregnant with her second child and had a long and scattered tale to recount. I found her much less tormented than she had been in college, and perhaps a bit depressed. Over the intervening years, Millie had been through periods of effort and daring in which she tried hard to organize her life as well as periods of drifting in which she floated along, hoping for something good to happen.

As she narrated her history, Millie had forgotten her late adolescent self who had wanted to "be a bum" and thought of herself as having had a straightforward goal during college, a goal resulting from the dream she had to prevent people from dying young of cancer. Her first job, which she took after six months of "bumming around," was in a biology research lab. She remembers her first day at work feeling "Look out world, here I come." But there she was asked to do what she regarded as dangerous experiments, being exposed to asbestos dust. And she deeply resented that a man who was hired when she was, who had graduated from college at the same time with the same degree, was being paid more. When she complained, the management of the lab was infuriated, regarded her as "hysterical," and she was forced to quit. "I had the wind knocked out of my sails," she recalled.

Disillusioned, she impulsively moved to Florida where a friend of hers was living and worked as a waitress and sales clerk—whatever work she could get. But she detested the drug-infested neighborhood where her friend lived and, fearing for her safety, returned home to Philadelphia. Still feeling lost, she began to drive a cab. At least in the short run, she could know where she was going. She drove the cab for four years, enjoying people's surprise at encountering a woman taxi driver. But she found herself often angry at the way people treated her and again feared for her safety. When she stopped and asked herself what she was doing with her life, she found herself longing to have an important, responsible position, but she couldn't envision taking the small steps that would be necessary to get there.

Finally, she decided to get some training to be a paramedical technician. "I really don't research things very well before I do them," she said ruefully, looking back. Working in an ambulance, which had seemed exciting and challenging, turned out to be overly demanding. The hours were too long and the stress overwhelming. She quit and took a job as a secretary in a hospital coronary-care unit. "I was not working up to my potential in terms of intellect, but it was fascinating." She felt appreciated and valuable. She stayed two years, and took courses in computer programming. In search of more responsibility and more money, she got a job with an insurance company, but felt the work environment there was "oppressive, demeaning to women and filled with stuffy people." When she became pregnant at age 30, she opted out of the work world.

Millie's story of relationships with men had been equally checkered. Through her twenties, she had many; each was unsatisfactory in different ways. She had met Phillip when she was 28 and they had a stormy time together. "We sort of backed into living together because we both were afraid of making a commitment." Worried that they would "chicken out," they married hurriedly. Once married, though, Millie could allow herself to feel "crazy about him." She felt that they were "linked psychically." She described Phillip as a "very solid kind of guy" who helped stabilize her emotional swings. But after their daughter was born, Millie felt the relationship teeter. "I feel more defensive about me as an entity, as a separate person. I find myself backing off from responsibility and decision-making, especially about how money is spent since I'm not working. I feel weird being dependent on someone else."

For the next three years, between ages 30 to 33, Millie had been channeling all her energies and aspirations into their daughter. "I worry about each stage, afraid I won't be able to handle it. But it's so nice to have someone who really needs me." She missed working, but didn't know what work she wanted to do and anyway couldn't bear the thought of leaving her daughter in someone else's care. She felt transformed by motherhood, more responsible, more conscious of her behavior, eager to set a good example. And her fantasies of success were threaded into imagining what her daughter might grow into. "I want her to excel in something. She's very bright and I think she could really do something, really make a contribution to whatever she wanted to do." These were hopes that Millie had not managed to realize for herself.

During college, Millie had stopped practicing the Catholicism in which she had been raised. This had been part of declaring her independence from her parents. As a mother, however, she was planning to raise her daughter in the church. "Religion is a good thing to have in times of need—a strength you can draw on."

At this age, Millie was also struggling with all the disappointment she had felt in friendships. She had expected friends to be like family. "It's like when you find out your parents aren't perfect. I believed that some of my friendships would last forever and I was really disappointed." Her world at age 33 was limited to her family. She had become closer to her parents, her siblings, her cousins and aunts. Millie seemed very much back where she had started from. Her parents no longer even regarded her as "the weirdo of the family" although they still worried about the side of her that might "cut loose."

Millie regarded herself as content with her life at age 33, filled with wonder at the intensity of her love for Phillip and her daughter. But her narrative was peppered with the words "disillusioned" and "disappointed," and she was mourning her failed occupational ambitions. Her quirky sense of humor and quick wit were much muted. Most worrisome for her at this time was that Phillip had been talking about moving to a different part of the country where his company felt there were good sales opportunities. Millie worried that although he felt like her "predestined other half," they might have to separate. She didn't want to leave Philadelphia again. But she was frightened to think how helpless she had become, "tied to my daughter's needs and Phillip's schedule."

At this interview, Millie also told me a poignant early memory that seemed to be a metaphor for her life: "I was in kindergarten. We were cutting out shamrocks. The teacher asked me to cut out the shamrock and I was so impressed that she asked me to cut it out. This was going to be the best shamrock the world had ever seen. I was being so careful that I was going too slow, and she ended up coming over and taking it out of my hands and saying, 'Okay, we'll let someone else do this.' I was crushed." Throughout her life, Millie could not translate her dreams of greatness into realistic action and, at age 33, she again felt that it was all being taken out of her hands. She had begun to drift and was trying to row toward home.

—*Age 43*   When I found Millie again at age 43, she related a continuing saga of wanderings and new beginnings. She had found herself, but in a way that surprised both of us. Phillip's sales work did take him far from Philadelphia and Millie felt she had no choice but to go with him. They lived in a succession of small Southern and Appalachian towns, each one "a greater disaster" than the next. Millie busied herself with trying to find adequate schooling for her daughter and making friends with people who "didn't like strangers" and regarded her as "the Yankee." She often felt she was living "at the end of the earth." It was hard even to find a doctor to attend the birth of her younger daughter. Both her family and Phillip's family were far away. There was no support and, in some desperation, Millie turned to religion. The local priest had said that he would not baptize Millie's new baby unless she regularly attended church; going to Mass became the only time she experienced some peace and felt part of a community. Phillip was equally unhappy with his work situation. One venture after another fell through. "We didn't do a lot of fighting, but we sure didn't do a whole lot of talking and I did a lot of stewing inside. It was getting to be unbearable."

Four years after leaving Philadelphia, when she was settled in a somewhat permanent situation in Louisiana, the priest mentioned that the church was looking for a Director of Religious Education. And Millie was filled with the idea that here was something she could do. "I wonder if it was divine intervention. It was very peculiar. In my normal rational mind, I would never have said, 'Oh, sure, do that,' but it was something that I can't describe other than to say that I felt called to it. . . . And that's how it all started. And once I got into it, I had to spend a lot of time trying to lead and talk to people and all that. It's just amazing. And it's a real big change—a positive change." Now Millie travels all over the country, grapples with the differences among belief systems within Catholicism, and manages to hold onto her own beliefs, while honoring and working with people of other religious bents. She battles "that occasional feeling of wanting to strangle pompous hypocrites," but she has mastered tolerance. Active and visible in the community, she struggles with separating the "truth of the faith from the personalities." In the course of her work, she has often felt that she has profoundly affected other people's lives, even that she has healed. "I feel that I am doing God's will," she says, "instead of fighting it like I normally do. I guess I'm a bit headstrong. I'm helping people and I'm learning so much in the process." She revels in her newfound strength, and continues to pursue an even deeper spirituality.

Phillip has converted and joined the church and this has added "a whole new dimension" to their life as a couple and as a family. Their marriage feels like it's getting better all the time. Now that the children are older, they again have time for each other and, Millie says impishly, more sex. Millie has become more relaxed as a mother and enjoys the fact that her children now have a sense of humor. "We can all wisecrack together."

Millie retains a warm, affectionate bond with her parents. "They regard me as a middle-aged lady," she jokes, but appreciates that the relationship is based on love rather than control. They worry that she "might become a Holy Roller" but are reassured that while her faith is deep, she is not a fanatic. "This must be a comfortable stage in my life right now," Millie said, nearly glowing. The words "disappointed" and "disillusioned" did not appear in this interview. She would like to have more personal discretionary time: she is still a mother first of all. And, thinking of her course in life, she says, "All I can say with certainty is that life is weird. I never would have imagined myself here, but my grandmother used to say 'Everything is practice for what comes next.'"

Looking back and reflecting on her life, she regards herself as having been wild in college, filled with lots of ideas and strong ideals, but she feels that this is the first real commitment she has made to herself and others around her. "It's a way to find yourself, giving yourself away. If you keep looking for yourself someplace in the mirror, you are not going to find it."[2] I thought that Millie was right here. Looking for herself in the mirror all those years, she hadn't found herself. But, by age 43, she finally had.

MARLENE

—At the End of College   Marlene was the only daughter of Holocaust survivors. Although she appreciated their love of her, their background and values offered her little as a guide for how to pattern her own life. As a teenager, she became sensitive to the views and styles of others, regarding everyone she met as a potential model for her own life. She chose a small women's college because friends a few years older went there. She decided to major in political science because she liked the people in the department. Feeling that "everything is debatable," she had no clear beliefs—but she agonized about everything. Although she had flirted with left-wing politics—SDS, socialist ideas—she came to dislike the people in the movement and disengaged herself from these groups.

Marlene acknowledged in her senior year interview that she had "trouble expressing feelings." She thought deeply and questioned most things, but it was hard for her to explain where she stood on most issues. In a period of feeling depressed, she had begun to see a counselor. But opening up issues frightened her, and she "dropped it like a hot potato."

Somewhat by accident, she joined a women's collective that ended up raising her consciousness about being a woman. She recounted trying to justify to a friend the fact that she ironed her boyfriend's shirts, but realized she had no rational explanation. This confused her. Marlene couldn't get clear on how to think of herself at this stage. "I feel the image that my friends have of me is not the image I have of myself and I felt I was being pushed into their image of me as nonemotional, practical, independent, reliable, trustworthy— a strong, cold image—and I didn't know if there was another side, and if there was, how to show it." Her search in college, then, was about how to *be*.

She felt bereft of models. She had gone through a period early in college of anger at her parents for having "ruined" her. They spoke Roumanian at home and hadn't taught her to communicate with others. They gave her "hang-ups" that made her feel isolated. Worse, they couldn't know her or who she was becoming. In a moment of courage, Marlene told her mother that she was sleeping with her boyfriend. This was an act of trying to disavow the fictional view she felt her mother had of her. At the same time, Marlene felt she burned her bridge to childhood. "I could be a child as long as I could preserve my mother's view of me as a child," Marlene said. But now her problem, having declared herself an adult, was what kind of adult to be.

Marlene had turned to her boyfriend to guide and teach her, but he disliked her dependence on him. Like a parent, he forced her to do things on her own. Closeness to other women in the women's collective helped, but Marlene was like a fawn struggling to get up on wobbly legs.

Although she was a very successful student who had a lot of pride in her intelligence, Marlene at the end of college was too afraid to assert herself and, not knowing what she wanted to assert anyway, planned to follow her boyfriend. She would go where he went and find something to do. She needed more time to get to know herself and she wanted to do this in the company of someone she trusted.

Although uncertain about what to do with herself, Marlene seemed eager to continue to explore. Keenly aware of how she acted in the company of others, she was in search of a picture of herself that could contain both her strength and her vulnerability. She was trying to get herself in focus. She felt far from a home she could not return to, from parents who seemed to belong to a different world. While she was hearing the call of new ideas—new definitions of women, of society—she didn't know how to place herself among these currents.

—Age 33   When I saw her again at age 33, Marlene narrated a long odyssey of search that was just then coming to resolution. She had followed

her college boyfriend to Boston and took odd jobs while he went to law school. But this relationship soon began to sour as he continued to feel too tied by her dependency on him, a dependency made worse when her mother died shortly after she graduated from college. Desperate for security, she painfully came to the realization that her boyfriend was not going to marry her and she would have to think about making her own plans. Marlene then began to consider developing some career goals. Why had she not done anything with her education? she wondered. But she didn't know what to choose. One of her close friends was enrolled in a library science program and Marlene thought that such a course of study might give her credentials that would get her out of doing temporary secretarial work. She had another friend in California and decided to move there and enter a library program.

Marlene liked the life in California—its openness, its freedom—and settled into a contented period of study and friendships. When she finished her degree, however, she was unable to find a job. She put together a pastiche of part-time employment, "on the margin of library work," but found that since the "California work ethic was much more fluid" than that of the East Coast, this was an acceptable kind of life. What was most exciting during this time was some volunteer work she was doing at a women's health center. Again she had turned to women's issues and to the company of women dedicated to a cause as a source of meaning in her life.

Marlene was now dating Ben, a man who had plans to emigrate to Israel to set up a residential treatment center for emotionally disturbed children. This reverberated with some old Zionist interests that Marlene had not thought about since high school. She found in herself a longing to reconnect with her extended family in Israel, many of whom she had never met. The more he talked about his dream, the more Marlene wanted to take part in it. The more she thought about "family"—a word tinged with longing and loss and hope—the more she realized that "family" somehow went with being in Israel. She decided to marry Ben and move with him to Israel. The future, at this point, seemed full of promise.

But the project in Israel was fraught with disappointment. Things didn't happen on schedule, funding that was promised didn't arrive, negotiations with the administering authorities were stalled. They waited for a year, living on a kibbutz. During this time, her father died and their son was born. Marlene had a mild postpartum depression, her emotions were out of control, and she felt terribly isolated and without support.

The Israel venture was turning out to be a disaster. Marlene had longed to settle down, to build a life of stability and community in Israel. Instead, the stress and frustration of not being able to accomplish what they had set out to do were putting them at odds with each other. They began to argue and blame each other. Marlene began to feel that Ben wasn't serious about making things work out in Israel—maybe he wasn't trying hard enough. After another six months, they began to see that they would have to return to the States.

At this point, Marlene was 30 and recognized that she needed to begin again. Uncertain of any direction, Marlene, Ben, and their son Simon began wandering around the country, staying with relatives and friends, trying to decide what to do. Visiting some friends in northern California who lived in a coastal town that charmed them, they impulsively decided to stay. Marlene found a part-time job in the local library, Ben got part-time work in a bank, and they divided the child care. Hoping now to establish the stable family life she had always dreamed of, Marlene and Ben framed their family with an increasing religious commitment, began participating in the Jewish community, and observed more holidays and traditions.

Eventually, Marlene began to volunteer again in a women's health center, and reimmersed herself in women's issues. After a year, the library lost its funding and Marlene lost her job. But the women's health center offered her an administrative job that, though far beneath her skills, did allow her to devote more of her time to a crusade that would help women take charge of their bodies.

All this time, her marriage was deteriorating. Ben quit work in the bank, tried some other things he didn't like, and eventually stopped working altogether. He spent his "work" time—when Marlene was watching Simon—playing music and hanging out in coffeehouses. Eventually, he decided to go back to school, but what claimed most of his attention was the opportunity to be involved with other women. Marlene felt that they were sharing nothing but child care. To use her words, "It was all falling apart. I desperately wanted to hang on to what I saw as my family, but it wasn't working out."

Fortunately, Marlene had been part of a women's support group and these women rallied to help her sort out her feelings and accept what she in some way already knew—that she would have to separate from her husband. The "What do I do now?" question was more serious than ever. But her friends helped her regard this new possibility with expansiveness rather than terror. Marlene sensed that it might be her last try.

She had always hovered around the edges of women's health and women's issues. Now she began shaping the idea to focus this interest and transform it into a career. She talked to a lot of people and investigated training programs. Finally, she found one that would train her to be a nurse-midwife, qualified to work in both gynecology and obstetrics, exactly what she wanted. The only problem was that the university offering this program was in New York. Could she leave her 3-year-old son that far away and for that long? How could she even think of taking him along? His father would fight it, and this was a very demanding program of study, too demanding for a single parent. One thing about Ben was that he was a wonderful parent. This was an agonizing decision for Marlene, but in the end she decided that the time had finally come to make decisions based on her needs. She could see her son on school vacations and in the summer.

"For the first time, I felt like I knew what I wanted to do. I remember in college feeling so envious of people who were directed and knew what they wanted to do. Then I suddenly felt that sense of direction at the age of 32, and it felt wonderful. Everything started to fall into place." She took the GREs, applied to the program, sold the house, took an anatomy course, and filed for divorce. "I was doing all these things and handling them well. I felt very in control." And off she went to New York.

When I interviewed Marlene at age 33, she was inundated with schoolwork that she was happily struggling through. She missed her son and worried about her relationship with him, but was optimistic about the future. In New York, she met a new man, Jerry, and was beginning to hope for another chance at making a family.

At this age, Marlene was very reflective about her growth and felt she could see now where she had been blinded and made bad choices. She felt she had been motivated by a desire to "hang on to security above all else" and had clung to one man or the other as though they were a life raft. She had hoped that her boyfriend during college would take charge of her, then relied on Ben to define a life for her. As she thought of her years during and since college, Marlene said, "I was floating here and there and bouncing off of what I was getting from other people. My attitude was 'why not' rather than the sense of what to do."

Marlene realized that she had been in thrall to her deep, often unconscious wish "to have a TV kind of family," the family she had never had. And she had been so afraid of a career interfering with that dream that she had "kept myself fluid" in order to be ready to mold into marriage and family. Only when she could mourn the dream of "perfect family" could she think realistically and clearly about how to fashion a goal. And her feminist women friends were essential to this—they gave her the support to help her "emerge." When she left California, they gave her butterflies as a symbol of her metamorphosis. This metaphor seemed apt: it felt to her as though she had been through a process of emerging, a competent, goal-directed self lying hidden, preparing hesitantly to show itself. "If I can perceive how someone else perceives me, it helps me to pull things together," Marlene said.

Ironically, moving ahead independently steered her into her worst fears—it disrupted her family, or, at least, her relationship with her son. But Marlene was hoping for another chance, a chance to "get it all in." Now it seemed possible even though, as Marlene observed, it would "require a whole lot of planning."

—*Age 43*   But she had mastered planning in all the turmoil she had endured. I found Marlene at age 43 still in New York, working as a nurse-midwife, married to Jerry, mother of another child, having realized most of what she had hoped for ten years earlier. But not without pitfalls along the way. The biggest frustration for Marlene in the past decade had been not being able to conceive and trying every hi-tech fertility method, but failing at all of them. This process had absorbed most of her attention and they finally adopted a little girl. They were delighted to get her as a very young infant, but disappointed that the adoption did not end their preoccupation with conception as they had hoped it would. Marlene felt that the infertility period was the hardest life crisis she had yet endured. By the time I saw her again, she was settled into the planning involved in raising a toddler, a teenager, and managing a demanding career.

On every front, Marlene had learned to use her new capacity to take charge of her life, to speak her needs and desires, and to pull her life into the shape she wished. Marlene's first job after graduate school "seemed like the best job in the world and it turned out to be a disaster—the wrong job with the wrong person. It was a dream job—setting up a women's health center. Looking back on it, I was ignorant of the political stuff and a little bit naive. So it was a hard experience, but it helped me figure out what kind of place I needed to be in. I left after six months." Given her hopes and dreams for her new occupation, this failure shook Marlene, but she was now able to reflect and change rather than to hold on at any cost or abandon her enterprise in despair. She found another, more suitable job.

Marlene's decision to stay in New York and marry Jerry meant that she and Ben had to work out a bicoastal custody of Simon. They decided to have him spend two years in each household, but, after some years, Simon had more of his own say in how he would arrange his life. Reworking their relationship was emotionally wearing and a brief period in family therapy helped. At present, Simon has enrolled in high school in New York, with a plan to continue. Marlene felt their greatest strength as a family was their capacity to talk together about things. She feels now that she and Simon have "a great relationship," that she and Ben are still working out the parenting with respect and harmony, and that Simon has settled into the blended family well. "But it's more difficult than anyone imagines—all the different dynamics of the different relationships."

Marlene at age 43 is content, but doesn't idealize her life. She no longer seems to require that life be perfect. Having a baby at this age is harder than she had thought, even though she badly wanted to do it. "I just don't have the patience I had—the patience I had even when Simon was little. And I'm having trouble with a toddler—the demands. And she's not a terrible kid, but sometimes at the end of the day, if I hear "Mommy," you know . . . I just don't feel like I have the patience I should have." Some of this comes from trying to juggle work and mothering. Marlene works three days a week and continued without a break after her daughter joined the family. But she feels the tug of her professional connection on the one side and her daughter's needs on the other. Daily she engineers judicious and painful compromises. "I feel all the things I wish I had time to do in terms of work and career. I feel I go to work and see my patients because that's all I can deal with. It's not what I thought I would be doing in terms of going to professional meetings, or things I wish I could do politically. I beat myself up for not doing this and not doing that and I'm completely exhausted."

Meanwhile, Jerry's work has gotten more involving and has been taking more of his time. That leaves more housework for Marlene and she often resents this and wishes he were more involved in the family—that he would lose himself playing with the baby for hours the way Ben had. But she basks in Jerry's love, so her complaints are dwarfed by her overall sense of his cherishing her.

Marlene's job has given her the sense of purpose and effectiveness she always wished for. "I feel like I can help really influence women's lives. Birth control, what are they doing to protect themselves from AIDS? Or they have a partner who is abusing them, who refuses to use condoms and what does that mean for that woman—How does he feel about her? What is that message? How does she feel about herself? I see a lot of women doing a lot of risky things. I think I can really work with people in terms of making some positive changes."

Having created what she had been searching for in her life, Marlene is even more in pursuit of her roots than ever before. She feels increasingly aware of the meaning she had in her parents' lives, and since they are no longer around to talk to, she has grown closer to her relatives in Israel. Only in this last interview did Marlene tell me that she has a half-brother there.

"My parents had such a different life. We didn't have a shared experience—they didn't know what it was like to be in school here or to grow up here, and I used to have this feeling like I was raising myself. Both my parents died years ago and even more so in the last ten years I feel how their [Holocaust] experience has shaped my experience, my identity. Well, some of it is positive in the sense that it was reestablishing a family again so I sort of carry the family line. And it feels like a responsibility I gladly take on, the heritage and the memories. My birth continued it on. A lot of it was kind of bad—that feeling I had of being cut off and them not sharing things with me. I don't ever remember them telling me about it, but I knew about it. . . . And now that my parents are dead I have all these questions about their family and my family and what happened and there's no way to get those answers, and it's become more and more of an issue in the last ten years. Part of it is having children, the other part is just trying to seek my roots. I also am at an age that I can remember when my mother was my age and I'm trying to grapple with what her experience might have been like, but there's too many holes and too many gaps and I can't quite fill it all in."

More certain now of herself and her own life path, Marlene seeks more and more to place her life in the larger context of her parents life and of history. This is one more thread not yet woven fully into the tapestry Marlene is creating. Revision for Marlene has been a process of letting a part of herself go, then pulling it back toward her when she can see a place for it. She put her intelligence and competence on hold while she sought a secure relationship with a man, then had to leave her son behind as she reclaimed her ability and prepared for a profession. She couldn't claim her parents or their meaning in her life until she felt a more solid sense of embeddedness in her culture and her life. For her, searching and integrating have been an ongoing process. But, at age 43, Marlene has a sense of having found a place for all the parts of herself.

Millie and Marlene had the most dramatic searches in this group. As they grow into and through adulthood, they exemplify what psychologist Jim Marcia has called a cyclical pattern of exploration followed by commitment followed by further exploration. Both women are aware of their own psychological complexity and it took them many false starts before they could get all the pieces to fit. Millie and Marlene stand in contrast to other Searchers whose college-age identity confusion was less intense and who were putting less of themselves at risk. Searching can take many forms—and the outcomes are highly individual. Other Searchers either settled down and had later periods of crisis, settled down psychologically close to home, or ended up engulfed by internal conflict.

NEW PATHS, NEW QUESTIONS

Both Theresa and Regina were unsettled and in crisis at the end of college, but had a greater sense of direction than Millie and Marlene. They were able to put away their anguished questions earlier, and both settled into patterns reminiscent of the Pathmakers. But, given their greater self-reflectiveness, emotionality, and idealism, they experienced more psychological distress.

THERESA

—At the End of College   Theresa, who I earlier quoted as feeling caught between two societies, a liberal and strict one, was guiltily tugging against the restriction of her Sicilian family but trying to maintain her connection to them. As the end of college approached, she was filled with energy and exuberance and couldn't imagine that there could be enough time in life to do all that she wanted. Theresa had idealized her mother's warmth and giving-ness, and wished to emulate these traits in her own life, but she also wanted life to be different. Never did she want to be under a husband's control or victimized by his resentment, as her mother was.

—Age 33   After graduation, Theresa married her high school boyfriend, who was Jewish—that would show her parents who was making the decisions! But she didn't go far from home. She took a job teaching history in the high school she had graduated from and, though living psychological-ly and physically close to her parents, thought things through with fierce independence, experiencing herself, like the Pathmakers, as captain of her ship. She disavowed religion, then later returned to it. She was ardent about her teaching, which she "loved," but was becoming excited about comput-ers and thought about changing into this field for another challenge. She had pursued a master's degree with almost enough credits for a doctorate. But she had scaled down her ideals during her twenties. When she started teaching, she had expected "all of the students to be eager to learn every-thing I could teach. Now I'm happy if a few learn 50% and the rest behave so I can teach." By age 33, Theresa had been told that she could probably not have children. Her husband had said he didn't want children anyway, and, although emotionally preparing herself for a childless life, she was still hopeful of having them.

Another way in which Theresa was proud of having sculpted her life in counterpoint to her parents' was that she and her husband had many friends. Where she had seen her family as insular and afraid of strangers, Theresa felt she had "made many opportunities for others to enter my life." She and her husband bought a vacation house in the mountains and usually had friends in as company. At this age, Theresa seemed to be energetically navigating along a path she had carefully crafted, free of the doubts and struggle that had occupied her during college.

—Age 43   At age 43, however, Theresa reported that her course had been upended. The discovery of a tumor (at age 38), which turned out to be benign, invoked latent, intense fears of death. "I really lost it. I felt for sure I was doomed . . . I felt, I can't die. There's too much for me to do still. I want to be around, to be part of what's going on. I want to participate with the people I know and love. I had never before been sick." She developed panic attacks, had to be maintained on medication for years, and struggled to keep her fear from dominating her life. Any minor physical symptom would torment her. Looking for a reprieve, she had sought divine miracles and moved into an evangelical sect of her church. She also entered psychotherapy.

In her early forties, Theresa continues to be in conflict about her work. She now teaches computer science in her old school, one that has become increasingly dangerous, and feels committed to her students beyond fear for her physical safety. She recalls breaking up fights, risking injury, "shaking for hours afterwards." "It's a very stressful job and I'm often tired at work. But I don't want to leave. I think kids need to see people who come across as not being afraid, of being tolerant and willing to work with them. I'm a bit unhappy but my morale is not low." She goes on to tell success stories about young people she has championed. The advantage of working where she had herself gone to school is that she understands what some of these kids are up against, particularly those with immigrant parents, and she feels she knows how to help.

When Theresa turned 40 and realized that the doctors were right that she would never conceive, they adopted two children. Theresa, at age 43, came to a new understanding of her husband's earlier reluctance to have children. Now she thought that he had just been trying to be supportive of her should she prove unable to conceive. He hadn't wanted her to think he was disappointed in her. When the time came to adopt, however, he was as thrilled as she was to enlarge their family. Somehow, having children lessened her anxiety disorder. "When we got our daughter, it allowed me to spread out. I don't focus on me so much."

Having children and being in therapy also led Theresa to rethink her own history. Although she had always idealized her mother, she realized how her mother's overprotectiveness had contributed to her sense of fear. "If she could have kept me in a glass bowl, she would have. That's how I was brought up. And I know that now. And I don't want to do that to my children. I'm more laid back." But the problem is that Theresa's mother is now living with them. ("My father died. Where else could she go?") Theresa is vigilantly trying to keep her mother from overprotecting *her* children. "We argue, yell, and scream, but it's still good. She's a great help. She does all the gardening and the cooking, and she and the children really care for each other."

Theresa also described herself in midlife as struggling against the "imposter syndrome." Even though she is acknowledged as a superior teacher and others revere her work, she says, "I often fear that I am fooling everyone. I come across as a very strong person and I keep saying if they only knew how weak I am and how afraid I am." She traces this to her relationship with her father, who rejected her because she was not a boy and always told her she was not good enough. She also relates her doubts to how contemptuously women are often treated by men in the educational system. She tries to laugh about it, but is finding that her external successes cannot still this voice of self-criticism.

Sometimes, she feels, she doesn't really know herself. Taking the medication for anxiety caused her to gain a great deal of weight and she looks in the mirror and isn't sure who she sees there. At age 43, despite having carved her own path and living it, Theresa sounds more like she did at 21 than she did at 33. Again, she is questioning, aware of conflicting parts of herself, understanding herself more, rethinking the past. In a period of renewed searching, she is redesigning her life.

REGINA

—At the End of College   Like Theresa, Regina used her occupational commitment to form a center of her identity in her early adulthood. Raised in a military family, she moved a great deal while growing up. Observing different cultures from her own experience, she became fascinated by sociology during college and proved to be a superior student. Her parents had changed religions when she was 12 without discussing what that meant to them. This left her uncertain what to believe. Similarly, her political beliefs felt confused. Most important, however, Regina was struggling with how to be in relationships with men. She found herself falling into a pattern of letting her boyfriend think for her, then breaking up with him to date others only to return and fall back into the same pattern. Her identity struggle in college was one of locating herself in relationships and in beliefs.

—Age 33   When I met her again at age 33, Regina had earned a doctorate in sociology and was developing an academic career. She had found a church that espoused a "spiritual humanism which meets my need to escape the emptiness in daily life when it lacks a centeredness, and provides a connectedness to others." Similarly, her political beliefs seemed clear as she became increasingly committed to a feminist orientation. At the end of graduate school, she had married Roger, a fellow graduate student, and they had, for two years, evolved a complicated commuting relationship while they worked at different universities. Through these years, Regina felt herself

clearly pursuing a path of her own making, a path that seemed promising and, most of all, right for her.

But after several years of marriage, she began to feel that Roger was not all that she needed. Although they were "best friends," their sexual life was sorely lacking. Roger was relatively uninterested in sex, not romantic, and Regina found herself craving more intimacy and passion. In her early thirties, Regina had a turbulent but secret affair that raised soul-searching questions about whether she wanted to stay in her marriage, whether it could be improved, whether she wanted to have children with Roger—or if she should leave and start again. After a long period of psychotherapy, she decided to stay in the marriage and try to make it work, but the doubts and discomfort never fully abated.

—*Age 43*   By age 43, Regina was more settled on a well-marked path. Now the mother of two children under 4, one of whom is seriously retarded, Regina's identity is grounded among the markers of work, family, and spirituality. Regina was promoted to full professor and had established a national reputation as an expert on women in the criminal justice system. And she has found good care for her retarded son and manages to meet his special needs. Her religious questing led her to convert several years ago to Episcopalianism, a religion that "offers me a deepening of my relationship with God. Religious practice is a way of opening channels within my self to broader spiritual experiences and broader connections with other people." She and Roger built a house in the woods. All the pieces of her complex and challenging life feel in place even though Regina has undiagnosable periods of intense fatigue—which might be Chronic Fatigue Syndrome or perhaps result from psychological causes. Despite frequent pain and tiredness, she manages to keep up with all she has taken on.

But Regina continues to experience internal cycles of searching, of thinking about redoing her life. At midlife, she describes her twenty-year-long marriage to Roger as "loving, committed, and stable, but profoundly unsatisfying." Looking back, she wonders if perhaps they married out of a need not to be alone. "We were pretty frightened, pretty anxious, and pretty defensive about life in general and maybe we thought that we could protect each other. And we did know each other pretty well at that point in time . . . I think we fit together as a couple much better now. We've made some major decisions in terms of having a family. I think we work better together in planning our lives, working out daily details, helping each other manage the details of everyday life." They have given up on sex altogether. Regina regrets that she lost the chance to really experience herself as a woman. "It's almost like I had to put everything else on hold if I was going to escape the kind of compromised life my mother had had," referring to her fear of being trapped into traditional female roles. But she is no closer to knowing what to do about her marriage. When I asked her why she has chosen at each period of crisis to remain in her marriage, she said thoughtfully, "I don't leave relationships easily. And the establishment of a home and family has provided me with a stabilizing influence. We work well together and are friends. But in a deep sense, I don't know."

From the time they were in college, most Searchers, like Theresa and Regina, struggle to balance often-warring parts of themselves. Outwardly, they may appear certain and committed; internally, they wrestle with inner confusion that, once quelled, only reappears and requires renewed resolution. Both Theresa and Regina have had markedly successful careers and stable marriages, but both fight against feeling like an imposter and labor to convince themselves that they are doing their best. For both, the deeper, knottier problems of identity lie in relationship, in belief, and in feeling at home in who they are. Their paths, now marked and clear, are nevertheless strewn with doubt and remain open to continual refashioning.

SETTLING DOWN EARLY

For some, the questioning, soul-searching period that flourishes in the college environment evaporates as they take their diplomas. Some of the Searchers found that, when college ended, the search seemed to end as well, so they headed home—emotionally if not also physically.[3] They had tried their wings a bit during college; once that ended, they sought firm ground and took the bus to what was familiar. Interviewing them after college, I often couldn't tell whether they were choosing on their own terms or fleeing into what seemed safe—and available. Instead of finding answers to the questions they had been asking during college, these women simply turned their back on them. They resolved the dilemmas emanating from the conflicts between their parents' expectations and their own desires by muting the part of themselves that was finding its own voice. They returned to the world of their parents, but with a small space carved out for their own decision-making.

NATALIE

—At the End of College   Natalie had entered college already engaged to be married, and, at that time, what she most wanted in life was to be "Mrs. Somebody." While in college, however, she began to think more in terms of being somebody of her own and broke her engagement. She was an editor

of the college newspaper and enjoyed seeing her name in print. She wanted people to know that she was a writer; her dream was to write a novel. She wanted both an exciting career and a secure home. But, like other Searchers, Natalie's ambition was clouded by other considerations. For example, Natalie had thought about how she would put marriage and a career together and felt that, if her husband objected to her career, she would probably quit. So she was still in conflict, still thrashing out the contradictions between her different needs and values.

Reflecting on herself while in college, Natalie felt that, up until recently, she had "always hidden behind [my] parents." Her former fiancé had helped her recognize this: "He made me stronger as a person. Now I want to be on my own and do things. I'm getting really sick of hanging on to my parents. I'm sick of being a leech. Maybe I'm afraid of growing up. I want to be an adult, but sometimes it's really nice to hide behind being a little girl." She was afraid of making deep commitments. "When you graduate, that's it. It's got to be something permanent. I can't say 'Well, I'll try it for a semester and if I don't like it, I'll switch to something else.' And I'll have to face the reality of establishing relationships to keep them." Natalie had changed friends often. She would become enchanted with someone, then lose interest. "I'm trying to overcome that flightiness I have."

In her college interview, Natalie described a recent dream: "There was me and another person who was a shadow. We were trying to get to the top of the mountain because if we got there it was supposed to be the most fantastic thing in the world—the view or something. Then we got there and then the fog started coming in and we were trying to come down the mountain. And we got lost, we got separated, and I was trying to find either him or my way down. And I'd go in these buildings . . . I went in this one building. It was the house where we used to live and there was a man sitting in a corridor who told me how to get out of the house. And I was still in a fog. At the end, I got down to the end of the mountain and it turned out the fog was a forest fire and everyone was packing up and leaving."

This dream epitomizes the Searchers' inner world as they came to the end of college. There is the hope of reaching the top of the mountain, the most fantastic thing. But with that goes the necessity of separation, even from the accompanying shadows of one's childhood. And does one go forward alone or cling to the shadow-person? Forging ahead alone brings the fog and the fear. And, in the fog, one could still go back home, even though that engenders the wish again to "get out of the house." And in the end, the fear is very real—one might have gotten burned in the flames. In any case, "home" is destroyed. This dream demonstrates the intensity of the psychological processes at work in the Searchers' struggle for individuation.

Natalie's own interpretation of her dream in college was that it symbolized "having a climax and having that person leave you," pointing to her ongoing conflicts about sexuality. She felt guilty that she had had sex with her fiancé and that it did not lead to marriage. But she also saw in her dream her need for security and fear of being alone. She understood that she went to the old house to feel sheltered.

—*In Midlife*   This dream presaged Natalie's choices after college. As in the dream, she returned home to live. She fell into a dull technical writing job where she has stayed for twenty years, and in her mid-thirties fell into an equally dull but secure marriage to a passive, quiet man. Of this marriage, she said at age 43, "I feel like I belong now. I didn't like being alone. This way you feel like you're in a normal relationship—you have a partner, feel like you are a team. Sometimes when you're single, you sort of float along. Everything is in twos. Now I feel like, oh, you're a normal person cause you're married. You've conformed to society's expectation. And I'm a nurturing person and a pleaser. So now I have somebody to please and that's very fulfilling. But I do feel it holds you back because you can't do exactly what you want. . . . He's very dependent on me, which sometimes can be a bit of a drain. He never goes out. He likes TV, likes to have his dinner. He's just always home and wants to do everything together. It even bothered him that I was coming here today. After a while I get sort of antsy, cause I like to do more things."[4]

Unable to conceive for the eight years of her marriage, she accepts this as fate. "But I still have a little glimmer of hope that it might still happen." And she thinks about the possibility of adopting an older child. Marriage narrowed her circle of friends, but she retains a close friendship at work. She collects antique china and enjoys her garden. While Natalie seems content and stable, the spark of questioning and struggle that flickered in her during college was gone from the woman of 43. She seemed to me to have opted for shelter.

Natalie herself seemed aware of the new fog she was in. "You start to realize you're out of college twenty years and what the hell have you done. Things I haven't gotten to yet." In the interview, she was trying to renew her motivation to write that book. Perhaps that more alive part of herself is quiescent but not yet lost.

LAURA

—*At the End of College*   Laura had felt pushed into college by her working-class parents, who wanted at least one of their children to succeed by this standard. Her being in college, she felt, was her mother's "one big accomplishment in life." Once there, she became interested in her studies and, as graduation approached, was thinking of applying to graduate school in public health. But this wasn't something she wanted to "rush into." She needed time to think it over. She had decided to work for a year to earn money for graduate school and be able to live on her own.

As she was graduating, Laura was at the beginning of a struggle for separation and autonomy that many of the other Searchers had undertaken long before. She was starting to break away from her mother, wondering how much longer she would continue to go to church to please her. She was frightened about sex, but curious and readying herself to define things her own way. She was clear, though, that she couldn't become sexually active until she left home. "I couldn't make love to someone and then go home to my own bed."

What was most troubling Laura as the end of college approached was that she had never fallen in love. Oh, she had had crushes and infatuations, but nothing ever grew into what she could think of as love. "I hope that one day it will hit me like a brick wall," but she was worried. Despite her talk of graduate school and independence, her frustrated wish for love seemed to be Laura's emotional center.

Laura's family had moved a great deal while she was growing up, and her younger sister had always been her best friend. More outgoing than she, her sister made friends and was willing to share them with Laura. Deeply and unconsciously, Laura seemed to long to repeat this sense of an intense twosome, bonded against whatever life disruptions might befall them.

—*Age 33*   Shortly after graduation, however, Laura did fall in love—with a man she described at age 33 as "an attractive man, a very nice man, a very quiet man, very much like my father and very much like me." They formed an ardent couple and married several months later. Laura was centered on her husband and very proud of their relationship. She boasted that they never had a fight and the only negative thing about their relationship was that they never got enough time together. "I can't imagine anything I would want of marriage that isn't there. I think in every area of my life my husband has a part. He is totally supportive of me in my personal life and with my work experiences. If I'm pissed off at work and can't stand it and say I want to quit, he says, 'Fine, quit.' We are open and honest with each other—if we have something to talk about, something we're worried about, something we're afraid of, we can go to each other and talk about it. We respect each other and that's a big part of why we're able to have such a good marriage."

They had decided they didn't want children. "We sort of baby each other," Laura said. After college, she had taken a job in medical technology, answering the call of a friend who worked there when the service was short-staffed, and was still there when I interviewed her at age 33. Laura had simply forgotten about graduate school. She liked her work, enjoyed the contact with patients, and felt effective by helping to calm them and getting them to cooperate in undergoing medical tests. But she hoped she would be in some other job in the future. Although her work was gratifying, it was often boring.

—*Age 43*   Ten years later, though, at age 43, Laura was much the same. Still in the same job, she was resigning herself to staying in it. She had briefly been made a supervisor, but then the administrative structure changed and her position was eliminated. Although "devastated," she was happy to be able to return to her old job. What was most interesting to me about Laura at this stage was that within what seemed to be a relatively constricted and conventional identity, she had developed the inner conviction to define her life on her own terms. Seven years earlier, her husband had gotten fed up with the long hours and pressure of his managerial job. "He decided to quit and was going to take a little break before he went back out into the workforce, but what happened was that we both really got to the point where we really liked him being at home. He's a wonderful cook, and all the kinds of things that one has to do at home—laundry, grocery shopping—I'm not really suited for that—I have some physical limitations which make some of those things kind of difficult for me. He didn't mind doing it and so he's still doing it. He works part-time doing odd jobs. This is really nice for me because I really don't do anything other than go to work. He does everything else at the house. I think at the beginning it was a little difficult for me because I was concerned what people would think of him, that they would think less of him. I wasn't concerned that they approved of the way we worked this out, but that they wouldn't think of him as highly as I think he ought to be thought of. He's extremely intelligent, he's a wonderful loving husband, and what some people might think who don't really know us—I know that people who know us understand what we're doing, but I didn't want people to think badly about him. I talked to him about this because we talk about everything and he didn't care what other people think. I'm rather happy with the way we've worked out our life and rather proud, to be perfectly honest. We don't feel that he has to go out and get a job so we can make big money. It's not what we're all about." Their needs are simple, they have most of what they want, and "expensive toys are not that important." Laura is glad to be free of any house chores and feels that she and her husband just grow closer over the years.

The rest of Laura's life revolves around helping her sisters who have had some difficult times. And they have two dogs that Laura feels have "helped me to become a better person. Simply because I'm aware that others have needs and I can satisfy these needs. I think they help me experience that maternal instinct that I never really felt otherwise." What she wants most out of life, now and in the future, is "to be a good person and to be and to have been a loving wife."

In her reading, Laura seeks out stories about women who have adventures and take risks. She admires them. But that is not what she wants for herself. Her major work has been her relationship with her husband—that's what she feels most special about.

Laura, like Natalie, simply turned off the quest. They returned home after college, recentered in their families, and stopped asking quite so many questions of life. In retrospect, from their thirties and more so from their forties, they remember college as a wonderful, eye-opening vacation that had little impact on the rest of their lives.

PERSISTENT INNER KNOTS

Two of the women who had been Searchers at the end of college found that their searches were hampered by unresolved inner conflicts that made it impossible to secure a comfortable place for themselves in the world. Their lives grew increasingly chaotic and contradictory; only with psychotherapy were they able to understand the internal chains that were imprisoning them. Both reached a dead end in their late thirties and then asked for help.

These are stories of women at odds with themselves, who thrashed about for many years trying to undo the knots. Both significantly rewrote their understanding of their lives in their late thirties, finding that they harbored enormous anger at their parents that had, in one way or another, taken over their lives.

SANDRA

—At the End of College   Sandra had grown up "a fat child" and later developed a serious eating disorder. In college, she was struggling to free herself from her parents' expectations. But in doing something of her own choosing, she felt she was disappointing them; doing what they wanted made her resentful. Having lost a great deal of weight, becoming slim and pretty, she craved male attention, but was frightened and enslaved by it. She was filled with self-doubt and self-hatred but didn't know where to locate its cause. On the one hand, she was angry at her father for his control of her. On the other hand, she was angry at her parents for not having provided her with more discipline, for having allowed her to be fat in the first place. In her col-

lege interview, she said, "Right now I feel very dependent on my parents. I love them very much and I don't want to hurt them. They've done so much for me. Especially my father. I'm trying to get away from them, but they won't let me. They want to keep me there forever. . . . I want to do something but I don't even know where to begin."

—*Age 33* By the time she was in her thirties, she had settled things a bit, but in a self-contradictory way. Just after college, she followed her mother's pattern (which she thought had been disastrous for her mother) in marrying a man twenty years older. She had replaced her father out of a wish to escape him. Not surprisingly, at age 33, she expressed great ambivalence about her marriage. Although it provided her with security, she felt romance and spontaneity were gone, and that her husband was "completely oblivious to my feelings." But she held on for the security and began to see other men. She doubted that she would ever want to be tied down to children, but hadn't yet made a final decision.

After college, Sandra began working as an administrative assistant in the business world, using her zealous conscientiousness to succeed. Although she held seven jobs in ten years, none was satisfactory. Either the pay was low, the people were unpleasant, or there was no opportunity for growth, so Sandra would move on. At this point in her life, age 33, Sandra still seemed to be searching.

—*Age 43* This search led her to psychotherapy, and, at age 43, Sandra felt that her therapy had been the most important aspect of her life in the past ten years. She sought therapy when she finally acknowledged to herself that she had been bulimic for years. She felt she had come to a new understanding of her life, which involved recognizing that her parents were "seriously deficient as role models. I just became really aware of what had happened to me when I was younger. My parents never beat or hit me or anything like that. They tried to give me everything I needed materially. My mother is a people-pleaser. And my father is a really angry man. I think at the age of 30 I was more of a victim than a person. I started seeing a therapist and I started finding out I wasn't a victim anymore. . . . I'm very aware. I just don't know how to act on a lot of it. I come from a family of denial, I come from a dysfunctional family, whatever . . . . I have spent a lot of time trying to pay back, I guess."

Sandra said that she is still unsure how to make use of her new awareness. After several extramarital affairs that ended badly, she values her husband more. But the marriage is now completely asexual and she still doesn't know how to make her peace with that. Worse, her mother lives with them now that her father has died. And this is a source of intense distress for Sandra. "She and I do a dance of pushing each other's buttons. I'm in the house for three minutes and I'm out of my mind." So her solution is to be home as little as possible. Given her Iranian background, she can't even consider not living with her mother. "In my culture, when parents get old, you take care of them," she said.

Sandra continues to get overinvolved in her work, staying long hours. "I'm a people pleaser like my mother and the office manager has to please everyone. It keeps my mind off my own problems." But she recognizes that her people-pleasing is often in the service of her anger. "I'm a very angry person," she says, "just like my father." She has since decided not to have children. She's too afraid of trying to raise them, too afraid of her anger.

At age 43, Sandra still hopes to find a way to anchor herself in something that will feel meaningful. Despite her therapy, it is hard for her to imagine being her own person rather than being like her victim mother or angry father. "I have struggled over the years to put my life together as best I can inwardly and outwardly. Outwardly I do a better job. Inwardly its tougher for me . . . I appear to be strong but every day it's a struggle. I have to fill my life up with all sorts of things to get me through. I work out, I have a lot of friends, I take classes, I do volunteer work. I put myself on a schedule. . . . Whatever it is I can fill up the time with, I fill it up. I am fearful of having any quiet time, because I don't know what I'd do with it. I don't know what it is to be relaxed . . . I think I've been lucky not to fall apart."

LESLIE

Leslie, by contrast, did fall apart. Although she drifted a great deal through college, Leslie seemed to have moments of trying to reach for a life plan and that is why I classified her as a Searcher. After college, she began to drift in earnest. She had eleven jobs in ten years, trying to position herself somewhere in the human services field, but either found the work unsatisfactory or got into squabbles and was fired. At age 33, she was working night shifts in a group home for mentally ill adults. She drank heavily throughout her twenties and had been throughout her life what she described as "morbidly obese." She had fallen in love with a woman she was then living with, but was trying to hide her lesbianism. She described herself as "completely dependent emotionally on this woman for acceptance and approval to help me get through the ups and downs of everyday living." She lived in fear that she was the more emotionally involved of the two. Throughout this time, she was also intensely close to her family and her life was enriched by involvement with them and her siblings' growing families. She looked to her mother to help her out when she was unemployed or broke. Her hopes for herself had diminished since college: "My goals have become less sweeping and idealistic in the last ten years. Then I wanted to understand why people did what they did; now my goals are to pay the bills and to do the best job I can from day to day. . . . It is better to change goals and dreams to what is possible than wasting time chasing after rainbows." In her early thirties, Leslie seemed to have taken charge of her life, trying to anchor herself in what appeared possible.

In the next ten years, things deteriorated. Leslie continued to fail in her work and found that her violent feelings were getting out of control. She made a suicide attempt and was in a mental hospital for several months. This led her to a long course of psychotherapy. During this process, she revised her understanding of her life history and recovered memories of both physical and sexual abuse. But this resulted in estrangement from her family, who denied that such things had happened and were furious at her new version of events. Through much anguish and torment, Leslie was finally able to separate herself from them. She felt that, through therapy, "I was able to free myself from the prison of my abusive past," and she set about remaking her life. This process took several years. With the help of a vocational rehabilitation program, she retrained in a data-management field and "graduated" at the top of the class. She liked this work and found that she could accommodate herself to it without the anger and distress she had always experienced in work settings. And she can see opportunities for growth in the field. "I regained a positive self-image," she said. She and her partner, after a turbulent time, acknowledged their commitment to a permanent life together and had a formal wedding ceremony. They bought a house together. They decided not to have children. Leslie has also chosen to keep her "private life private." Leslie's interview was rich with insights, a document of all she felt she had learned in this crisis at midlife.

UNPREDICTABLE PATHS

Still in quest of themselves when college ended, the Searchers' adult passages toward identity are more varied than those of the other groups. The Searchers make more changes, both internal and external, as they try to match what the world offers with what they discover about themselves. But this is not surprising, since the searching state is an unstable one. It *should* lead to one of the other possibilities—either making commitments, returning to the secure structures of childhood, or drifting.[5]

Some Searchers, like Laura and Natalie, as we have seen, start out more like Guardians, staying close to a childhood self, but leaning over the precipice of individuation just a little. They experience the questioning that accompanies a search for independent identity, but they try to muffle it, to keep it in bounds. As they move into adulthood, they have access to less diversity in their life experiences, and less support for their exploration. Their perspective narrows and they become less able to tolerate ambiguity. Psychologist Jane Kroger (in press) refers to this process as a regression of rigidification. Choosing more-or-less conventional lives relatively close to their families of origin, they nevertheless put their own stamp on at least some aspect of it. They feel they have made their own choices, but have done it by quelling those more daring parts that might have sought something else. Unlike those who began as Guardians, these women do not seem to experience a midlife awakening to forgotten aspects of themselves. They seem content to glide along the paths they have already made.

Other Searchers, like Sandra and Leslie, are tied in emotional knots that keep them from finding a place of respite. For them, what seems to be struggle about identity may reflect deeper and more pervasive emotional conflict. After college, they begin to drift. They are caught in ambivalent struggles with their parents from which they cannot extricate themselves. Enraged, consciously or unconsciously, at those they love and depend on, they cannot disentangle themselves so they can follow their own stars. Their lives get caught in trying to redress their childhood or avenge their wounds. Kroger (in press) understands this as a regression of disorganization in which personality becomes less structured due to unmanageable stress or trauma. In these two cases, at least, psychotherapy was of great help.

But most of the Searchers did, sooner or later, find themselves, and they became, at midlife, much like the midlife Pathmakers, albeit with more continuing ambivalence and self-doubt. They began, we recall, as more self-reflective women.

Searchers who continue to search after college face a more difficult task than the Pathmakers who charted a life plan during their college years. The world is a much larger place than college, and the supports that are available in the college atmosphere vanish once college ends. At the close of what Erikson called the moratorium period, society expects that the young person will declare herself and the path she will follow. And when young people try to delay such a declaration, society may turn its back on them or, worse, label them negatively. Millie's family, for example, had given up on her, called her a "weirdo." The Searchers who didn't form a plan at the end of college often faced a world that took them for who they ever-so-tentatively said they might be. Even if they had wanted to retain control of their own course, the Searchers often felt cast adrift. The ties to others who might support them and help them steer often disappeared. Possibility became more and more abstract. It was hard to know how to implement other choices and their anxiety increased.

The world of work was one that each of these women was eyeing somewhat warily. They were often full of ideals, but confused about how they might translate these into reality and uncertain how or where they might be able to succeed. Only a few of these women had any real idea how to enter the work world or match their talents and interests with occupational demands. Most "fell into" first jobs and either decided to stay for lack of a vision of what else to do or began bouncing from job to job. They were hard workers and were ready to apply themselves to a task, but they were lacking in information about the politics of the workplace for educated women.

Unlike the Pathmakers, few Searchers had formed relationships during college that could help them secure and support their quests in the wider world. This made the struggle to individuate from their parents much more onerous. They felt too alone to exert much effort in the service of their own shaky desires. Some returned home psychologically just to feel anchored. They needed a holding environment that could "be there" for them while they grew.[6] Some, sooner or later, were able to obtain the support they needed. Marlene found a women's support group to back her and cheer her as she gingerly tested her right and capacity to claim a path of her own. Millie found strength through reclaiming her faith and sense of community in religion. Theresa and Regina could fall back on their husbands, while Sandra and Leslie relied on therapists.

More self-conscious and self-doubting as young women than the Pathmakers or the Guardians, the Searchers required that others be there to buttress their ventures. They could dare, but not for long, and not without support. Lacking this, they crept to safety or drifted aimlessly.

Throughout their lives, Searchers lived closer to their emotions than the other groups. They are more expressive and more reactive, which leads them to more intense joy in small pleasures and greater pain at frustration. The greater emotionality of this group of women may in part account for their having more psychological symptoms and physical problems than the women in the three other groups combined.

The Searchers are also a more spiritual group than the Pathmakers. Their idealism and openness to experience lead them to value the connection with forces greater than themselves. Still opposed to external authority of any sort, they strive for personally defined religious experience rather than religion based on rules. Many of these women have crafted personal forms of religious expression, often in small groups of like-minded others.

The Searchers, despite the divergences in the course their lives have taken, continue their college-age pattern of self-criticism and self-doubt.

Many of them describe a propensity to "beat up" on themselves, to excoriate themselves for not being able to do everything or do it perfectly. They make a point of taking stock of themselves, of evaluating their progress. As a group, they tell me that they are too emotional, too unkind, too intolerant of others. Regina, in trying to sum up her progress in identity, wonders if she has done as well as she might have. "If my life had to end right now, I would say that I've covered all the important bases for myself already. I have done some things I have felt to be really important in life. I have friends who I think truly love me, I have maintained good family relationships, and I have a husband who really loves me, and I have retained the relationship with him through some daunting ups and downs in recent years. I have begun to raise two children, who are exuberant and happy children, I have accomplished quite a bit occupationally in terms of becoming a full professor and having a good publication record. I think I've made a genuine difference in some people's lives—students who refer to me as teaching them everything they knew. I've had a rich inner life, a life I've been able to share with other people from time to time. I've been open to my surroundings and had moments of beauty on a daily basis. I've paid attention to my spiritual life and my connection with the broader world around me. My biggest criticism of myself in recent years is that I wonder if I've become too selfish, too self-centered, too much time examining my own navel and not enough responsiveness to the outside world. But I know I have done some things, some service that has made a difference. I think I have faced some challenges that I worked with the best I could. And maybe I wished I would have made other choices, now looking back on it, but I did do the best that I could do. I think in times of stress, people always try to do the best that they can. And maybe looking back on it, you wish the best would have been better, but that you always have to recognize what you have done at the time as the best you could. Maybe I'm not always sure of that, but, in my better moments, I feel that I've tried to do the best I could." In their striving for ideals, in their self-criticism, the Searchers retain the fundamental orientation of their college-age selves.

Revision over the course of life for these women has often been focused on tempering impossibly high standards for themselves in the face of which they could only feel inadequate. As they age and grow, they learn to accept themselves as less than they might have dreamed they would be, yet still value what they have made of their lives.

All my life I've wanted to be somebody.

But I see now I should have been more specific.

Jane Wagner, The Search for Signs of

Intelligent Life in the Universe

7 THE DRIFTERS

Unlike the Searchers, the Drifters in college were not struggling to make commitments or plans as they approached the end of college. Nor were they juggling the pulls of the past and the promise of new forms of experience like the Pathmakers and the Guardians. They had simply stepped out of their pasts and were living only in the present. The future seemed like a far-off world as they floated on the currents of the moment. Responsive to their immediate world, open to its novelties, they were expecting to fall into an interesting rabbit hole and lose themselves among its wonders.

The social climate of the late 1960s made just about anything possible. It gave the Drifters as college seniors the space and the permission to lose themselves. They could give free rein to their impulses. They could "drop out," accept being labeled as "hippies,"[1] and their elders, although perplexed and chagrined, regarded this as typical of the times. In every age, there are ways to drift.

Although some Drifters seemed charming free-spirits, on closer examination they were really less in control of what they were doing than it might have appeared. Instead of anticipating the place they might take—even a countercultural one—they were expecting that life would somehow happen to them. They mistook the relatively protected world of college for the larger reality of living in the adult world and were at a loss for what to do next. They were avoiding, rather than undertaking, the work of forming identity.

The women in this group are very different from one another. They were all rather lost as college seniors, but lost for different reasons. Some regarded themselves loosely as "hippies"; others were simply having a good time. Still others were angry or merely sad. The future was something that would arrive someday, but they regarded it with neither fear nor hope. "When the time comes, I'll do something," Debbie explained. They lived as if the present would never come to an end.

Some seemed to have fairly serious psychological problems that prevented them from taking on the work of identity formation. Others were evading their own developmental task, absorbed in being critical of society or wishing that the world would change.

Other psychologists who have studied these four groups have found the Drifters to be the least psychologically healthy on a variety of psychological measures. The Drifters score highest on measures of anxiety and, in general, show themselves to be most likely to withdraw from situations that are frustrating or difficult.[2] Psychologists have regarded this as the most worrisome of the identity pathways, but we have known little about what becomes of these women.

Following them for twenty years, I find that they continue to be a varied group but are alike in becoming women who feel somewhat battered and chastened by life. They have had the most to learn, the most adjusting to do. Their lives make the most interesting stories because they have lived closest to the edge and have undergone the most unusual experiences. Often, their early adult histories center on an episode of something important in their lives exploding and then having to put out the blaze and get things right again. Yvonne's life story at age 33, for example, was centered on the trauma of having been abandoned by her partner after the birth of their child who, born prematurely and very ill, died several months later. Erica married a much older man whom she knew was dying because she felt she could bring joy and meaning to his last months. Evelyn has been living in a turbulent and violent lesbian love triangle. But the drama in their lives has come at the cost of much suffering.

By the time they are in their early forties, the Drifters' lives are more settled, some because of their own choices, others because the currents have carried them to where they are. "I still don't know what I really want to do," mused Donna at age 43. "I just go on doing this and that." It is in this emotional state where I found most of the midlife Drifters—doing *something*, but not at all certain it's what they ever wanted. Yvonne and Erica came so close to emotional collapse and poverty in their thirties that they are grateful in their forties simply to be able to be "making it." Many Drifters in their forties are still very much anticipating that their real lives will yet begin and are once again starting over, hoping for better outcomes. Only Jennifer, among the Drifters, is contentedly following a well-defined path, although the contours of her life are largely drawn by her husband.

In their early adulthood, through their twenties, the Drifters made often hasty choices that they spent their thirties regretting. Why did I have these children? they wonder. Why did I never find a partner, a career, or something to believe in and work for? Or: I used to have friends—where did they go? By age 43, they look back ruefully (if asked to), aware of missed opportunities, trying not to think about it. They are saved by their capacity not to ponder too much. Instead, they live each day, much as they did in college, but now, as adults, making the best of what they made—or didn't make— of themselves. As Yvonne put it, they try to accept what they will never be.

The Drifters as college seniors were enchanting in their unwillingness to travel the well-marked paths, but their lives later are tinged with a tragic propensity for getting lost. At some point, these women wake up and are astonished to realize how old they are. And they wonder how they got where they are.

The Drifters, each time I reencounter them, are always full of surprises. More than the other groups, this group conjures the unexpected. Their lives are the least continuous, as if each period is a new incarnation. Their capacity to forget the past is alarming. They live, in effect, outside their own histories.

While they were in college, this was particularly startling. They had forgotten or were trying to forget their past. As they spoke about themselves and their experiences, it was often as though they had been born only in their late adolescence. The sense of their childhood or their parents was distant from them, irrelevant. But, in abolishing their past, these women obliterated a core part of themselves, leaving only a space, an emptiness, a receptacle to be filled with whatever they might find.

Most of these young women went home as little as possible during college. They might stop by for a brief visit, but emotionally they had written off their homes and their parents. They were living "free"—either out of choice or anger. Few at this time could say much about what their parents were like. Their parents seemed to be shadow figures, ghosts without qualities; they were there only to be escaped from.

After college, most of the Drifters dispersed widely, went on the road to encounter the world. By their early thirties, two had returned to live at home.

And by the time they were in their early forties, five of the seven women in this category were living within a quarter mile of the home in which they had grown up. (A sixth, Donna, lives an hour away from her parents but next door to her husband's parents.)

The Drifters headed home when they found themselves at a dead end, lost in the vastness of choice. They went home to "create a more organized, planned life," in Vicky's words. Their hope was to be able to touch outside of themselves the structure they could not build internally. In midlife, all these women speak of feeling a sense of clarity and control at home. Although consciously many returned home to be near people they are attached to, there is also, often unconsciously, the hope that things would be more settled, less anxiety-provoking. At a deep level, these women returned home to reconnect with something in themselves they had lost, to restart, to recapture a missing center. They were desperate to find the very structure that the Guardians were liberating themselves from during their adulthood. The struggle to get in control of themselves seemed more likely to succeed if they could do it physically close to home.

THE DRIFTERS AT THE END OF COLLEGE

The Drifters as a group were defined by what they lacked—exploration or commitment in regard to identity. That they were doing neither of these things resulted from an inner world that didn't hold together, was made up of pieces that didn't seem to fit, and they had a lack of concern about this inner fragmentation. Perhaps it seemed to them that everyone felt that way. On the surface, however, the Drifters appeared in different guises.

They were alike in being unable to make plans or take a stand. As Vicky said, "I just want to leave things open so anything can happen. It doesn't matter if I made plans anyway, because I'd just change them." Every choice, every circumstance seemed unique and unrelated to everything that went before. This was particularly apparent in these young women's inability to define any sort of sexual standards or principles for their behavior. "It all depends on the situation, the kind of environment you're in," said one. "I just get a feeling for a person and go with it," said another. Pressed to explain some pattern or logic as to who she decided to have sex with, one woman thought for awhile, then said brightly that she *did* have a standard: "I wouldn't sleep with anyone who is fat."

At pains to bring their behavior in line with some inner guidelines, they rationalized what they did; if they felt any guilt, they repressed it quickly. Jennifer, for example, spoke at age 21 about a time when she slept with a man she had just met, then wondered the next morning whether it had been a good idea. "I kissed him and then I figured that if I had gone that far, what difference did it make." When I asked what this incident meant about her standards or values, she said she felt that if it was right at the time, then it must have been right later and it's silly to feel guilty.

Unable to trust themselves, these women had given up the idea of trying to commit themselves to beliefs or goals. After all, they had learned, they'd just change them anyway. Better to "leave things open," waiting—and hoping—for circumstances that would somehow make things come out right.

As a group, the Drifters were among the most talented and privileged women I have studied. As children and teenagers, they all did well in school. They were high achievers who recounted histories of getting A's or being recognized for their artistic talent. Of the seven women in this group whom I continue to follow[3] from my original sample, four attended a highly respected private women's college. Their "drifting" in college was not for lack of talent or skill. They were women of promise who had the opportunity to choose their future.

The Drifters often felt wishes and dreams stirring in them, but the voices of their inner selves were unintelligible and hard to translate into the language of plans, beliefs, or goals. If they imagined a future at all, their hopes were fantasies rather than being linked to any action that might translate them into reality. It took Vicky twenty more years to put her feelings into language, when she said, "I feel like an artist without a medium." Indeed, this description would hold for many women in this group. Several were in fact majoring in art in college. But all the Drifters had the sensitivities of an artist, seeing the world from a somewhat different perspective, alive to their own responsiveness, but unable to structure this knowledge into identity. Instead, they set about realizing themselves in impulsivity, in the pleasures of the moment, even in the pleasures of despair.

Unlike the other groups, I find that if I try to write a clear sequential history of the early life of the Drifters, I simply can't. They have the most discrepancies in their life stories—their stories of the past change. Their development remains mysterious because at each point in their lives when I talked with them, they tell a somewhat different version of their histories. Even the facts of their early lives are transformed as they experience themselves differently. But this rewriting of the past is not integrative and expansive, a result of deepening insight, as it is for the Guardians or the Pathmakers. Instead, the Drifters' life histories are cut to the fashion of the moment. Pieces are stitched into place to make sense of the present. Old selves lie dormant; selves that no longer serve well fall away and with them the stories that sustain them. The sense they were making of their lives at age 33 is erased and overwritten by the narrative of age 43. Even past traumatic events may fade from importance, as though they never happened. Vicky, for example, as a college senior, told of spankings as a child and of her terror of her father. But when I asked her directly at age 43 if she had ever been treated in a way that she might now consider to be physical abuse, Vicky said that she could remember her younger siblings being beaten but never herself. Similarly, Yvonne recounted having been raped on a date while she was in college, but could not remember this event in her interview at age 43. Donna told me a story of growing up in an idealized close, warm, loving family. At age 33, she thanks her mother fervently for "having an open and liberal mind which has enabled me to be receptive to new ways of thinking and doing." By midlife, she describes her family only as having been distant and cold, never really understanding her.

Without roots or clear direction, these women often seem like corks bobbing on the waves. Their lives are picaresques, a series of adventures that they are often at pains to link. After college, they continued the project of trying to have a good time, but the good times started to fade as their friends began to get deeper into loss of control or settled into commitments of their own. Sooner or later in their twenties they reached a dead end. As Debbie put it, she felt "exhausted and fed up" with the world as she found it and hopeless about making it change. Vicky, at age 33, said poignantly that she realized that above all she needed "some stability" in her life. The need to attend to the practicalities of living—to earn money, to find something meaningful to engage themselves in—had crept up on them. They noticed that others seemed to have "a life," but these women were often unsure how to create one of their own.

As a group, the Drifters, in their twenties, changed their address, held more jobs, had more abortions, tried more religions, and used more drugs and alcohol than the women in the other groups. They continued to drift— in and out of places, relationships, and projects. Still unable to find meaning on their own terms, Drifters dealt with their early adulthood by allowing themselves to be buffeted by whatever life brought, waiting to be claimed by something. They followed whatever took hold of them—a religion, a man, children, a bureaucratic structure. They had little sense of making choices, and their life stories at the age of 33 were narratives of things that "happened" to them, things they could lose themselves in.

THE ENIGMAS OF DRIFTERS' PATHS

No matter how hard I struggled to make sense of their lives, the Drifters presented a haphazard sequence of events in which logic and motivation were difficult to discern. The dynamics of decision-making, where choice grows out of what one already is, were obscured. I could not make out why they had made one choice instead of another and I suspect that this reflected their own puzzlement in making their lives cohere. Often, in thinking back on why they did something, they would draw a blank—"It made sense at the time," they might say, skipping over the space for memory of motivation.

Yet I was surprised to find that by their early forties, these women had settled into a life that felt to them more stable and understandable than ever before. Often, those who had seemed most disorganized in their twenties or thirties redirected themselves and found meaning; others, who at age 33 seemed more secure and satisfied, were lost again later in their thirties. Still, most of them made some new beginning around age 40, a beginning that seemed to them more solid and authentic than the many other fits and starts of the earlier decades. By age 43, they felt they had learned some important things about life and this knowledge helped ground their identity.

As I try to understand these women in their early forties, I often find it hard to tell if they are still drifting or not. So frequently, what had seemed to be a commitment in the past proved later to be only a short-lived fling with a passing whim. Many of these women appear to live their lives in different terms from those in the other groups. Their inner psychological structure is different, although outwardly they may resemble the others. Dealing with a core emptiness that was with them in college, the task for them is to structure rather than revise. Less clearly defined internally, they are more responsive to the context in which they find themselves, taking on, like chameleons, the colors of their surroundings. Knowing their "true colors" is then difficult for the observer—no less than for themselves. Locating "core" pieces of themselves becomes for them a hard-won achievement.

There is no simple or single explanation for why these women lacked internal structure and came to the end of their adolescence so unformed. For each, there were unique circumstances of their childhood, poor "fits" with their families, that left them unable to take in what the women of the other groups were engaged in modifying.

VICKY

—At the End of College   As a graduating college senior, Vicky seemed like one of the most psychologically disturbed women in the group. She was depressed and angry, unable to control herself well or make much sense out of her life. She was questioning deeply, thinking about herself and her feelings, but nothing was adding up.

I began the interview with my standard question: "If there were someone you wished to know you, what sorts of things would you tell them about yourself?" Vicky replied, "I'd tell them the way I was feeling at that moment—my mood and why I was in that mood—the way I'm reacting to the things that are happening to me now." As is typical of the Drifters, she defined herself in the moment. Vicky seemed flooded by inner conflict, wallowing in emotions that she could neither master nor interpret and gaining respite from the pain by following friends into drugs, sex, anti-war marches, and generalized protest.

Vicky had been a high-achieving, obedient, and compliant Catholic girl until she went to college: she returned after freshman year looking like a hippie and espousing the virtue of the youth and drug subcultures. She worried about what the neighbors in her small rural town might think of her, but decided not to care. Vicky became increasingly estranged from her large family. They could not understand her. In turn, she was angry at her father for his tyrannical demandingness and her mother for her docile acquiescence to his rule. At the same time, "I was afraid to leave my past." She told me she had stopped going to church, then spoke of how much she really likes hearing Mass.

Vicky's way of experiencing these contradictions in herself was very different from the psychological phrasing of the Searchers. Where the Searchers *felt* their conflicts as parts of themselves in opposition to one another, the Drifters experienced contrary feelings that didn't seem connected to each other. Vicky felt "afraid to leave" her past, for example, but was unaware of any way in which she was holding on. "I live day by day," she said, by way of explanation. Recalling herself in high school, she described herself in one part of the interview as having been "obnoxious. I never got punished equal to how bad I was." In another part, she said, "I always did everything right." In college, she felt she behaved in too many different ways to adequately convey except to say, "I always have a sense of unhappiness. I wonder if I'm happy to be alive." Unable to reconcile these many parts of herself, she kept them apart and lived with her confusion and a sense of emptiness. In psychological language, this is a form of dissociation—parts of the self are maintained separate from other parts, and this form of functioning is typical of the Drifters. Unlike Searchers who feel and articulate their conflicts, Drifters offer me fragments, which I then find impossible to assemble.

Throughout college, Vicky would become deeply involved with a group of friends, but then would feel that she was losing herself and pull away from them. Much of the time she felt lonely. Majoring in psychology as a way to learn about herself, Vicky toyed with the idea that she was mentally ill. She wondered if she were really any different from people in a mental hospital and daydreamed about what it would be like to be in one. As she was about to graduate from college, Vicky seemed to me to be headed for disaster.

—In Midlife   To my surprise, however, Vicky pulled herself together. At age 44, she feels centered and certain and reflects on how much she has learned about life. She had a long and somewhat scattered sequence of jobs in the human services field and now holds an administrative job in industry. After college, she got a job in a mental hospital and realized, in retrospect, that she had hoped to change the world, or, at least, to change the way mental patients were treated. By the time she turned 30, Vicky had been continually disillusioned with how things were in the reality of the world of work as she found it. She had also become disappointed in her communal living situations where people would seem to have the same values as she, but turned out to be unreliable or behave in ways she considered unfair. She also had two love relationships that ended badly. She couldn't understand why her partners acted the way they did, couldn't communicate her wishes to them, and, in the end, simply left or was left. Lost and confused, Vicky decided to return home in hopes of finding some stability.

She took a "desk job" temporarily while she set about "researching possible occupations" in an effort to take charge of her life. In this "temporary" job, however, Vicky gained a mentor. Her supervisor, a woman, recognized her managerial talents and encouraged her. More than this, however, this woman validated Vicky's sense of how things were in the world: that people did cover up and pretend, that organizations often overlook mediocrity and shoddy work, that the best people don't always rise to the top, that people behave irrationally, and so on. Each of these was a hard-won insight. For the first time, Vicky understood that things she had in some way known about the world matched reality. Knowledge that had seemed forbidden or in error could now be aired. Vicky felt enormous relief to have someone else, someone she admired, confirm what she had always at some level known to be true. She could at last claim her own sanity. And, with this, Vicky was also able to recognize that in her family no one was ever allowed to say what was what. No wonder she had felt so confused.

Living near her childhood home gave Vicky a sense of security and structure while her mentor provided her support and validation. As a result, Vicky began to revise the way she saw the world. She recognized that she had talents and began to try to think clearly about how her skills could intersect with the world. She began framing her questions in narrower terms and plotting her goals in more achievable units. She stopped thinking that her painful run-ins with colleagues and supervisors were all her fault and began to be able to identify the source of her boredom or dissatisfaction.

In her early forties, she is still very much working through these insights. Vicky dislikes the environment at the company where she works. She feels that "it is male-dominated and insensitive to the legitimate needs of workers." She resents working for a manager she considers incompetent and rails against the fact that (her) good work receives no more recognition than half-baked, dashed-off work of her colleagues. She takes the role of the "outspoken" one at work, the one who complains, who challenges authority, who questions policy and fights for change. At the same time, she realizes that this makes her unpopular with some and that she has to put up with the tension of interpersonal conflict. Occupationally, Vicky still doesn't feel committed. Like her previous jobs, Vicky regards her current one as a necessary way to make a living. She has stayed with this company because she had grown weary of changing jobs every two years, but still thinks of finding a way to express her skills in some work that would be truly meaningful. She loves physical activity: perhaps she would like to direct an exercise gym. Perhaps she might start her own business, parlaying her talent for sewing into designing clothes and selling them. Perhaps she might try to live abroad, leading hiking tours of remote areas.

Although Vicky's work is not the center of her identity, her sense of competence at work made it possible to take herself seriously. "I feel like an unsung heroine" she said at age 43. And what she has learned over the past few years, as she has entered her forties, is the valor in being able to appreciate and accept the "small changes." No longer interested in changing the world, what is most significant to Vicky is that she has lost weight, stopped smoking, finds time for the regular exercise that she enjoys, designs and makes her own clothes, helps her mother care for her now-disabled father, has learned to ski, and grows wonderful roses. She has learned to speak up and gain the courage to say what she feels and believes. "Some people regard me as a renegade," she says at age 43, "but I regard it as living in the reality that I perceive—and not denying things." And that is what Vicky finds has been most heroic about her.

In her late twenties, Vicky had begun living with a man, an old high school friend, who traveled a great deal in his work. She said, at age 33, that her ideal relationship was a "commuter" one. She jealously guarded her own freedom and was fearful of too much togetherness. By the time she turned 40, Vicky felt certain enough of her self and her own boundaries to marry him. She said she valued him particularly for giving her a lot of space. Their understanding when they married was that she would remain free to pursue whatever career she wishes even if it means they will live apart. (He, too, has uncertain career goals and has been employed in a number of different areas.) He is her companion in the hiking and backpacking she enjoys so much and they are partners in carefully choosing elements of their living space and remodeling their house. Theirs is a fully reciprocal and equal relationship—they share in chores and responsibilities. They have little physical or emotional intimacy, but she feels she can always rely on him for support. She recognizes that she can be demanding and persistent and difficult to live with and is grateful for his acceptance of her. Neither wanted children. Vicky felt she had done her mothering in raising 10 younger siblings.

Also in her early forties, Vicky joined an Episcopalian church that she values because of its openness and freedom from the rigidities of her Catholic girlhood. At the same time, she enjoys the familiarity of the Mass and the ritual. She actively participates in church community activities and sees herself as an advocate for women's rights. She has also worked on political campaigns for women candidates in local elections and sometimes wonders if she too might like to run for office.

Vicky feels interested in her own growth. Often in the interview, she used the phrase "it's really interesting" to mark the changes she has observed in herself. She still likes to analyze herself, to consider herself in contrast to others. By age 33, Vicky had actively moved away from what she came to think of as "the soul-searching I did in college," regarding it, in retrospect, as "an exhausting waste of time. I don't think there are permanent answers, though there seem to be permanent questions." And Vicky became able to live with that ambiguity, keeping herself in check for the next decade.

All in all, Vicky regards herself, at age 43, as content. The main thing, Vicky reflects, has been gaining more control of herself. For her, it has been "a devilishly persistent process to identify *my* values and make my own choices free of the institutions that earlier in my life had more authority." But Vicky is still casting about trying to center herself. I would expect that 10 years hence, Vicky will be living in yet another version of herself, another rearrangement of the pieces.

In some ways, Vicky is still drifting; in other ways, we might think of her as searching, now with a clearer idea of herself, trying to find a place to express herself that will appreciate her. She has increasing stability and control of her life. She now has some anchors—her spirituality, her marriage, and her understanding of the world. Her sense of identity is taking shape as she has learned both to communicate and to compromise. She doesn't know yet if she can find a place for herself in the occupational realm that will suit her, but she feels more certain in her understanding of how she intersects with her world. What she wants most—and has fought hardest for—is to be heard.

THE PERILS OF AWARENESS

The Drifters' approach to life is a fundamental openness to experience. They are more "aware" than any of the other groups. They read more widely, take more courses for personal enrichment, have many interests, and are more likely to be "pulled" by new ideas or fads. Opening themselves to experience, they are poised to respond to what may be "out there." More than any of the other women, they are likely to speak passionately in their thirties—and more so in their forties—about political issues. They take more seriously than the other groups their commitment to values such as "honesty" or "dignity" and respond angrily when others are being mistreated. Like Vicky, many have come to see that women are passed over in the workplace or denied legitimate needs. Many are strongly pro-choice and concerned about women less privileged than themselves. In general, the Drifters, from college through adulthood, remain more challenging of authority, more willing to do battle with the status quo, and more willing to up and leave when they get angry.

Many of these women ground their sense of identity in thinking about life and gaining insight into the world. The narrative of these women is an epic of struggle for greater understanding of people, of relationships, of the structure of the world. Often they speak of having felt naive, in the dark, not knowing what they would find in the world. Those who became mothers all say, in one way or another, "Why didn't anyone ever tell me what this would be like?" All who are working for pay felt they had been unprepared for the realities of the work world. Growth is synonymous with greater knowledge of what the world is like—not just intellectually knowing, but deeply grasping in a way that permits a fuller orientation to reality.

The Drifters are a group of vital women. They remain responsive, encountering the world through their senses and their feelings. But while everything seems interesting or possible, they lack an inner template on which to base their choices. What would they say "no" to? Searching, when there never seems to be a match between outward possibility and inner goals, can itself become another form of drifting. When they do make choices, they tend to make them in an all-or-none manner, throwing themselves full force into whatever it is, leaving nothing of themselves in reserve. Each time, they hope that they have found "The Answer." As a result, their histories, at least through their thirties, tend to be accounts of wrapping their lives around a pursuit or a relationship, abandoning it, and then being swept off into yet another all-absorbing center.

Erica has spent her life since college selflessly giving to others, moving about, alighting when she is drawn by someone's needs—not by her own design but by circumstance. She takes care of others for low pay, adopts stray animals, finds friends who are troubled and need her help, and finally married a man who was ill and for whom she could be a "savior." She claims herself by losing herself in others. Most recently, she has married a man from Bangladesh and plans to move there with him to help him in whatever he does. (Significantly, however, Erica confided in me that she is not quite sure where Bangladesh is.)

Yvonne and Donna had rooted themselves by age 33 in religious commitment. Yvonne had converted to Catholicism and listed Christ and her priest as the most important people in her life. Most of her recounting of her life at this point was with reference to her religious commitment, which was at last a belief system that helped her make sense of her life. By the time she was 43, however, this involvement had lapsed. She rarely went to church and thought that other Catholics would probably now consider her a heathen. But she wasn't quite sure how it had gotten away from her—it had just faded.

Donna had found a spiritual commitment to an Eastern religion after her life had veered completely out of control in her late twenties. Lost in drugs and sex, with her second marriage in danger of collapse, she found a "spiritual leader" to whom she could turn to make all decisions for her. She found peace in giving him the responsibility for her life. By age 43, however, Donna's commitment to her spiritual life was a part of her life but no longer its center. She tried to maintain spiritual discipline, and saw this as a framework for her life, a set of ideals to aspire to, but it no longer completely ruled her life. She did not look to her spiritual leader for all the answers, and had even joined a Methodist church as another outlet for both her spiritual needs and her wish for community.

It is not until they reach their forties that the Drifters organize themselves more clearly, anchoring themselves in something, then adding other bits until a whole is shaped. But then, having arrived at this new arrangement, they are often haunted by past actions that don't fit with their new understanding of their lives. Even when they find themselves in the present, they are at pains to come to terms with who they were. This is one source of their pervasive sense of regret. Donna, for example, is tormented by guilt over an abortion she had before she came to follow the spiritual path. "I was different. It was a different lifetime. How could I have done that?" she anguishes. The Drifters continue to want to disavow those parts of themselves that feel inconsistent with the present, still trying to shed the past which they remain unable to integrate.

The unsteadiness of their own identity complicated the Drifters' relationships with others. At times, they swept people into their lives who would define them; at other times, they kept people away for fear that they would.

Only three of the seven Drifters had children (although two of the remaining four, even at age 43, consider that they may yet be mothers). All three Drifters who became mothers began with the assumption that they would continue some kind of occupational involvement as well as pursue their other interests, but they gradually allowed themselves to be absorbed by the needs of their children. In varying degrees, all felt that they had lost themselves in this process. The task in their forties became, once again, one of redrawing their boundaries, finding themselves yet once more.

DEBBIE

—At the End of College   As she approached the end of college, Debbie was the most *aware* of all the women I talked to. She was very much a child of her era, epitomizing the stereotype of that time. She didn't think of herself as a "hippie," for that was a label and Debbie rejected all labels. She wanted to be fully herself, whatever that was, and in quest of this self, she experimented with everything—mysticism, sex, and consciousness itself through mind-altering drugs. Her quest was to feel intensely alive, living her inner experience and her feelings. Finding a place in society was not on her mind. Asked if she planned to marry or have children, she said, "I don't think about it—it seems so far away. But I wouldn't like to live by myself for the rest of my life." In regard to occupation, Debbie said, "I don't know what I want to do—join the circus, a gypsy camp, I don't know." She was majoring in English literature because she liked to write. But she was very critical of education as she had experienced it, and she had some strong ideas that education ought to be more conducive to creativity. She thought she might like to start a day-care center in Vermont and run it according to radical methods of education. But this was a fantasy, not something she was trying to make happen. "I'm terrible at planning," she said. "I don't do long-range things very well. When the time comes, I'll do something."

Debbie had spent her junior year in England and met other seekers who both intrigued and influenced her. What fascinated her most was the opportunity to play with her sense of self. "In England, I could be anyone I wanted to be. I kept changing my name." Most important to her was that she felt that she learned to trust her instincts; she spoke about this intuitiveness as central to her identity.

Raised in a highly traditional Irish family in Boston, Debbie had followed the strict rules of her parents until she left home for college. Her parents had high expectations of their four children and Debbie's older brother and sister were both very successful. But Debbie was always careful to differentiate herself. She didn't want to be a carbon copy of anyone. A successful businessman, Debbie's father was dominating, critical, and demanding and was unhappy at her lack of goals. Her mother was a devout member of their church and active in church matters, devoted to her children and their well-being. Debbie thought of her as always being very good, never doing anything wrong. "She always thinks the best of people. She was a good mother, a good wife, everything." The extended family all lived in the same neighborhood. Her grandparents were next door. She barely knew, growing up, that there were other ways to live.

When she came to college, Debbie threw off all the ties of her childhood and seemed to do this without guilt. She felt she wanted to "make a Debbie which has nothing to do with my mother or father." To use her words, "I said to myself, 'I'm just going to be me.' I'm going to start with a clean slate. And what I started to put on it were all new ideas and all these ideas were ones opposite to what my parents believed and slowly what's happened is that I'm feeling incomplete and I realize that what's happening is that I'm adding on a lot of the things which they've told me and I'm taking them as my own and coming more together with them."

This last statement is a lovely description of the adolescent process as we generally understand it; it is to some extent true of many people's sense of what their adolescence was about. In Debbie's case, it was more true than in most. She leaned farther out over the edge: there was little that she didn't test.

Debbie thought that her parents would both have "heart attacks" if they knew about her sexual experimentation. Her parents thought she should save herself for marriage and assumed that she was still a virgin. Debbie, on the other hand, resisted having any standards about her sexual behavior. "This sounds terrible. It's like it's just not that big of a thing anymore. Making love is just a different level of communication. I make love with lots of different people—it's different with each. I just trust my instincts. Sometimes I think rationally the next day that that was a silly thing to do, but I never have regrets or feel guilty."

At the same time, Debbie was nostalgic for structure and order. She thought of her grandparents, whom she deeply loved. "Sometimes I feel I'd like to be Irish like my grandparents are. Then I'd have something to hold onto. I don't really feel like an American. Like when they talk about the Revolutionary War and they're always saying 'Our forefathers' and I'm thinking 'not my forefathers—they weren't here until a little while ago.' So I can't relate to American history. . . . Like when I was in England, people could say, 'I am Norwegian' and it seemed so comfortable and secure, all being Norwegian together, but I don't feel that way when I say 'I'm an American.'" Even her nationality, a basic building block of identity, was for Debbie open to question—and to disappointment.

Debbie did articulate the way in which she defined her identity at the end of college: "That I'm honest. I think I'm a good person to have a relationship with because I'm an honest person." And I concurred. There was an essential honesty in Debbie. She wanted to see life and see it clearly. She noticed hypocrisy around her and resisted forcing herself into prearranged roles. She held onto her voice and her own perceptions, no matter what.

For Debbie, Eastern religion and cosmic consciousness held great appeal. She had met a woman in England and came to idealize her; she felt that if such a wonderful, gifted, and mystical person could like her, then she, too, must be worthy. "I experienced the unified cosmos and we're part of it and all there is is to love each other and I was really feeling it—feeling at one with trees." In trying to find herself, she experimented with fusion and loss of self. Back in America, however, she felt that the mysticism she had sought was cheapened and commercial. "In India, people go up in the mountains and for years they try to reach these heightened states of consciousness. But in Berkeley, for the mere price of $149.95, you can go home and practice biofeedback. Your alpha level can go right up to your potential. You just pay your money and *you* are going to reach Nirvana. It made me feel foolish to have believed what I did. I just became more cynical." Debbie realized that she had to ground herself in something other than "my own reality." But she wasn't sure where to put down roots.

Debbie had always had many friends. People liked her and were drawn to her. In college, she lived with "four guys who adored me and made me feel special." She had no single "best friend" or "boyfriend" through the years—she was close to different people at different times. And in this, Debbie always felt aware of the dichotomies—"whether to be a collegiate or a freak, loud like my father or soft like my mother." She felt she could be any of these.

Reflecting on herself in college, thinking of the distance she had come, Debbie cried when I asked her to think about who she would like to be like. "I'd like to be like my mother. She's sure of herself, but in such a different way. She just has a basic formula on what life is all about. She's quiet and doesn't argue with people. She's peaceful, calm." I understood Debbie's sadness as her awareness of how she could not go back, could never again join her mother in this secure, calm, peaceful place. "In the old days, it was so easy. Either you were going to get married or you weren't going to get married. You were going to be a teacher or a nurse. But now you can go anywhere and do anything and there are so many possibilities that—I don't know. I could be doing something I couldn't name because I don't know it exists yet."

For Debbie and other college-age Drifters, the future was filled with possibility, too much possibility. The freedom was both exhilarating and frightening. These were women who seemed to have shed the past like an old coat that had been warm and comforting but oppressive and useless in this warm climate. And, knowing that they have removed the coat and were now exposed to so much that is new and confusing, they cannot simply put it on again.

But Debbie and the women who were drifting as she was were all somewhat lost without exactly knowing that they were. Even though they had confidence in their own perceptions, they were unable to articulate their voices in anything the existing society could recognize; they therefore had nowhere to make themselves heard. Their unspoken wish was to be free spirits, to live their feelings and impulses, to take risks for the thrill of it, to contemptuously but politely defy their families and the social institutions that seemed so mundane and impoverished. They felt their selves to be in parts: they could do and be anything, but lacked conviction that any particular thing to do or be was better or more authentic than any other. They wanted to experience without having to commit themselves—to preserve or dispose of aspects of their lives at will. At the core of herself, Debbie located her honesty—that much she was sure of. For this animated and intelligent woman, however, the problem was what else to make of herself.

—*Age 33* I expected that I'd have a hard time finding Debbie twelve years later. Fortunately, I had her mother's phone number and she told me that Debbie had moved to San Francisco. I found Debbie at age 33 ready to tell a picaresque of adventures that constituted her past decade of living. She felt, at this age, very removed from her college self, which seemed to her now to have been quite "naive."

Although marriage had seemed "so far off" to Debbie in college, she in fact married a year after graduation. She met Brett when they were both doing LSD. "That's the kind of relationship Brett and I had. Everything was very magical and energized and everything very high—very all possibilities and everything was very adventurous and open and everything was like sparks flying and nerve-ends opened and life happening (sigh) . . . and then what happened I think is that we both began to grow—and during the next two years I began to grow in a different direction. Brett was an artist and he was a quintessential artist—a mind-expanding drug-taker, limit-destroying life-adventurer, and I became tired or something, and I didn't want to be smashed into a million fragments and didn't want to stay up all night and take drugs and didn't want to have sex with other people and in groups, and I didn't want Brett to have sex with other women." And so, after several more years, they eventually separated and divorced. While together, she and Brett lived in various cities, here and abroad, always with a life full of intensity. "It didn't seem to matter whether the intensity was in the direction of pain or joy. The intensity was there and I felt that was real."

But the more traditional Debbie still hovered in the background, asserting herself from time to time. They had married in her parents' church, for example, and Debbie wore a white dress. When it became clear to her that she could no longer join Brett in his limit-seeking, Debbie was pained to find that she harbored traditional ideas about marriage that made divorce a wrenching decision. Although the relationship was frustrating and disappointing, she didn't want to end it. She did everything she could to try to make the marriage work. They separated and got back together. Brett nearly died after an auto accident and she nursed him back to health. Then he was imprisoned after a drunken fight and she visited him in jail. After more separations and reunions, they finally decided to divorce. This was a very painful time for Debbie and she cried as she spoke of it. "I felt I was separating myself not only from Brett but from my family because Brett was my family. I also felt that I was symbolically separating myself from my original family because they could not accept divorce."

In all, the marriage lasted six years. After their final separation, Debbie felt she had nothing but herself. "I had no job, no friends, but I felt I needed to stay and resolve things by myself. I started with me in this one-room apartment and I felt very broken and I felt that I began to make myself anew."

Through her time with Brett, Debbie had been employed on and off in a number of jobs. Just after college, she worked in jobs that were related in some way to psychology, mainly in social welfare agencies, which she felt were jobs of form with no content—where they asked her to do meaningless and irrelevant things. During this time, she felt much more involved with "living my life" and work was a necessity to get money when Brett was not selling his art. She was a waitress, a cab driver, a supermarket clerk. After their divorce, Debbie got a part-time job in a "hippie" boutique selling counterculture posters and clothing. But what she really felt she was "doing" during this time was reading books, meditating, writing in her journal, doing Yoga, recording her dreams, sitting in cafes, and "making one or two friends."

One of these friends was Bob, who was a very close friend to Brett. He was also an artist but more settled and less self-destructive. After some time, she moved in with him.

When I met Debbie at age 33, she had recently married Bob. They were living in St. Louis where Bob was studying art and she was teaching part-time in a Montessori school. She liked her work in that she felt she was trying "to guide children toward the creation of their own selves." She was teaching 3 year olds, and she felt that her work required "a lot of energy and patience, trying to make the best parts of myself available to the children. I really love relating to these children—they are some of my best friends in this new city. They are some of my most meaningful relationships. I also enjoy myself—it gives me a chance to be spontaneous creative, open and loving. It's great fun." For the first time, Debbie seemed to have found work that was meaningful. She had persisted in her effort to make something of herself. But her commitment to her work remained tempered. When she thought about her future, she thought she might like to continue teaching in a Montessori school or run one or teach others how to teach. But, she adds, perhaps she might be a parent and not working, or perhaps she might be doing something "I haven't even thought of yet."

I was fascinated with these words and how they echoed what Debbie had said in college. Perhaps the future would hold something she hadn't yet considered. Despite being more settled, trying to live within the structure of her marital and occupational commitments, Debbie held on to her sense of unknowable possibility. She could still have a life she couldn't even imagine.

The decision to marry Bob had been a difficult one. She keenly felt the sense of having made a vow before that she had broken. "I found it hard to promise forever again. . . . I asked Bob if he'd mind if I told the judge that I'd do my best instead of these absolute vows." So Debbie still had her honesty and her insistence on her voice. She had not capitulated to others' definitions. She still wanted to think things through on her own terms.

It was not Bob that she had doubts about. She felt that they communicated very well and shared values. "We both feel its important to remain open and questioning and honest with each other and honest with our own selves. We are both interested in exploring with life in general and our own lives in particular." I noticed how Debbie stressed the friendship and mutuality in her relationship with Bob, omitting any mention of the intensity she had experienced with Brett. At the same time, the idea of exploration, looking piercingly at everything, taking nothing for granted, was still at the core— so far from anything I had heard from any of the Pathmakers or Guardians.

The reason Debbie agreed to marriage was that she was beginning to feel ready to have a child. And she knew that her parents could never accept her having a child outside marriage. Her mother was so traditional that she still hadn't told anyone at home that Debbie was divorced. And, of course, she could not bring Bob home as long as they were just "living together." So, with a more traditional aspect of herself again surfacing, she and Bob married.

Debbie had begun to try to get pregnant, but without success. She worried that the four abortions she had may have prevented her being able to conceive. But she knew what she wanted. "I want to be a mother, to experience myself with Bob and a child, to experience family anew."

When I asked her who had been most important in her life, she still named her mother. "She was my first teacher in so many things, directly and indirectly." Also Bob, "because he is my life-partner." Debbie also spoke about Mark, her closest friend in San Francisco, who had supported her through the hard times and whose generosity of friendship she knew she could count on. She felt particularly close to her sister with whom, although she was far away, she experienced a deep sharing. Debbie continued to feel estranged from her father—she felt he had not changed in the past twelve years. He was still full of disapproval, hardly ever listening to her, never approving of anything he did hear. But she seemed to accept this. She maintained a sense of closeness to her family through her ties to her mother and her siblings.

At age 33, Debbie was trying to settle down, within the boundaries of her own choosing, still attempting to live life in terms of her own inclinations and instincts. She was deeply internal, committing herself not to "be" a role or a job, but committing herself to fully living her experience, whatever it might be. She was still awaiting the emergence of future, possible selves. "Although I am 33," she said, "I remain somewhat vague and unknowing as to what I may 'be' in my future." And yet, I thought I heard in Debbie a fundamental strength, rooted perhaps in some complex tie to her family, which allowed her to take risks with herself, to play with merger and intensity, with other states of awareness and consciousness, to ground herself in some basic reality while taking flight with her feelings. Reflecting on herself, she said, "I feel that in the past five years or so, I have become more conscious. Before that, I feel that I was following some kind of path, but it was dimly lit because I was moving in a particular direction, moving toward something, but I don't know if I could have described what that something was. I was using some inner senses for direction, but using them not very consciously." The theme of feeling more conscious, more deliberate, more in control of her destiny is what Debbie highlighted at this time of her life. And she sounded mellowed. Still lively, still questioning, but more willing to accept. As she got older, alternatives got more concrete for her. She had the same goals, but understood them in a new way. She was clearer on what action would be required from her to get to a new destination. Life felt more embodied, less magical.

—*Age 43*   Ten years later, it was again only through her mother that I found Debbie. And I was astonished to find her living just around the corner from her family home. Had she just "gone home" again? I wondered. After all that? And, in some significant ways, Debbie has.

Within a year of my last meeting with Debbie, her daughter Miranda was born. Being a mother has been the dominant story of Debbie's last ten years.

Having Miranda was a major turning point because it opened a new part of herself—and, we might suppose, provided the first role that was clearly defined in terms of its demands. "Because I was a mother—it's so clichéd, but it was for me a very profound, very meaningful experience. I decided I wanted to be a mother who was home. That was a choice I made. This made it difficult for my husband. We had both worked part time. We each liked to do other things, so we made sure we didn't work too much, but what happened was that I was home *a lot* with Miranda, like 24 hours a day as happens with mothers who decide to stay home, and he worked a lot and what happened is that we got into traditional sex roles. That had never been our style previously. So having Miranda changed me in a number of ways and it changed my relationship with Bob. I resented being the person who was home all the time, although that's what I had chosen when I said I would not work. I hadn't clearly seen the picture of what it might mean.

"Having a daughter was an experience of falling in love with a whole new person. It gave me the chance to love someone unconditionally. She didn't have to do anything but I just loved her. I liked to hold her, sing lullabies, watch her all the time—it was wonderful but it was also overwhelming. Again, it was my own personal style. One doesn't have to do this 24 hours a day but I didn't know another way to do it. I chose to do it in this way—it was exhausting, because you don't sleep. Then it's like you're sitting in your house all the time alone with a baby."

Debbie thus describes finding herself in a "trap" of her own making. She clearly and consciously chose to be a full-time mother, to give herself fully to this role—24 hours a day. And at the same time, she deeply resented having to do this. She regretted losing her friends. None of her friends had children and Debbie found that childless people had limited patience with spending time with an infant or toddler. And Debbie wouldn't leave Miranda with a babysitter—she only wanted her to be with people who loved her. As Debbie talks about this, she speaks with a combination of ruefulness and defiance. She was both critical of herself for ever having thought in this way, but also proud because she wanted to cherish and protect Miranda so completely.

In part, Debbie dealt with her loneliness by joining a support group for mothers. At least, as she put it, she had someone else to sit with.

The hardest part was how strained her relationship with Bob became. "All the sudden you've turned into a parent and that's not what you set out to do. You start to feel like you're a married couple like your parents, and that's not what we ever tried to be. It's how many tasks can you do and how many can I do and somehow you get it all done." And although they tried to talk about how things had become, neither could find any solution and eventually they each just hoped that somehow things would get better.

They moved back to San Francisco where Bob knew more people and felt he would be better able to fulfill his role of earning the money for the family. And they had more friends as well as his family there.

But by the time Miranda was 4, Debbie felt like she was "drowning. I felt I had no life, I was being sucked up by being Miranda's mother. It was my own choice—you don't have to let a child suck on you—literally or anyway else. I see other mothers. I guess this is how I wanted to be a mother—who knows maybe it was my own need to have that kind of a mother—come here, take anything you want from me. Miranda breastfed until she was 3—

it was a very physical manifestation—here take whatever you need as long as you need. It was also very wonderful—wonderful to see someone take from you what they need and look up at you all happy and smiling but it's also overwhelming if you don't have things coming in to renourish you."

And Debbie felt she had almost nothing coming in. Her marriage was getting progressively worse. She and Bob rarely spoke. Debbie was always with Miranda and, when she and Bob did have time together, she felt they "really didn't like each other that much anyway." Debbie felt angry all the time, but didn't know who to be angry at. She spent hours wondering how she had gotten trapped. Finally, she entered therapy to figure out what could be going on.

Debbie didn't really come to understand why she needed to box herself in as she had, but her therapist did help her recognize that Miranda could survive with less attention and constancy from her. She began then to think about what some of her own needs and interests might be. She knew she wanted to do something creative, perhaps to write. For the first time since Miranda was born, Debbie got a babysitter and enrolled in a writing class.

As she wrote her stories, Debbie realized that she was using her writing to look at herself and gather different pieces of herself. But there was no magical happy ending here. Anne Sexton fought her way out of drowning in motherhood by writing, but hers is perhaps a Cinderella story. For so many women with talent, the road to making a living through creativity is blocked. Debbie's writing was, like that of so many others, good writing with no welcoming audience.

When she thought about returning to school, the old rebellious part of Debbie intervened and objected. "School was the straight world. I was going to make *myself* into something. I wasn't going to get another degree to say who I was or who I could be." Again she returned to the idea of "making myself into something" and again she was stuck on how to translate this amorphous idea into something tangible and realizable.

"I asked myself what I had made of myself so far. And the answer was: I had this child, I loved the child. I didn't like my husband, we never talked to each other. What was I doing? I didn't know. I didn't feel like I had made myself into much—or maybe I started to feel like, okay, you made yourself into a mother and you've done it very thoroughly for four years and now what else?"

For the next couple of years, Debbie tried to solve this by focusing on Bob and helping him clarify his goals. Blocked in thinking about what she might do next, it was more comfortable to be concerned about what Bob should do. She could see that he, too, felt trapped, hated his job, hated his life. Eventually, instead of starting school herself, she persuaded Bob to go school part-time to earn a teaching certificate.

Debbie missed her mother and sister, began longing to move back to Boston. She wanted Miranda to grow up near them. She hoped that once Bob was qualified to teach, they could move back there—which is just how things turned out. Just weeks before her fortieth birthday, she and Bob and Miranda packed up their possessions, and Debbie went home.

They lived with her parents for the first year, then bought a house down the street. Reflecting on this move, Debbie thought that an important part of her wish to go back home was an urge to confront many unresolved issues with her father that had emerged in therapy. She realized how much she had always feared her father and his disapproval. He had always yelled a lot and that frightened her. He was never physically abusive, but his rage was absolutely terrifying. She revealed now that she has always suffered from psychosomatic stomach problems related to her father's raising his voice. Part of what she termed her "conscious" decision to move back home was a wish to finally feel comfortable around her father. She has always felt like the "black sheep" of this high-achieving family and hoped that, at last, she could be accepted. "I got divorced, I looked like a hippie. They always had jobs, I never had jobs—I worked as little as I could so I could have time for myself—I'd be a waitress, I worked in a bar, I was a Montessori teacher, but only part time"—she could spell out her father's dim view of her.

Debbie had always enjoyed being with her mother and sister and brother and now everyone is, in some ways, back where they started. Like Vicky, Debbie was able to use the structure of home to rebuild herself. When Miranda began first grade, Debbie felt ready to think seriously about her own next step. At first she tried running some mother's support groups, helping new mothers think about issues in mothering, something she felt she had come to understand quite well. She soon came to see that if she wanted to make some money or be taken seriously, she would have to get a degree. Both her siblings are social workers and both are therapists. Debbie decided that she, too, would work for an MSW.

So, twenty years later, Debbie returned to school. And she began with much fear and trepidation. Would she be able to write the papers? Could she manage to pass the tests? For the first time, Debbie's doubts about her own capabilities were clearly visible. Now it was not her rejection of "the system" that was at issue, but her fear of "the system's" rejection of her.

It has been hard for Debbie to adapt to the traditional orientation of graduate school. In the first year, she had all A's but felt as angry about that as she had in college. "Schools give you A's for saying back what the teacher says. All schools say they want you to be creative but they really don't. For a long time the reason I didn't want to go back to school was that I felt the structure and the way schools teach was not what education means. I want to grow more psychologically. I didn't want a bunch of information. I wanted it to come from inside of me." But Debbie is, at least at the moment, maintaining herself in the educational system, despite her criticisms.

She has also made compromises in her expectations of marriage. "Bob and I never had a marriage made in heaven. When things don't go right, I want to talk about it. What is going on here? Bob's way is that relationships have ups and downs and it will pass. It's so archetypal. I hate to even say 'I want to talk' because he ways 'You always want to talk.' But sometimes I get so angry or so sad that I have to. I can't believe that he can't see the need or that he doesn't think that its better after. It's like one of those books—I have to do the emotional work for him. Just recently, we've had one of those. I feel at rock bottom and I bang on him, pull something out of him, something out of me and then I feel better." She realizes that Bob has a difficult life as well. He hates being an entry-level teacher, misses his artistic life that he enjoyed but recognized he could not make a living doing. Debbie realizes that he, too, feels in a trap of his own making, much as she felt in those early years with Miranda. They have frequently discussed separation, but decide to continue to work it out, particularly because of Miranda. Perhaps one day she will walk out the door, she thinks. For now, she stays.

One of Debbie's great disappointments in her marriage is the lack of physical closeness. She feels more erotically alive and sensual than Bob, who is usually too tired or too distant for physical intimacy of any sort. Debbie thinks about having an affair. She wouldn't shrink from this on moral grounds, but rather from fear that it would complicate her life.

Their marriage limps along, sometimes with contentment, sometimes with intense anger. "Maybe I don't know what love means. What the hell is loving? He respects me, he lets me be who I am. He supports me, he seems to respect me in any way I want to grow. That seems important to me. Does he pick me up and twirl me around when he comes in? No. Is that important to me? I don't know. Would I like someone who gives back massages more? Probably. I could ask him more and I do, but then I get mad at him that I have to ask."

Miranda continues to be the keystone of her life. Debbie gets tearful as she describes her. "She's a wonderful child—she's intelligent, curious, and kind to the other kids—she's creative." And to describe her daughter as "creative" is, as we know from following Debbie this long, the highest accolade. Expression of creativity is what Debbie has always sought—in her effort to be her own creative product ("to make myself into something") and now in her effort to nurture Miranda.

But as Miranda grows, the relationship gets more complicated. It was hard for Miranda to adjust to Debbie's being away and not available whenever she wanted. Miranda expressed her resentment and loss in a number of ways that were painful to Debbie. Now 10, Miranda is beginning to explore her own independence and often does this secretly, refusing to allow Debbie to know what she is doing or thinking. Most difficult, however, is for Debbie to realize how often she is angry at Miranda for not being how she wants her to be. "I'll ask, 'So how was camp?' 'Fine. Mom, please don't ask any questions. You ask so many questions.' She's kind of rude sometimes. That's hard. I don't want her to be rude. But I don't want her to be stuck being a nice little girl. I don't want her to be a good little girl like I was but I don't want her to be rude either." Debbie hated her father's criticism of her, yet she recognizes that she hears herself being hard on Miranda. "Because I have other things to do, I don't want her dumping her books anywhere. Or take a shower—hang up your towel." So now Debbie is struggling to find herself as a mother of an independent daughter.

She tries to think about what in her life has been for herself and what for others, but gets lost in the intricate maze of this question. How can she tease them apart? Relationships have always been central to Debbie. "Loving people and being connected to people are very important to me and a lot of what I've been doing in the past is that." And Miranda helped her access treasured parts of herself, gave her the right to "be funny and silly and creative." But now, having a husband, having a daughter, Debbie says with great passion that what she wants to do is "to work on being in the world and being what I want to be besides those things. I want to be a mother and a lover and also something else. . . . I'm trying to wake up and try to figure out who the hell I might be and certainly having relationships is part of that."

Debbie has had less time to express her spiritual side since Miranda was born. She talks to her daughter about faith and continues to feel that life is soulful. She feels an intense interconnectedness and sacredness in life. Yet her life seems too full of the practicalities of homework and schedules to allow for meditation.

Thinking back on her primary family from the perspective of her forties, Debbie concludes that "enmeshment was the mode of being." Individuality was treason and independence was desertion. "Boundaries are not heard of in my family. If I go to my parents house and ring the doorbell, my father is insulted. 'Why are you ringing the doorbell? This is our house—all the houses are supposed to be like our house'. I had to go away first because I felt like I was going to suffocate here, like I couldn't be myself so I had to get away—I felt too confined here. I had to put miles between us. And now I want to come back so I could understand how to do it and be right here and be separate *but* I don't want to be separate—I want to be attached. . . . I love the connectedness—this is what I grew up with. I loved the cousins and the aunts and uncles and I know what a sense of strength and belonging comes from all that. But I'm me and I'm separate. I'm not them." And she has come to tolerate that they see her as the failure. At this point, Debbie gets confused. Perhaps she sees herself that way, too. "You know, I would have called it—a hippie or a rebel and I don't want to be 'straight' and I don't want the letters of a degree. . . . The people I know in San Francisco see me as all the different things people see me as, but in my family that's who I am."

Thinking of her future, Debbie hopes for yet more control of things. "I'd like to become more conscious of myself, to make some more conscious decisions. I'm a pretty intuitive person—I've gone along my whole life kind of like on my feelings. I'd also like to add to that some conscious choices as well."

JENNIFER

Jennifer is the least typical of the women in this group if, given their diversity, we can identify a "type" at all based on external characteristics. She is the most content, the least troubled of the women who began their adulthood as Drifters, but it is hard to know if she has made the "conscious choices" Debbie is grasping for.

Raised in a "high-society" Southern family, the daughter of a Lutheran minister and a strongly pro-feminist mother, she was, in college, scattered and diffuse in her identity but untroubled about it. She mentioned, for example, that she had a "coming out" party at age 18, then refused to talk about it. She said that she hoped to do something "significant" in the human service field, but was at pains to explain how her major in music might relate to this. Jennifer seemed to be playing with her sense of herself during college, enjoying her impulsivity, and relishing being "irrational." But, looking back, I wonder if she was secure in knowing that she would return to a safe environment where her powerful parents would clear a path for her even though she was not acknowledging this. "I don't ever want to be settled," she had said at age 21,"because that connotes stagnating."

After college, she returned home where her parents found her work related to their own, work she engaged in happily until she married a man who, like her father, was a Lutheran minister. But even this she regarded as accident, coincidence, not deeply connected to what she already knew or was. ("The chemistry was terrific and it just so happened that he was also a minister. . . .") There followed a period of many moves as her husband established himself professionally, a time during which Jennifer continued to find human service jobs, some volunteer, some paid, but always work that challenged and excited her. Mainly, though, she was absorbed in organizing their life through all the stresses of moving, stresses that increased after their three children were born.

As time went on, Jennifer found the demands of being a mother and a minister's wife consuming all her time. "The last move was a really tough one. It took me two years to unpack the boxes. I just never had the energy to do more. My time is filled up with kids and some part-time volunteer work. I could tell you about that, but that isn't really that important." Throughout her thirties and into her forties, her life has been structured around "an incredible partnership" with her husband. And her interview is dominated by stories about interpersonal intrigue in the church community. Someone gets a divorce and it falls to her to calm everyone down. But Jennifer reads "women's books" and wonders about her own life. She is amazed at how many years have passed since she left the work world and fears that her children will think of her as the house cleaner and the gardener. It is difficult for her to reconcile her life with her view of herself as "a feminist." She worries about whether she could have the skills that are valued in the job market; anyway, she is uncertain of what she might like to do. Jennifer is like other Drifters in that now, as a middle-aged adult, when trying to recount her life to me in response to my questions, she only just begins to see its contradictions, the places where images of herself clash. With Jennifer, it is impossible to say whether she has made her own path or not. She attributes her choices to circumstance, one situation leading to another; her decisions arose from external necessity rather than inner direction. She seems happy. She is living a stable, busy life and is no longer, as in college, floating about among varied self-experiences. But the "feel" of her identity is different from those who had started out as Pathmakers, Guardians, or Searchers. Like the other Drifters, she seems more to have *responded* to life instead of having tried to shape it, catching a ride rather than being the driver.

TOWARD GREATER CONSCIOUSNESS

Growing into greater consciousness and control is a central theme of all the Drifters' adult lives. As young women, they had regarded themselves as intuitive and "not very rational." As they age, however, they experience themselves as gaining in conviction and becoming more stable and committed. None "fell apart." As time passed, they organized their lives more and more. But the Drifters' paths are checkered and complex. They start in college by throwing off all that might bind or contain them, and spend the next twenty years trying to feel in charge of themselves. Many, like Debbie and Vicky, return home in search of a lost part of themselves, hoping to find a feeling of calm where last they experienced it. Perhaps their propensity to physically return home is some effort to reclaim the past, to relive it, and this time to take in something they can keep for their own. The challenge for the Drifters is one of taking hold of some kind of life, in Arthur Miller's phrase, of finding some foundation from which to start.

More than any other group, the Drifters live in midlife with a sense of regret, a feeling of having missed so many opportunities. "Do I want the second half of my life to be the same as my first?" Evelyn asks herself. "I don't . . . I keep setting up the same dynamics. I don't want to do it again." They look back and often can't really understand why they did the things they did. "I look back and I can't believe it," Vicky said. "I wish I had done some career planning in college," sighed Erica. Or Yvonne: "A lot I put way back in my head and shut my head on it. I think about where I've been during this time. Where's my artwork been? A lot of those years were just lost. I'm not disappointed. Sometimes I am, but life goes on." For all their talent, three of these four who are employed outside the home are working in relatively poorly paid jobs, often with no benefits, doing work that feels unfulfilling and not equal to their potential.

Donna, one of the mothers who felt ensnared by motherhood, loves playing the organ in church and is proud of the Christmas village she designs and builds for her town each year. But she talks of her fear that she has lost the real achieving part of herself, feels that her work life got away from her as she tended to the needs of her children and her husband's business. And although she has made some efforts to do correspondence courses or community college retraining programs, she finds it hard to find her way back into the work world. Others of her age seem to be already so far ahead.

If their work lives are largely disappointing, their intimate lives are also less fulfilling than they may have wished. Intimacy is more difficult for the women in this group. The Drifters both crave and fear intense closeness. Less certain of themselves and their own boundaries, Drifters both long to lose themselves in another and are terrified that this may happen. Only Jennifer speaks of having a marriage that is balanced, vital, and centrally meaningful in her life. Her husband is a full partner and her life feels enriched because they create it together. The others have all had intense struggles in being close to another.

Many of the Drifters' partnerings have a somewhat Gothic quality, unlike those of the other groups. Yvonne was jilted and remains unmarried. Evelyn is more or less in a lesbian relationship with a woman who is not sure what she wants, and Evelyn thinks this relationship is probably over. But, she says, she so desires a committed and stable relationship that she will take whoever comes along first, man or woman.

Of the five who are married, three are married a second time. Both Donna and Jennifer married men they had known only two months. Erica first married a dying man, then wed a foreign man who had rented a room in her house. Vicky married an old high school friend after he proved not to threaten her freedom, and Debbie married her first husband's best friend. Except for Jennifer, the Drifters have marriages of companionship and mutual support, but their links with their husbands are somewhat distant and often tenuous. Their marriages seem less intimate, less fully resonant than those of the other groups. They value the feeling of being "in it" with someone and having someone to share the chores. Some speak of valuing the sense of being in each other's families, feeling grounded and connected in that way. Only Jennifer mentions that sexuality is important in her marriage; among the others, sex is infrequent or unfulfilling. In general, this group feels they need a partner to manage better and they value their husbands for "accepting me the way I am." "I am not an easy person to live with," said Vicky. "I need a lot of space and time alone. He understands that—and that's special about him."

Friendships are similarly complicated. Part of what sustained Drifters in college was their network of friends. Most of them were highly involved in what their friends were doing, and looked to them for structure and to clarify their own feelings. As they proceed into adulthood, friendship becomes more difficult and less stable. Most talk poignantly of losses and disappointments in friendships. As they get older, people come to seem unreliable: they often feel let down and abandoned. Yvonne, the only Drifter without a partner, was centered on the intricacies of her friendships in college and had since made some other friends. But, at midlife, she feels quite alone and wonders how all her friends have vanished. It seems that she must do all the phone-calling and she is gamely trying to adjust to life as a loner. Donna had a close friend recently to whom she poured out all the confusion and loneliness she had been experiencing. Being close to this friend was making Donna feel that perhaps she could remake her life when, without warning, the friend pulled away. Drifters very often find it hard to understand what is taking place in their relationships. Others' motives are opaque to them; things just "happen." The Drifters need a lot from others, just as they are vulnerable to being swept away in others' needs of them. As in other aspects of their lives, it is arduous to find the balance.

We are still left to ask what led these women to this particular path of identity. Why has their course been so painstaking? Why has it been so hard to structure themselves? The diffuseness of these women's identity is different in each instance. Yet they all share an early history of troubled identification with their mothers. Some had a mother whom they idealized, yet each, at some point in her adolescence, discovered that she was completely unlike her mother. Debbie regarded her mother as goodness itself. But in her docility, her selflessness, her weddedness to family tradition, Debbie could find nothing of herself. She was left to feel that she had to make herself all on her own.

Jennifer also idealized her mother, who was a high achiever and highly respected in the community and in her profession. (Jennifer is the only woman among the whole group I have followed whose mother graduated from college. Jennifer does not work outside the home and is the only nonworking mother content to be at home full-time.) But Jennifer couldn't see herself living up to her mother's accomplishments or energy. And she was aware of having felt emotionally abandoned by her mother in childhood. In retrospect, she feels her mother gave her too little structure and left her too much on her own to figure things out for herself. As an adult, Jennifer's resentment continues; she is now angry that her mother isn't more of a grandmother, doesn't help with her children, and doesn't always remember their birthdays. Jennifer's investment in motherhood is, for her, perhaps a way of doing motherhood in the way she wished her mother had.

The women who did not idealize their mothers had the opposite problems. They had mothers in whom they could see nothing to prize or emulate. Vicky regarded her mother's life as being about the care of eleven children and submitting to a tyrannical husband. As the second oldest, Vicky was forced into the role of mother's helper; her main goal in life was to be completely unlike her mother. Her adulthood flourished only when she found a woman mentor to show her another path. Similarly, Erica's mother was angry and depressed for most of her life and Erica, the only Drifter living far from home, just wanted to get away.

Drifters regarded their fathers as despotic, disapproving, physically absent much of the time, and emotionally uninvolved with them. These women could find nothing in their fathers to internalize or adopt for their own. What they took instead was a vague feeling of being unloved and unacceptable, for reasons they couldn't understand. (The one exception to this is Jennifer, who had an available, involved, and loving father. She married a man very much like him, a solution that, as we have seen, has worked out well for her. Of this group, she has the happiest marriage, which organizes her life.)

This is only part of an explanation of how the Drifters set themselves adrift. The identity problem is more difficult for them because they internalize so little of their childhood. The task then becomes inventing themselves, rather than reshaping bit by bit. With so much possible, nothing becomes very realizable. And with so little taken in from the past, the building blocks are not there. They get stuck in the sense that they *could* be anything. There is nothing inside against which to match or test external possibility. Being one thing or another, believing this philosophy, or following that religion—all are equally likely. They experience no inner demand to connect their experiences or make themselves consistent. "Instinct" and "feeling" seem to be reasonable sources of action. As a result, the self remains at the mercy of inner impulses and external claims. The yearning later in life to return home is in part a wish to reconnect with lost parts of themselves. Only when Drifters accept some limits are they able to phrase the identity question in terms they can maneuver. By midlife, they make important discoveries about themselves and they adapt, but much later than the women who had a clearer sense of themselves at the end of college.

For the Drifters, getting stuck initiates the real process of identity formation. Once they feel the contours of their world, they can think more clearly about how to modify it, about what they need. Control—or consciousness, in Debbie's phrase—comes paradoxically when they recognize what they cannot control: they can't control illness and death, can't control others, can't change the world. They recognize that life proceeds in small steps and this makes it possible to discover what is in their control—and then to act.

In her interview at age 43, Debbie is no longer supposing that she might make herself into something she hasn't yet imagined. Her world is now defined; she has accepted its terms. And this seems true of all the Drifters. There is both tragedy and beauty in this change. The tragedy lies in the tempering of youthful desire, the filing away of fantasy and glorious dreams, the falling to earth and finding that it is just life. At the same time, there is courage in coming to terms with reality, which requires enduring the pain of disappointment, grieving the loss of what might have been, and seeing clearly. As Vicky says at age 43, "There is a lot of deal-making and compromise—I guess that's what a lot of life is about."

The major revisions in the past decade for the Drifters have been about accepting themselves and their histories. These changes are not so much in behavior, but in awareness. They come to think differently about themselves in relation to others, to their expectations, to their hopes, and to time. All are tempered. Goals become more sharply defined, less magical, more within reach. Time seems more a reality, something to work within and not deny. They accept a finitude about their lives, trying to recognize that there are only a certain number of tomorrows, and what happens tomorrow grows out of what one does today rather than arising by magic. And in discovering that society offers only rare opportunity for the intense experience they crave, they become more able to tolerate the commonplace. But they still live poised for change, maintaining a tentativeness about the commitments they are trying to cleave to. Although they live with the present, they still feel another life is ahead. Where the other identity groups may say, "Here it is—here is the life I have made," the Drifters seem to say, "Here is the life I've made so far—Here is what I'm doing now—But the future could be still quite different—at least, I hope it is." Only the Drifters talk about "growing" as an *activity* they currently engage in.

As they grow through midlife, most Drifters are reinventing themselves. Most are hoping their occupations—occupations they have yet to find—will give them an opportunity to be recognized, to feel of value. Debbie is in school, Vicky is still trying to find a career that will suit her. Donna wishes she could reclaim the achieving part of her life that got washed away by family responsibilities, but doesn't quite know how to do this. Jennifer plans to reopen the work chapter of her life some time in the future. Evelyn longs for a stable relationship with someone of either sex. Erica is headed for a new life in a distant country, using her new marriage to open unimagined possibilities. Yvonne is lonely and stalled, relieved to be scraping by, hoping for something to come along to change things. There is a man that she is fantasizing about and . . . who knows?

CONVERGENCES: WHERE THE PATHWAYS LEAD

Launching themselves differently, women follow different trajectories in shaping and reshaping their identity. The "entry point" to adult identity—the road taken—colors and contours how life unfolds. In part, this is because the entry point is determined by personality structure, the conflicts and dilemmas from childhood that define the way in which women approach their identity riddle. By midlife, however, these routes converge and most of these women arrive, psychologically, at similar places. There is no "best way" to form identity; I can offer no prescriptions here. Other longitudinal studies of women's development have similarly found a general convergence at midlife between women who began their adult lives very differently.[1] But the beginning foreshadows a certain consistency in the psychological challenges each group faces, and presages a pattern of emotional growth that differs among the four groups.

Those who began as Pathmakers or Guardians tended to grow by enlarging the frame of their lives, increasingly making more room for the expression of their growing awareness of self. For them, creation of their identity involved continual modification of a firm, clear, but often confining internal structure. The Searchers and Drifters, by contrast, often dramatically burst through what had enclosed them in childhood and had to try to build their identity painstakingly from new components that they forged over time, doing their best to keep internal chaos from overwhelming them.

The Guardians sculpted their lives emotionally close to home and only over many adult years did they do the internal psychological work of individuating themselves from their families and their childhood selves. The Drifters, at the opposite extreme, tried to shape their identities with brand new elements, at great emotional distance from their past; their stories are quests for structure and stability. The Pathmakers, the most pragmatic and balanced group, grew in increments, integrating the new with the old while the Searchers, many of them asking for more than any of the other women, caught between the pull of the past and the call of the future, more self-reflective but plagued by greater self-doubt, struggled longer and harder to find what is right for them. But, in the end, despite the great variety in the lives we have observed here, all the paths lead to similar places.

After twenty-five years of working with these four groups, I ask myself if this system of categorization has been a meaningful one. On balance, I believe that it has. I think that these categories frame the themes of development that differ across the groups. For the Guardians, the themes of growth involve knowing themselves better, giving voice to what they had silenced in the interest of gaining approval, security, and certainty. The danger for them lies in constriction.

For the Drifters, organizing their inner life and adapting to reality as they find it is the more perplexing challenge, the pitfall being that of falling into confusion, fantasy, and loss of direction. The Pathmakers, between these extremes, have lives marked by themes of balance—between what they find in themselves and what opportunities for self-expression the world offers. The Searchers, those in an unstable state of conflict during adolescence, eventually fall into a pattern similar to one of the other three groups—reclaiming their old selves, like the Guardians, integrating old and new parts of themselves like the Pathmakers, or containing their contradictory fragments like the Drifters.

By midlife, though, all these women have found or made a path. They are both different from their adolescent selves but also recognizably a product of them. At the crossroads of midlife they meet, resembling each other in where they are, even though they may have arrived from different directions. For them all, progressive growth in identity means finding room for many aspects of themselves, not so much as a matter of taking up social roles such as worker or mother, but of feeling meaningfully connected to action in the world.

Although each woman has unique aspects to mold into identity and motifs that are prominent in one life may have no place in another, nevertheless there are themes that unite them, ways in which all of these women are, in effect, in search of the same thing. Having considered the differences among these women, in the last section, I want to discover commonalities. How are these women alike and what may that mean for all women? What forms the core of identity in women?

Some women seek lives of public effect, wanting to make real changes in society as they find it. Others carve out a quiet corner of existence, content to touch only a few other lives. Some women live carefully defined lives, clear on their commitments and priorities; others are more receptive to what comes along. Regardless of what sort of path a woman travels toward identity and despite the shape of the identity she designs, she will have had to discover along the way both her competence—the regions where she can be effective and do things of value—and her connection—the people whom she chooses to make important in her life.

Identity resides at the intersection of competence and connection: this is where people feel most fully themselves—and are most recognized by others as being who they are. Adult crises in identity among these women have most often involved the struggle to keep the experience of competence and connection in balance. While these themes of competence and connection seem to be in some ways a restatement of Freud's comment on the poles of work and love as the pillars of human life, they are broader and, I think, more inclusive of what women weave into their core sense of themselves. The words "work" and "love" carry with them connotations that are more bounded and specific and are, perhaps, more descriptive of male identity. For women, competence goes beyond but may include their work; connection transcends partner and children and doesn't necessarily imply either sexuality or motherhood. A woman's identity rests on her sense of how she is effective in the world and how she is linked to others. Most of the time, these themes are interlaced. Competence includes the sense of having meaningful import in others' lives and connection embraces skill in making deep and abiding ties.[2]

Growth and revision in a woman's life involve rethinking her competence or her connection or weaving them together in an altered way.[3] As women move through life, they continue to explore both these aspects and how they do this affects the shape of their lives.[4] In this part, I will describe what I have observed about how issues of competence play out in women's lives and then do the same for connection. The final chapter will consider the issue of revision: What changes in women's lives as adulthood progresses? Are there definable "stages" of adulthood for women? And what propels and supports growth and change?

Women . . . need exercise for their faculties and a field for their efforts.

Charlotte Brontë, Jane Eyre

8 COMPETENCE

What Vicky likes best about her work is "having to deal with all different people in the company." Recently, she set up a training program that involved training managers along with their secretaries in computer use. For this, she received a lot of criticism—she was mixing levels, forcing communication among people of unequal status, allowing secretaries to see their bosses' mistakes. In her work role, Vicky is concerned about the relationships among the people in her company and finds that this is not well received among those in charge. But she is beginning to despair of finding a more humanistic work environment. As long as she has the energy, she says, she will keep trying to make the system change.

A woman's sense of competence resides in her sense of effectiveness in the world. Although the expression of competence is a central anchor of women's identity, the experience of competence is not synonymous with participation in the work force. Many of the women whom I have interviewed are vitally engaged in their careers and draw from their paid work a sense of mastery and effectiveness that is crucial to their well-being. Most report feeling capable and skilled in their occupations; they are often stressed by meeting all the demands, but successful in doing so. Feeling "good at" what they do, however, is not the same as finding meaning in it. And where meaning is not to be found, being "good at" does not translate into a valued sense of competence. Nor does it become an abiding anchor for identity. Among these women, competence derives from an awareness that they have done what they set out to do. Competence implies feeling that one makes a meaningful mark on the world, but there are many domains in which a woman may make this mark.[1]

WOMEN AT WORK

Unlike men, these women did not grow up in a society that taught them that the standards by which they would value themselves (and be valued by others) would be found in the name of their occupation and the size of their paycheck.[2] Therefore, they had to create their own terms, their own ways of thinking about what their work meant as an aspect of their identity. They came of age in a social world that was wrestling with how to regard women who worked. Society in general wasn't sure if it was acceptable to ask a woman at a social gathering what she "does." Parents wanted their daughters to be able to support themselves until they got married, but were rarely concerned about how they did this. As is still true today, society was uncertain about whether to count a woman's ambitions or occupational success as part of her attractiveness as a woman or a mark against it.

Women of this generation entered the workforce as "outsiders." They came into this new world through gates previously closed to them. And while they were eager to test their skills and to feel a meaningful part of the public sector, they were asking what this new world offered them. They were deeply aware, at least initially, that they were *electing* to join this exclusive society. And they brought with them hopes and needs that differed from their male counterparts. Because "work" wasn't delineated for them by entrenched social definition, women of this age sought a variety of meanings in work. Therefore, work as an aspect of identity is very different for different women. For some, it is highly important; for others it is tangential. The issue here is about the self-defining value a woman places on her success in the work domain.[3] What does she hope to derive from her work? What does she in fact receive?

Before there were opportunities for women to take serious responsibility in the work world, a woman's horizons and hopes were bound to marriage. The shock of recognition that marriage is not all that they thought it would be has been a major theme of the record of women's lives since literature has concerned itself with women's experience. Throughout history, women of every generation have had to come to terms with the fact that there is no "happily ever after" in marriage; they have felt their rage (usually against their mothers) and their disillusionment (usually in society) that what seemed to be a promise of their girlhoods was not fulfilled. Fairy tales were filled with princes, but women's life stories were about how they coped with living with frogs. This has now become so banal that it is no longer of much interest. And, in this age of modern fairy tales, belief in princes has gone out of fashion.

I think a similar process has occurred, at least for the group of women I have studied, in regard to work. This was a generation that was imbued with the idea that career would be some sort of Answer. The fairy tale they heard from the swelling voice of feminism as they grew into adulthood was: Get educated, get a briefcase and an income, and *then* you will live happily ever after. But they had only vague ideas about how this might be realized or how it would feel. And what I hear from these women at midlife is similar to what their mothers must have experienced, but in a different quarter of their lives. *Their* complaint is about their disillusionment in work.[4]

Earlier studies of women could divide their participants into women who had careers *and* families and those who chose only to raise children. Among my participants (and among college-educated women in general) this distinction is no longer relevant. Only three of the women in my study are not working outside the home and one of those is in graduate school. Most educated women today seek some return in the public sector for the investment of their skills and talents.

I think that the issue for women is no longer *whether* they work outside the home but *how* they work—with what meaning, what investment, what expectation, and what reward. The reason I choose the word "competence" instead of "work" for the more instrumental, active, task-related pole of a woman's identity is that the concept of competence reflects a woman's sense of how she engages the public goals that she sets for herself. Unlike many men, few women defined themselves as "a manager" or "a teacher." Occupation may be what she "does" for many hours of her life, but is seldom what she feels she "is." The degree to which occupational endeavors are assigned prominence in these women's identity is a function of whether or not she witnesses waves emanating from her work that are meaningful to others.

Alice, one of the women for whom work is a firm anchor of her identity, was voted Teacher of the Year in Wisconsin. She is a high school science teacher in the small town where she lives and energetically drafts imaginative courses that engage her students in experiments. She drives an old painted van that is distinctively hers and easily recognized by whooping students happy to see her. Driving around town, she knows how much she matters to them and that she has an impact on their lives. But Alice values her work to the extent she feels her influence on her students. She is not interested in "moving up." Alice has turned down all offers of administrative jobs, which have been many. She knows herself—she thrives in the classroom, with her students, has no interest in a desk job, or going to meetings or haggling about policy. Alice feels that she sees her options clearly and knows what she wants.

Feminist writings concerned about promoting women in the workplace warned me that women would hesitate to speak of success and accomplishment, that women fear achievement as being unfeminine.[5] But I had no such experience. My participants forthrightly told me of their ability, their work triumphs, and their mastery of their tasks. And they spoke of these accomplishments without hesitation or shame.[6]

I asked the women I have been following to tell me what about their work they found to be the most satisfying, what in their work gave them the most gratification, and what they felt was most difficult. These otherwise very diverse women, with widely ranging occupational assignments, described in a consistent voice what meant most to them in their work. Nearly all located meaning—and identity—in their work relative to the impact they felt they had in the lives of others. They wondered about what their work really meant, whether it felt essential, whether it really mattered to someone that they were doing what they are doing in the way that they are doing it. They were asking themselves hard questions. It wasn't enough to be "good at" their job. They wanted their work to have effect, to mean something.[7]

When they feel effective in their work, work is more likely to feel part of their core sense of identity. How this process plays out in a woman's life is shaped in part by her own talent and ambition, but much is affected by forces beyond her own skillfulness. The responsiveness of the environment is a powerful factor in determining whether or not a woman's sense of competence in her work will blossom and thrive or wither and perish.

These women ask, foremost, to be generative in their work. They bring what used to be thought of as "maternal instinct" in their wish to offer to others what is good in themselves. However their job description might be phrased, these women translate it into generative terms, and they feel competent when they feel they are having positive effects on others. When I asked the women I have studied to tell me about the greatest satisfactions of their jobs, they emphasized their gratification in interactions with others. "When I help a patient through a difficult procedure," said Andrea, the doctor-researcher. "Working with the kids—and it's really gratifying when the kids come back to see me," said Gwen, echoing the sentiments of most of the teachers. Those in corporations spoke of the pleasure of their clients in receiving good service.

A quite poignant example of this wish to see one's effects on others comes from one of the Drifters, one who is least successful in her career among the women I have followed. Yvonne works as a sales representative for a clothing manufacturer and always feels in danger of losing her job in this depressed economy. For her, satisfaction comes when she goes into one of the small towns on her route and sees someone wearing something that she has placed in the stores. Then she has the sense of having pleased someone, having given something to another. For all the women that I interviewed, feeling that they have done something meaningful in the lives of others, done something that others would be grateful to them for, was the central theme of what makes work matter.

The eighteenth-century notion of the distinction between public and private spheres seems to have vanished in this phrasing of the experience of work. Beyond the feminist cry that the personal is political, these women have made the political personal in bringing what used to be considered "domestic" values to the workplace. For them, success is measured in human terms. Power is sought in order to be of use to others. Effect is measured empathically rather than numerically.[8]

Although most women also mentioned, somewhere along the course of my conversations with them over the years, pleasure in pure mastery, this feeling seemed at its peak when the task was new. Younger women or women taking on new challenges were most likely to speak of their struggle for confidence in themselves or their anxiety about being good enough to do well. By midlife, most of the women I spoke to regarded the effort to achieve proficiency in their work tasks as being far in the past. They felt successful; they knew their jobs. They could plan and accomplish. Many, especially among the Guardians and the Pathmakers, had received awards and other special recognition. Few aspired to reach the pinnacle of their organizational ladder. They had gone about as far as they wanted to go. They took their ability for granted and felt their ambition satisfied. It was as though they were saying, in effect, "I have no doubt that I *can* do this well, but what does it *mean* to be doing it at all?"[9]

I was surprised by how few of these women mentioned income or status as a major gratification of work, although nearly all depend on their income for maintaining their lifestyles. The need for money may require them to work or force them to continue in a particular job at a particular time, but it is not what gives their work meaning. As a result, even where they are well compensated in dollars for their efforts, women may still not derive the sense of competence they wish from their work and, to that extent, their work feels less a central thread of their identities.

THE REALITY BEHIND THE FAIRY TALE

I interviewed Emily, a judge from the Guardian group, in her chambers. This involved some complex arrangements since tape recorders are not permitted in the courthouse. So I was examined and escorted by myriad officials until I finally arrived at her chambers, all the while building an impression of her importance in the world. Emily allowed me to use her private bathroom, and, with calm authority, asked her secretary to order us some sandwiches and coffee. She offered me a seat and took hers. I found myself facing a petite, pretty woman with long blonde hair, dwarfed by her enormous high-backed chair, with her black robes hanging on the wall to the side. I asked the first question of my interview: "Please tell me about what, over the past ten years, has been most significant for you?" Without even pausing to consider, Emily said emphatically, "My husband."

Now, for someone who has been studying identity in women for twenty-two years, I suppose I should not have been surprised by this—yet I was. There was something about the chair, the robes, the private bathroom that led me to expect that she would begin with her apparent professional success.

But Emily has struggled with a lot of disappointment in the occupational realm of her life. "The glamour wore off after two months," she said. In her judicial role, it has been hard for her to feel that she has positive effects on others. "The hardest part of this job is that there is not a lot of expressed gratitude. You have to look for ways to feel good about what you do. In all my years on the bench, I've had only three thank you notes."

The first time a litigant filed a report against one of her decisions, Emily felt almost ready to quit. Forbidden to defend herself publicly, she felt helplessly exposed to media ridicule. She realized she had to get used to it, but it was painful.

"Nobody is smiling in this job," she says. "You see a lot of the reverse. . . . I find it hard to deal with uninformed people who don't understand the judicial process and think they can just call me up and explain the situation, and when I don't take their calls, accuse me of arrogance." It's hard to become emotionally tough enough to put a minor miscreant in jail especially if it's the day before Christmas. "You have to use a lot of energy to make people see why you're not unfair," she says. "And then you have to deal with the fact that there is this man out there furious at me and there's nothing to do about it."

One issue that had provoked notoriety and censure came from an area in which Emily felt she could affect people. Sensitized to the intricacies of the pain of divorce from her parents' experience, she became strongly sympathetic toward displaced homemakers—women in their fifties or older who have been at home all their lives, whose husbands left them and wished to be free of the economic burden for them. Emily has special concern for these women left without marketable skills or means of support and feels that they deserve to be compensated for their years of working in the home. Consequently, there are some powerful men in Missouri who have had to pay more in divorce settlements than years of male judgeships may have led them to expect. And Emily has come under a great deal of fire for this. But she keeps on; her sense of connection to these women is greater than her pain at the criticism. Here are people she feels she can help

The State Supreme Court often praises her opinions. She is regarded as a "good judge" and on people's mental list of those who might be promoted to a higher court. But this recognition does not compensate for the more direct response, the "smiles" Emily misses.

When women find it too difficult to feel their positive effects on others through their work, they begin to disengage or despair. Emily is already thinking about retirement. Her husband is nearing retirement age, and she might like to move to Florida to be nearer her family. And she doesn't necessarily see herself staying in law. "I'm a good judge, but its a happy thought to think that I won't be doing this forever. I'd [like to] do something else. I've always been passionate about interior design—I love to decorate my home, pick out fabrics. Perhaps I would do something like that. It wouldn't be that difficult to give all this up and do something completely different." Being a judge is certainly a part of Emily's identity, but it feels to her like a mutable part, a part she could shed or change without losing her core sense of who she is.

Emily's experience, although perhaps more clearly stated, is not very different from that of the other "most successful" women in my study. Grace, the other judge, and Andrea, the doctor, similarly enjoy their success, but wonder what it means; their goals are to move outside of work demands rather than assume more. Grace takes pleasure in deciding a difficult matter in what she believes is a fair way, but she suffers from the burden of all the responsiblity she carries and longs for more time with her children. Andrea enjoys contact with her patients, maintains her passion for research, but wearies of all the hassles with insurance companies and funding agencies and hopes to cut back her work time in the next few years. (Only Regina, the college professor, among the "most successful" women, looks toward future horizons optimistically, but she has the freedom to define her projects to suit herself. I will return to her later.)

The workplace is a structured world that demands that people narrow their skills, exercising only a part of their capability and often doing tasks repetitively, while other aspects of what they could do or accomplish lie fallow. As we have seen, a number of the women I interviewed never found an acceptable niche in the occupational realm for the abilities they find in themselves; they feel themselves to be, as Vicky phrased it, an "artist without a medium." Natalie, for example, one of the Searchers, complained in both her later interviews about the lack of space for creativity in her job. At 33, she said of her technical writing job, "I feel I am not living up to my full potential. Having an artistic and creative nature, I feel my current position does not satisfy this portion of my life. . . . It is difficult some days to get up in the morning knowing that a boring job lies before you at work. But, that's life!" Still in the same position ten years later, she said with more resignation and less anger, "When a job goes out and it is perfect, it gives me satisfaction. They come back and say thanks. But it's not creative at all. You have to give them exactly what they want, can't make suggestions to improve things." She has learned to live with the tediousness, but she has not found a way to bring her creativity to her employment.

Many women, particularly Searchers and Drifters, bounce among jobs for a time, growing more and more disenchanted with the work to be done and the working conditions they find themselves in. Often these women despair of finding work that engages their creativity or provides them enough autonomy to exercise their talents. People like Debbie or Millie, for example, among the brightest and most articulate women, remove themselves, at least for a critical time, from what they feel is an uninviting occupational world.

Less than half the women I interviewed seemed to be vitally engaged in and enthusiastic about their work.[10] Only this minority of women wished to be doing the same or related work ten years from now and were optimistic about their occupational goals. The rest were in various states of disillusionment or disaffection, either surrendering themselves to what they felt was unchangeable or still pondering how they might improve—either themselves, their work environments, or their occupational choice.[11]

The Pathmakers (and those Searchers who later made their own paths) differed from the other groups in terms of being most likely to engage meaningfully in work and find identity-forming satisfaction in it. Each was able to recognize that her first occupational plan did not suit her and to devise a more thoughtful and, usually, intricate new plan based on a greater understanding of herself and her interests and talents. This required courage, perseverance, and a basic belief in themselves, as well as a highly developed capacity to learn from their experience. They are women who were able to analyze what they needed and where and how to find it, and they continue to regard the work world as one they will negotiate with to gain the conditions they need to be effective. Guardians, by contrast, are more likely to adapt to the conditions they find, still doing what they are "supposed to" do and submitting to authority, unless they reach some critical brink where they feel they cannot compromise further. At this point, as we have seen in the case of Fern, they are likely to harness their fervent moral energy to the cause of change.

Professional women who grew up in families where their parents had not gone to college also seemed more satisfied with their work careers than those who came from more privileged backgrounds. In many cases, they achieved more and had more pride in what they accomplished. Perhaps, having come farther, they had a greater sense of attainment. They succeeded against greater odds, stretching more tenaciously toward what had seemed out of reach. The women who grew up with greater privilege found it harder to win the thrill of success, even when they accomplished quite a lot. They were more critical of the work world as they found it, expected and demanded more, and were therefore more likely to be disappointed.

I was surprised and puzzled to hear so much disenchantment and distance in these women's experience of themselves at work. Colleagues with whom I discussed my findings were often dismissive—perhaps I had an unusual group of women here, they suggested. It was not until I interviewed Regina that these issues became clearer. Regina is a sociology professor, and her way of talking about herself and her identity at work was both different from the others and more familiar to me. Like her, I am a college professor, and most of the people who I know well are in the academic world. "Work," as my colleagues and I know it, contains a great deal more autonomy than what is available to most people in the work world.

Here is Regina describing her work: "I very much enjoy my job as a professor. My job has changed form over the years. Each year it seems I make a conscious decision about just what kinds of things I'm going to do. During the 1980s I did a great deal of editorial work—I served on four editorial boards and, toward the end of that period, accepted a contract to edit a book. I also served as an associate editor for one of the professional journal's regular columns. I'm tired of that, though. I did that for a number of years. I'm moving into a period now where I am also tired of the line of research I've been involved with—I'm heading into some new directions, but I'm not yet sure what it is, what I'm going to be doing differently. I'm beginning to do more service work related to the university—issues about women on campus. I also get a great deal of satisfaction out of serving as an advisor to women students—and a few men—although with women students, my relationships tend to be particularly intensive, I suppose, much more of a mentor relationship than with my male students. And many of my students over the past ten years have become close personal friends of mine. The most important professional gratification very much depends on what I do, I suppose. I get a great deal of satisfaction out of my writing projects. I tend to choose projects that I have a personal interest in. One of my reviewers for promotion to full professor said that I seem to have a special gift for translating theoretical and empirical work into implications for other professionals. And maybe that's true. I view it as an extension of my teaching role, a role that is inextricable from who I am as a person. I'm communicating part of myself as a person."

Regina's experience of "communicating part of myself as a person" and having the freedom to choose the direction of her work based on her personal interests is what sets her—and her work—apart from the experience of most of the others. She represents an extreme of autonomy. And it does seem to be true that those who have more autonomy at work, those who feel more authorized to express themselves, are those whose work is closest to the core of their identity. But this is atypical. For most participants, coming to the end of a project means taking the next one off of a pile created by someone else rather than, like Regina (or like me), having the luxury to creatively plan their next direction. Being "tired of" doing something does not usually relieve the necessity of doing it. The opportunity to be creative at work, when it is bestowed, is what seems to meld personal and work identity. In these all-too-rare instances, work becomes a true expression of self. This was perhaps the wish with which most of these women took up their work roles in the first place. They hoped to work in a way that is "inextricable from who I am as a person," to communicate their inner self in a public role valued by others. Few found this a realizable goal, however, and often concluded, like Natalie, that not being able to bring one's passion to one's work was "just reality."

WOMEN IN ORGANIZATIONS

By the time they were about to graduate from college, all the women I interviewed had internalized a deep work ethic of striving and taking responsiblity seriously. (Even the Drifters, who weren't necessarily oriented to achievement, valued the idea of working hard at something.) Years of study and the pressures of college academic demands had schooled them in applying themselves. As they imagined the future, some had clear ideals of the good they wished to accomplish: "I want to help people" was the most common phrasing. For others, work promised simple occupation—a field for effort. "If I don't feel I'm accomplishing something, I go crazy," said Evelyn.

Later, however, as adult women with experience in the workplace, many felt stymied by bureaucratic rigidity or the unresponsiveness of their organizations. Many believed they were neither helping others nor getting anything of worth accomplished. Investing themselves in their tasks, instead of just trying to move ahead in the hierarchy, often ended in frustration. For many women, the challenge was to achieve a sense of competence within an organizational system that limited their autonomy and self-expression.

Vicky described the company where she works as "a very male-dominated company. I think it's a very difficult environment in which to survive. If you don't play the game right, you are quickly alienated." In a management position in the personnel department, Vicky crusaded to have new people initiated into the company more carefully and sensitively. "I feel a lot of what I've been doing is struggling with issues with the higher management. As long as I have the energy, I'm willing to do this, but other times I get really tired of trying to create an environment that's positive, where people are really able to do a good job in the sense that people are given the tools that they need and the respect and whatever it is that is necessary that allow for good performance. Obviously if you are in a male-dominated environment, there's a setup that you are not going to be able to win at. And I've had my own immediate problems with the people I work with, particularly with my supervisor who is paid twice what I am paid. A very difficult person to get along with. We have very different styles. And I just see it as—I'm in a position where I am being managed by someone who is incompetent and can't give me what I need. And what I need is a professionally competent role model who has skills beyond what I have and can help me develop my skills and that really doesn't exist where I work. And I see that I can do that on some small level to other people who I work with. I can be a mentor, trainer, encourager with some of the people I work with. But its hard to commit to that role when you're not getting what you need to renourish and restore yourself."

Vicky has had a number of positions in different companies and summarizes her work career in this way: "I've realized that what might be a critical factor is the people I am working with or for—their values and their way of doing business. Once I get going, I tend to be very intense and very focused. I tend to do things very thoroughly, to do a good job and move forward, not to do the same thing again and again. I think a lot of times the work environment I'm in accepts really mediocre performance from people. You do a good job and it receives the same recognition as a shoddy piece of work. People are not willing to recognize that you perform well because it makes a statement about themselves. Having to deal and interact with all these things forty plus hours a week is hard work."

When these women were unable to make the system change, they withdrew either physically or emotionally. We recall that Fern, the physical therapist, left her well-paid and high-status managerial job when she found that the hospital administration cut back her department's resources so much that she was unable to do her work in a way that felt "ethical" to her. Or Debbie, who left her first social work job telling them that it was "a job of filling out forms with no function." Alice, when she was in her late twenties, decided to switch careers because she had come to a dead end as a department chair of occupational therapy in a hospital. At the time, she said, "My job has become little more than a paycheck to me. Administratively, the hospital is one screw-up after another. After 5 1/2 years of sticking my neck out to try to improve matters, I finally gave up because nobody else seemed to care enough to listen anyway." As soon as she could, she retrained as a teacher, a career in which she feels she has much more latitude to have positive effects.

But no specific career seems exempt from these sorts of suffocating restrictions. Where Alice found teaching freeing and gratifying, Harriet, who has been teaching emotionally disturbed children for twenty years, thinks it stultifying. She was distressed when the superintendent's office issued a new edict about how special education teachers must conduct their work, and insisted that they work in a way that Harriet is certain will be much less effective. She found that she has much less autonomy than she supposed in doing her work as well as she can. Gwen, also a teacher, similarly complains about "all the changes the state is requiring. I feel like a lot of the things I thought were really important—the social enriching things—we don't have time for anymore. It's just test, test, test. Too much pressure on kids these days. They don't have time to be kids. And I find that difficult. The state is making so many changes and so many demands that I am looking forward to retiring. I don't want to quit working, but I'm ready to do something different." The issue, then, is not the specific career, but the organizational systems people create in which to work.

Andrea, for eleven years, has been struggling with the department chair in medicine, a "difficult man" who has tried to control her, even attempted to appropriate *her* research funds. She has tried to resign herself to the fact that working where she does, a place she otherwise enjoys, simply means continually doing battle with him. Where women might once have told tales of their frustration with their husbands, they are now more likely to feel caught in quandaries with the people they work with.

Other women became disillusioned with the "work" aspect of their identity when they discovered that occupational competence does not necessarily bring rewards. Budgets are cut, administrative changes occur, and they feel how unsteady the occupational ground they have tilled really is.

Brenda, one of the Pathmakers, was in a high management position in the company where she had worked for twenty years. At age 41, she experienced a work crisis in which she learned, painfully, that she "shouldn't trust the company so much." "I had always been rated very highly by all the bosses I worked for. Even though I was rated highly, because of the money I make, you can get cut very easily if they have to cut the budget." The year before, shortly after receiving a special bonus for high performance, her position was eliminated. Even though the company found her a lateral position, Brenda describes herself as having been "devastated." She felt her loyalty had been misplaced. Despite her age and experience, she somehow deep down still believed that if she did a good job, she would be rewarded. Now, at midlife, Brenda is counting the years to retirement. "My loyalty isn't quite what it used to be," she said. "I still do my job and put in whatever time it takes, but I just don't feel as comfortable the way I used to be." Now her emotional investment is more clearly in the things she really enjoys in life, like boating and biking with her partner.

Over a third of the women I interviewed used the word "devastated" to describe work-related disillusionments (and many others expressed the same sentiments without using the word). They felt their self-esteem toppling in the wake of demotions, firings, being passed over for promotions, or prevented from doing their work as they thought best. Or they experienced their co-workers or superiors as being unappreciative of their efforts and psychologically withdrew. They turned to other aspects of their lives for a sense of competence, maintaining themselves occupationally, but with their hearts no longer in it. Their work became what they "do" rather than a part of what they "are." The dream of fulfilling themselves "as a person" at work had tarnished.

THE DEVELOPMENTAL COURSE OF COMPETENCE

As they grow from late adolescence to midlife, women gain in self-confidence and knowledge, as we might expect. But this perception evolves slowly and erratically and, depending on a woman's experiences in her work, leads her either to a sense of generativity in her work at midlife or a feeling of stagnation.[12]

Young women—women on the threshold of their adulthood—tend to regard the work world with both hope and trepidation about the place they might take in it. As I listen again to the earliest interviews, I hear both the eagerness and the worry as these women prepare to enter adult work roles. If they have selected a professional door on which they wish to knock, they are apprehensive lest they be judged not good enough to enter. Will I be accepted? is the foremost question. They feel their youth and their inexperience, and they wonder about whether they could ever be taken seriously—as a teacher, a lawyer, a physical therapist. The first years after college, for those who are in earnest pursuit of work goals, are filled with skill development, through graduate training or on-the-job apprenticeship. Their twenties decade is devoted to learning the ropes and evaluating their progress. They still regard the work world as an extension of the college framework—learning and performing, being tested and trying to earn an "A."

For some women, their twenties are a period of further search, of deciding perhaps that the first career choice doesn't suit them and making another. The Pathmakers all made second choices. But, by their early thirties, even the women who were exploring the most thoroughly had settled on a career. Regardless of whether they stayed with their first commitments or entered renewed periods of exploration, all these women throughout their twenties were gaining a sense of what they could do in the world, learning that they could be taken seriously, that they would be acknowledged for what they were asked to do in what they had previously regarded as the "grown-up" world.

By the time I saw these women again in their early thirties, they had come to respect themselves for their abilities. They were women who knew how to do something in the world and were proud of it. They had gained a sense of competence and, in most cases, were proud of it and engaged in its exercise. Those on defined career paths felt responsible and looked forward to greater responsibility. They believed they were competent in what they did, but they were still challenged, still in the process of increasing their skills. Now they were less concerned with being evaluated by others and more focused on defining the horizons of what they might accomplish with their abilities.

At some time in their late thirties, those women on defined career paths were most likely to have a crisis in regard to their work—usually centering on generativity. Certain now of their skills and abilities, they began to ask themselves if the rewards of their work were worth their efforts, especially where they found themselves enclosed by walls that precluded them from growing further. (And these women seemed to feel more troubled by brick walls than glass ceilings.) It was at this point that the rewards of being with their children or hobbies and other interests began to look more attractive. Professional women at all levels seemed to ask themselves what really they were accomplishing at work and if it was worth the investment they were making in it.

Feelings of competence are related to a sense of mastery, and mastery is most intense when challenges are new. A task, once mastered, no longer provides a burst of triumphant feeling. As a result, many highly competent women feel themselves stagnating in the face of inescapable routine and repetition. Some women were fortunate to be in organizations that allowed them to grow and develop by expanding—or even changing—their responsibilities. Brenda, for example, who was managing a purchasing department of a large corporation in her mid-thirties, found that she had reached a dead end. "I was bored—if I tried to make any improvements to make things easier, I was vetoed. So I felt I couldn't do any more to benefit the people who I basically worked for and none of the people under me were learning anything new. I wasn't learning anything new." Fortunately, another department recognized her managerial skill and offered her a position, so she was able to take on new, and therefore more challenging tasks.

Oddly, among the women I have interviewed, the ones who seemed most vitally involved in their work at midlife were not necessarily the ones who accomplished the most, but those at the threshold or in the early stages of some new endeavor. I interviewed Clara just weeks before she was to start a new job (her first full-time position) and I caught her excitement and optimism—feelings I rarely heard from the others. "A lot of what I will do seems like fun," she said. "Ten years from now, they're building a new space for archives and I'd like it to be mine. I'm not interested in administration, I'm not looking to move up. I'd like to move sideways into what I like to do most." On the threshhold resides the energy of hope.

At the same time, many women didn't want to imperil the familiar and the certain for the new and the risky. Many spoke of being in line for higher management or administrative positions that they feared were either dubious in terms of job security or uninviting because of the headaches that accompanied the role. Andrea, for example, evaded an opportunity to head a department of medicine because she decided that "it wasn't worth the hassle." "I'm not interested in status," she concluded, "I like doing what I'm doing." She felt still enthusiastic about the clinical and research work she was engaged in—or, at least, more so than the prospect of administrative headaches. For others, the midlife work crisis often emerged as a choice between comfortable stagnation and risky advancement.

The developmental challenge for these women has been to stay emotionally engaged in their work. They entered the occupational world with the starry eyes of idealization, with hopes phrased in terms of being able to do some good for others or accomplish something "worthwhile." They mature into their work roles by learning to become more realistic about what they can effect. In general, they learn that it is not so easy to help others or improve others' lot, values that had been a bedrock of their identity. The trick is to absorb this lesson without despair, to manage to feel generative even in the face of unresolvable problems. As Marlene said of some of the women she tries to counsel about safe sex and birth control, "A lot of the time I feel like I'm talking to the wall, but I talk to the wall and whatever gets through gets through." She maintains her sense that, overall, she can make some real difference in others' lives, despite the failures, despite the odds.

Managers, those in organizations, are likely to feel most competent when they feel themselves empowering others or resolving interpersonal conflict. Success for them, too, is measured in terms of its interpersonal effects. When Brenda assumed her new higher management role, she found herself charged with supervising "two warring factions. I watched them become people who work together as a real team and I think I facilitated that. That's been the most rewarding thing—watching them work together. At this point, if they don't make their deadlines, it's not because they were fighting with each other—there's another reason."

How women cope with what they come to learn about the realities of "doing something" in the world in large part determines how they connect themselves to their work.[13] Some remain vital and engaged and deeply feel themselves to be "a teacher" or "a manager" or whatever their job title is. Others go through the motions, but their real selves are elsewhere. They are able to remain productive in the sense of complying with what is expected of them, but they don't feel generative; they are "good workers," but not personally enriched. They work without the engagement that comes from feeling that they are fully bringing themselves to what they are doing. This sense of alienation from the work itself often brings the greatest disappointment.

This all may be equally true for men. But I think that because these women bring a deep sense that they are choosing to work, that they are a first generation pioneering high-status roles for women, they demand more from what they are doing.[14] Unlike men, they don't see themselves, in most cases, of "having" to work in order to "have" an identity at all. Paychecks are welcomed, but not a source of meaning or gender identity. These women don't seem to value themselves based on their income level; many, in fact, mention that they could be making more money in another sector of their fields. They work in hopes of self-realization and a feeling of effectiveness. When this is thwarted, the whole enterprise of employment is opened to question. None, however, considers "just staying home" a psychologically realistic alternative.

COMPETENCE AND RELATIONSHIPS AT WORK

Identity in work goes beyond exercise of faculties, however. The material world is easier to conquer than the relational one. With enough effort and skill, the systems analyst will make the computer system run, the designer will draft the plans. Relationships at work, by contrast, are convoluted and unpredictable, offer endless challenge, and are critical to the experience of self-at-work. Women derive their sense of competence (and, therefore, identity) from within an interpersonal web. For a woman to have real identity-forming engagement in her work, she needs to feel interconnected with others in a way that seems meaningful and personally enhancing. And this is true from the very earliest stages in which women form a plan for what they might "do."

As college students, women are very much in need of mentors and models, people who will notice them, react to some unique proclivity in them, and encourage them. Those women who found such mentors, either in college or shortly after, are those most likely to experience and express their sense of competence in their work and make that work an important pillar of their identity.[15]

All the professional women I interviewed felt shepherded by people in their fields—mentors—who taught them or cheered them on. Most important, these senior people seemed to invite the young woman into the field and to have conviction that she belonged there. Sometimes mentors evolved from supervisors, graduate school professors, or organizational superiors. These mentors served the crucial function of buttressing these young women against their self-doubt and hesitance on the threshold of their occupational commitment. They were often models for how a career might be mapped out. They provided wisdom about the political realities in the occupational scene. They became like surrogate parents in the work world who helped a young woman come of age professionally. As a result, these women felt a personal link to the occupational world that helped to orient and bind them. Most often these mentors, who were equally likely to be men or women, became friends as well.

After a woman fully entered her work role and gained the first gusts of confidence in it, other people at work continued to catalyze (or dampen) her ongoing occupational growth. Usually the people that women named as important "influences" in their forties were different from those they had learned from in their twenties and thirties. The people change, and the specific way in which they are important changes, but women continue to need others to stretch them and validate their efforts. As women mature in their work, their need for mentors evolves into a need for stimulating colleagueship, shared investment in a task that enables enthusiasm and growth. Where women are working with people they like, the nature of the task seems to be less intrinsically important. Or the task and the relationships become enmeshed and inseparable. The identity-related piece of work, then, may be less an identification as "a nurse" and more one of being a nurse in a particular community. Engagement in the work task grows out of group cohesion and enlivening relationships with others that are, in turn, rechanneled into work goals. Maria, for example, cherishes the "wonderful staff" she supervises. They are a cohesive team, "brainstorming to be creative, always pushing and shoving for our projects, getting involved in the community."

The sense of cohesion and closeness with a work team can also make up for lack of interest in the work itself. Laura speaks of being bored with her work as a medical technologist, but she so much enjoys the people she works with she hardly notices that she's tired of the work itself.

Women work in a relational context and relationships with co-workers are central to how "work" is threaded into a woman's identity.[16] Most of the women I interviewed draw their friends from their workplaces. Consciously or not, they try to weave an unbroken pattern of connection that embraces their work and the rest of their lives. The workplace then becomes more than a place to work; it has largely replaced the marketplace or the backyard fence as a center for a woman's sense of community. The workplace has become an arena of sharing with others who become meaningful and essential to a woman's sense of well-being. Emily, for example, spoke of her sadness at her mentor's upcoming retirement. "It just won't be the same," Emily sighed, "I will really miss him." In the next sentence, she began talking about retiring herself, as though unconsciously she were thinking that without her trusted friend and advisor, her own involvement in her work might be lost.

In their colleagues' eyes, people see their competence reflected and validated. Simply being sought for informal advice is identity-enhancing and adds to a woman's sense that she is respected and has something to offer. When this is absent, work can become intolerable. Natalie, who has been in the same technical writing job for twenty years, had been asked to assume an acting directorship in another department. But the women there, resentful of an outsider being brought in, began to "act like girls in junior high school." They would whisper in her presence, make snide comments about her clothes, refuse to include her in their conversations, and jeeringly call attention to every mistake she made. After a month of this treatment, Natalie requested that she return to her usual job. The sense of comfort with others she worked with mattered more than the opportunity for promotion.

Conflict and tension in the interpersonal world of the workplace can override identity-enhancing gratification in work.[17] Clara worries about this as she takes on her new job—she's had enough experience in organizations to know about interpersonal destructiveness at work. "The down side of [this new job] is that the Library has been a dysfunctional place. A lot of people despise each other and undercut each other. The new director is ambitious and insensitive—working for her unnerves me and that will be hard. She's one of these people who tells you ten minutes before she wants something. I'm stepping into a hornet's nest. Some of the people wouldn't support me for the position because I was friends with someone they didn't like. I was so naive—didn't realize I had enemies. It really came as a shock to me. When I began to feel I was involved in something political, I got so angry it made me even more determined to get this job." Clara has her eye on the work she wishes to do, but worries that the interpersonal politics will derail her.

Many women are reluctant to make job changes when this means giving up a work environment they feel is warm, convivial, and supportive. Ambition and status are less appealing to most women than feeling oneself to have a valued place among others. Women weigh the interpersonal losses before putting themselves in line for promotions. They are unlikely to seek advancement at any cost. In wanting communion and community at work, women tend to shun competitiveness that might lead to alienation and estrangement from those colleagues they feel close to. Women prefer to work in collaboration and mutual empowerment, fearing being lonely at the top, finding pleasure in work that requires joining together.[18] Maria, who has forged a collective group of nurses who work well together, is wary of the pitfalls of climbing ladders. She wants to be sure that she would have autonomy to effect change (for others) if she were to move up and that she would work with people she could like working with.

One of the hardest transitions for Emily, when she became a judge, was losing a valued group of colleagues. She had been a state prosecutor and worked with a group of bright young lawyers very similar to herself; she applied for the judgeship without any expectation of getting it. Although she and others thought that the Governor might be ready to appoint a woman at last, Emily was young and relatively inexperienced and thought she had little chance. "I didn't know what I was getting into," she said, "but it was the sort of thing I couldn't pass up. Once the Governor chose me, I couldn't say that I changed my mind." Once in her new office, she found herself now surrounded by elderly male colleagues with whom she shared absolutely no interests. "It was like being with eighteen fathers," Emily said. "But some of them were great, gave me a lot of help and support." She allowed them to teach her how to enjoy televised golf. She, in turn, got them to take seriously the importance of remembering and celebrating each other's birthdays. But she still missed her friends in the state's attorneys office with whom she could now no longer socialize. And she missed the sense of "working on cases together." "The judicial life can be lonely," Emily learned.

This emphasis on competence in collaboration, however, does not supplant these women's sense of competence in a job well done. They savor the sense of mastery and effectiveness that derives from the accomplishment of the task itself. Emily feels proud of writing an incisive judicial decision and enjoys the approbation of the State Supreme Court when it upholds and compliments her work. Clara relishes her skill in restoring an old book. Each woman cherishes the skill she has acquired for its own sake. But the overall, abiding, deepest sense of competence for women is the feeling of competence in connection to others. At least, this is what women tend to emphasize in reflecting on their experience of themselves in work.

Psychologist Carol Gilligan has pointed out that society, in dividing mastery and relationship into different realms, often offers women a double bind in which to pursue achievement means to disavow relationship.[19] The women I have studied steel themselves to resist this dichotomy, translating their pursuit of mastery into relational terms and combatting forces that seem to coerce them into sacrificing one for the other. This is often at the price of advancement and status. Efforts to make their work reflect collaboration instead of competition are not valued in settings designed to facilitate power and hierarchy, but these women nevertheless try to work within such systems. If they question the system itself, they find themselves quickly subdued.

COMPETENCE AND SUPPORT

The sense of competence as a pole of identity is never won, of course, once and for all. To some extent, the search for it is renewed each day and maintained by the encouragement of others. In this group of women, the mainstay of support for competence derives from husbands (or partners in the case of the two lesbian women). Contrary to popular mythology, husbands are allies rather than foes in the reach for competence.

Nearly all the women I have interviewed maintain that, more than anyone else, it has been their husbands (or partners) who have cheered them on (as well as cheered them up). Emily says that she could never have borne the stresses of her judgeship without her husband's presence in her work. He understands legal issues, reads her opinions, and offers useful ways of thinking. And he comforts her when she feels stung by criticism.

When the hospital where Laura works was reorganized and she was demoted, her first thought was to be with her husband. Only he would fully understand, she felt. He had supported her through her promotion, through learning how to be a manager, listening patiently as she considered each new situation and how to respond to it. Only he could know what the loss of this position would mean to her.

Clara's husband supported her decision in her early twenties to give up the teaching career in which she felt she was "rotting" to devote full-time to book-binding, which had been a hobby. "I stumbled into where I've gotten and he has been the most direct and indirect influence on everything I've done. Partly by his love of books, which has always nurtured in me my own love of them. And his support in terms of taking care of the children and helping me with the papers I've published." If anything, Clara said, as her career has progressed, he has pushed her to take on more than she felt ready for.

Helen is married to a high school principal and his involvement in her decision-making as a teacher makes for a lively interchange. She enjoys her competence even more in being able to share her successes with someone who knows well how to appreciate them.

Evelyn was first drawn to her partner because it was she who seemed to believe in her and encourage her to take on more work responsibility and seek promotion. "This woman gave me the confidence that I could do these things, anything I could put my mind to. A lot of it was because of her. She just gave me this feeling that I could do anything."

The examples could continue. Everyone succeeds for someone. By this, I don't mean to imply that women can't "do it alone" and shouldn't try if they don't have someone encouraging them. But it is clear from what these women have told me that having an intimate partner invested in their career success is a major boost to developing a sense of competence.[20] Doing it alone is a much harder road, and I think that it is time that we as a society acknowledge this.

WORK/FAMILY CONFLICTS

If husbands support rather than oppose women's sense of identity in competence, what about work/family conflicts? These do exist, to be sure, because these are women who are, in many instances, taking on enormous responsibility on both fronts. Each woman finds a way to balance these aspects of her life, juggling, improvising, and engineering creative solutions as the needs arise.[21]

Several of the women I interviewed made job changes in their twenties to accommodate their husband's careers. Because these were often their first professional jobs, they saw themselves as equally able to begin in one place or another. None of them had to make mid-career changes because of a husband's career advancement; this formidable set of dilemmas and difficulties is not represented among this group.

Collisions between needs of the family and work needs differ, of course, for mothers and non-mothers. Those with young children have the hardest task. Grace, I believe, speaks for all the women who have both careers and children when she says, "It's a constant struggle every day of having to make maternal decisions over professional decisions. You have to jockey which is more important at the moment. The most important of those two things is being a mother, but sometimes the professional is more important and I don't think the [balancing problem] will ever change as long as I am working." Grace makes a centrally important point here, in stressing that the conflicting demands between work commitments and mothering are never "resolved." Rather, they are analyzed and decided again and again, day after day, sometimes several times in a day, with each situation presenting somewhat different dilemmas. The life of a working mother plays out as an endless series of "I can't schedule a meeting at that time because that's my son's school play . . . I can't take you to the orthodontist at that time because an important client is flying in from California," and so on.

The burden of organizing the responsiblity for children still falls to the mothers; they have to find a way to balance their career interests with their parenting. Of the thirteen working mothers, only Grace (a judge) and Regina (a professor) have worked full-time in a male-dominated field while raising children. Both had their children after age 30, when they were already established professionally. Grace, however, is hoping to resign her judgeship for work she can do on a more time-flexible basis. Of the remaining eleven, four are teachers who were able to make use of liberal leave policies and "school day" hours to aid in combining work with mothering. The others worked part-time, studied, or took time away from work when their children were small. Clara is starting her first *full-time* job now that her youngest child has entered school.

Some of these women chose careers or particular jobs *because* they offered the possibility of combining work and family life. This was especially true among Pathmakers who, because they were clear early on that they wanted to have both careers and families, retrained in careers that would make it easier to mother as well. Three of the four Pathmakers who became mothers rethought their career goals in light of their wish to raise a family. Maria, for example, studied nursing while her children were infants, in order to have a career that would allow her flexible work hours. And Clara, the bookbinder, used her children's earliest years as time to study and apprentice.

Watching themselves balance so many responsibilities, these women are proud of themselves. They are busy (Alice gets up at 4:30 A.M. to do her schoolwork), but they make their lives fit together. They don't think of themselves as "Superwomen" nor do they resent having such a load of responsibility. If anything, some of them say that the more frenetic their lives are, the more they get done.[22]

Those women who are not mothers are not necessarily more focused on their careers than those who have children—this is another cultural myth. Maria, for example, the nursing director with two children, sounds every bit as invested in her work as Andrea, the doctor-researcher who does not have children. And Regina, who has two children, has work that seems more centrally important to her than Emily who has no children (but many other interests). The non-mothers also achieve a complex balance between their occupational ambitions and their other interests in life. But since most of the working mothers are in some branch of human service (none are in the corporate world), comparisons become confounded.

All in all, the working mothers are happier with their work than the non-mothers. They live in "high gear" and relish the variety of experience and interaction in their lives. None say that they could have done more or achieved higher status if they had not had children; they have accepted and lived within the social constraints—the fact that most professions do not allow women part-time work or marginalize women who do work part time, that quality day care is hard to find and, even if found, still exacts an emotional cost. Although thirteen of these thirty women have found a way to pursue meaningful work and still raise children, they have done it in the context of a society that itself has not figured out how to parent the next generation while still allowing women to realize their full occupational potential. They have each found individual, unique solutions. There has been no simple way, but once they have created a workable structure, they tend to understate the complexities.

All these women took as a given their need to take part in the public adult world and express their competence, to whatever degree possible, in work. They feel they are more fulfilled individuals, more interesting partners, and better mothers as a result. The energy and planning required are often daunting as they use all their resources to realize themselves in both worlds (and they derive a sense of competence and pride from being able to organize well and "get it all in"). None say that their families interfere with their work, although they clearly make work decisions based on their families' needs. Work that involves a lot of travel is off limits to those who are mothers. Several, especially teachers, are delaying or foregoing further education or training because the time and financial demands would overburden their families. But these losses tend to be mentioned rather than stressed.

If anything, as Clara said, realizing their dream of family often motivates them more intensely to accomplish their work goals. "Somehow the fulfillment of having wonderful children and a phenomenal husband let me move ahead and do things that are satisfying intellectually and professionally," Clara said. Before having children, Clara reflected, she had been "floundering a bit, unsure which direction to go. I was working part-time and wasn't very focused. It came as a kind of counterpoint to the family and partly because taking care of small children is not the most interesting thing in the world. Intellectually it's deadening, but there is such a huge emotional satisfaction in nurturing and caring and loving. It was like this strange way in which I could let go and allow myself to move forward." So Clara felt that having children helped her to be *more* focused on her career. Among the Searchers, the group who seemed at the outset to be asking the most from life, those who at midlife are most engaged in their work are the ones who also have children.

These women do not experience family as keeping them from their work, but work often feels to them like an interference with their family investments. Many wish they had more time to spend with their children, but it is the draw rather than the demands of children that produce the conflict. In part because they do not feel imprisoned with them, these women enjoy their children and are reluctant to give up the fun of being with them.

Although none of the nine married non-mothers says directly that she did not have children because they would limit her career aspirations, several indicated that they delayed having children because they wanted to preserve their dual incomes long enough to ensure a certain standard of living. Implicit in this reasoning was a belief that having children would involve giving up or paring down of the career they were pursuing, reflecting a certain despair about being able to "have it all."

There was much diversity among the women I have been studying in terms of the balance of work and family concerns; each woman achieves her own combination in a unique way. Emily, for example, feels that she has the best of both worlds because her husband travels a great deal in his profession. That allows her a chance to get her work done and still be completely available to spend time with him when he is there. For Andrea, who works long hours, it is a struggle to coordinate her schedule with her husband's equally demanding work so that they have any time at all together. In Laura's case, she has become the wage-earner while her husband manages the home front. Betty does her work half the year and the family travels the other half. While Theresa relies on her mother to tend her children while she works, others use nannies and day-care centers. Both Maria and Marlene had husbands who shared the child care, taking charge of the children while they worked. Harriet's husband took six-month leaves after Harriet's leave ran out following the birth of each of their children. Given the idea that there used to be a "single plot" for a woman's life, the current variety of life structures that women design is astonishing.

Some women want to feel "in charge" at home despite the press of professional responsibilities. Others are more ready to share this authority, even though to Harriet, for example, it still "feels funny" to have her husband do all the cooking. These are, after all, daughters of homemaker mothers; what they find is that "doing it all" doesn't necessarily encompass doing *all* that their mothers may have done.

What they give up to "do it all" tends to be housework, exercise, friendship, and hobbies. Most say that they have learned to live with lower standards of housekeeping than their mothers may have had; they have too much else to think about than to be bothered about impeccably clean floors. More painfully, however, they regret not having time to read or sew or garden or exercise, activities they long to do. Their jobs and family could consume all available moments.

I think that one important difference among people that we seldom focus on is energy level, yet it was a clear distinction among the women I studied. There are those, like Alice, who can get up at 4:30 in the morning to do her schoolwork, work all day, be with her family in the evening, manage the house and the meals, and then go to bed at 11 P.M. Other women, especially those without children, do much less, sleep more, but still feel themselves without enough time to get to all they want to do.

Husbands help, of course, some more than others. But this was seldom a source of complaint among the women I interviewed. Most have worked out some kind of sharing arrangement; if not an equal division of labor, it is at least manageable. And they do not hesitate to ask for renegotiation of tasks if their load gets overwhelming.

These women are proud of what they have accomplished and look forward to accomplishing more—again, not necessarily in terms of advancement or income, but in effects on others and in feeling themselves taking part in the larger world. But it is rare for women to put their work lives at their center—as most significant or core in their identities. We distort women's identities when we adopt masculine conventions and label them as "a lawyer" or "a nurse." This is only a part. Women, of course vary in how they create their unique interwoven tapestries. Some make their occupational lives more central than others. And some find their real sense of competence outside work.[23]

OTHER SOURCES OF COMPETENCE

Myriad pursuits outside their careers claim the imagination and energy of the women I studied and offer them the pleasure of competence. For many, pride springs from the houses they have created. Houses are a project that allow for the limitless expression of creativity, with no superiors or organizational rules to hinder them. Finances are a constraint, of course, but the challenge is to work within these boundaries and make something of beauty and comfort that reflects their own uniqueness. Harriet was eager that we sit for our interview in a lovely room that she and her husband built themselves. She wanted me to notice the brickwork, the painted mural, the choice of shelving and furniture. This was a room that she had made to express herself and she was proud of it. Other women whom I interviewed in my office brought me pictures of their houses, especially of those parts that they had themselves restored or built. One might regard this as simple nest-building, but I saw it as a form of creativity, of making something of themselves by making something for themselves. "We built our house in the middle of four acres of dense woods," Regina told me. "There is lots of glass, and deer come on our patio. We recently put in skylights to better see the trees and the sky. This has been a real joy for me. Watching the seasons change while playing with my children. This is more than just a place to live, but a way of being in contact with nature."

Other women found important expression of their competence in domestic activities. Emily loves to give parties and enjoys her growing reputation as an excellent hostess. Sandra makes all her own clothes and cherishes being known for her unusual wardrobe. Natalie hybridizes daylilies. "I took the prize at the last Garden Club show, but there is this one color that I'm still trying to get. . . ." All this gets lost if we try to fit women into the "career" box. We cannot adequately depict women's lives without recognizing that some of the most intense identity-related feelings of competence well up outside the workplace.

Donna, who is not following a career track, is shy in telling me about the pride she derives from building the miniature village for her town at Christmas each year. After all, this is not paid work, and it seems to her that I, a university professor, wouldn't think that this is really "doing something." Yet she spends months working on it and enjoys the pleasure of the children of her town in seeing it. I think she imagined in me a reflection of our new cultural expectations about what is fit work for women. In fact, I was quite impressed. I would cherish having such artistic talent. And I was saddened to the extent that professional women, in claiming the right to our own accomplishments, may deprive other women of their pride in talents not oriented to career advancement.

Non-career sources of competence also serve to relieve stress for those who are "doing it all." Most women seem to need some comfortable activity they can retreat to when they feel overburdened or underappreciated. Vicky, who is intensely disappointed in the lifeless nature of her administrative work says, "I think about those life maintenance things, like doing laundry or grocery shopping. I can't say that 100% of the time I'm into doing them. There are times when they are still chores, but at times they become like a medication or whatever—they're just different. You can be very much in the moment. You're creating in some ways. Its interesting because some of those things are very rote, but that's very different for me than having to sit in a chair all day and having to do the same things over and over. Maybe because I personally choose to do them."

For Betty, when stress gets too much, she can escape to the ski slopes and find that she can still do some complicated maneuvers. Other women do crossword puzzles as a way of savoring a moment of unfettered mastery.

Many women also express their competence in a concern about health and healthful ways of living. Issues of diet emerged in many interviews: giving up caffeine, cooking without red meat, experimenting with low-fat recipes, and so on. Again, these were expressed as issues of competence—discovering what is good and working to achieve it.

FEELING COMPETENT IN RELATIONSHIPS

"I wish I had a book of *Right Answers for Every Situation*," said Millie. "I'd like to be sure I'm being firm when I should be firm and soft when I should be soft and not vice versa." Of all the regions of their lives, the place where women most yearned to feel competent was in their relationships. But this is a realm of competence that is harder to evaluate. How does one know if one is a "good mother"? How can one be certain that one is a "good wife" or a "good friend" or a "good daughter"? Yet these are what the majority of women most long to "be," despite their own unclarity about what it really means to be "good" at motherhood, marriage, friendship, or daughterhood. For women, the feeling of competence may remain elusive or erratic precisely because, in reaching for success in relationships, women are rooting their self-esteem on shifting ground. On the other hand, the experience of mutuality and resonance in small interactions and the solidity of ongoing devotion and care bring an intensely pleasurable—if often fleeting—feeling of competence and well-being. What is sought is the pleasure of another's smiles.

I asked these women to tell me about their sense of accomplishment at their current age and also to imagine themselves at age 80, looking over their lives and thinking about what they would be most satisfied to have accomplished. Nearly all spoke in terms of having made their mark in terms of relationships to others and hoping to continue to do so. Many counted among their primary successes the length of their marriages, their devotion to the well-being of another, and their capacity to inspire fidelity in return, and they hoped that, at the end of their lives, they could look back and see an even longer happy connection. The first hope of all the mothers was to have raised happy, productive, well-adjusted children. And reflecting on what of their existing accomplishments gave them greatest pride, the mothers were again most likely to speak of their children. At the same time, these mothers articulated the dilemmas of competence in motherhood, the challenges that lie far beyond feeding and diapering, the enigmas of relationship.

For the mothers, competence involves doing their best to ensure the well-being of their particular children. Betty has had to make herself an expert on learning disabilities to try to help her son, while Marlene is researching the effects of adoption on children to be sensitive about helping her adopted daughter understand her origins. Helen has had the challenge of assisting a daughter who is sightless in one eye and Regina worries about what the future will hold for her retarded son. For the mothers who have children without special needs, managing their children's school adjustment, planning activities that will be enriching, struggling with making rules about or responding to adolescent behavior—these are all just a part of the complex and ever-changing role of taking care.

As I help my about-to-be-licensed 16-year-old daughter learn to merge onto the highway, craning my neck from the passenger side, I remember holding her tiny hands as she tottered toward her first steps. With some irony, I realize that I am doing another version of the same thing. But more, I think at this moment, this is the track of motherhood—from steadying a toddling baby to counseling about high-speed merges. Sara Ruddick (1989) points out that although, as a society, we use the nursing mother as the metaphor for motherhood as a whole, in fact, nursing is one of the easier tasks a mother has to confront. The real emblems of motherhood, Ruddick says, are keeping the rambunctious toddler away from the poisons in the pantry or soothing the child who wasn't invited to the classmate's birthday party. Every mother has her own list. The striving to be a better mother, to fashion a response to the changing demands, to understand more, to yell less form an essential core of these women's efforts at competence. And within this, as many women told me, the real success is being able to keep perspective and retain their sense of humor.

What do we live for, if it is not to make life less difficult to each other?

George Eliot, Middlemarch

9 CONNECTION

When I first began this study back in 1972, at a time of fervor in the women's movement, I wanted to "find" identity in women in the same terms that Erikson described male identity. I began my 1972 interview by asking, "If there were someone who you wanted to know you, what sorts of things would you tell them about yourself?" I hoped to invite each young woman to explore what aspects of herself she held to be essential to her sense of who she was. And I was surprised and chagrined when so many offered such responses as "I'd tell them about my family and my friends," or "I'd tell them about the people who matter to me." This wasn't "real" identity, I thought. Given my schooling in the existing theory of the times, I had expected them to tell me about their occupational aspirations or their ideological positions, the things Erikson said are central to identity. But what all these young women seemed to want to talk about was the people in their lives and, at the time, I still thought this was somehow inferior or dependent or quintessentially female in a shameful way.

This pattern continued. As I asked, at each interval, What changes have there been in the last ten years? most began with what has happened to and with the people in their lives—new intimacies, losses or illnesses of people they loved, births of children or changes in their needs, or conflicts in relationships with those dear to them. Over the course of years, these women did not change in how they think about what matters most in their lives. They still begin an account of themselves with a recounting of changes in relationships with those they love. What has changed is that I have come to a different understanding of what this means.

In the intervening twenty years, both I personally and psychology as a field have come a long way in our understanding of women. Psychoanalyst Jean Baker Miller, proposing a new psychology of women, grounds her thought in the observation that for women, a sense of personhood is rooted in motivation "to make and enhance relatedness to others."[1] These are precisely the terms the women I have followed have used to define themselves in their ever-changing and complex interplay with others. Identity in women is fundamentally relational. We have come to grasp that, because they are mothered by someone of the same sex, girls grow up feeling more continuous with and less separate from others than boys (Chodorow, 1978). And we have also come to recognize women's relational embeddedness as a strength that has been deprecated in patriarchal society. I now go back to those early interviews and hear them differently. I hear young women trying to locate themselves with others, to realize themselves in interconnection and create a "self-in-relation" as Jean Baker Miller has described the course of women's selfhood. As they grew older and I grew older, I began to perceive more carefully how this locating of self shifted over the years. I learned that their fundamental orientation of themselves in relationship to others only grows richer and more complex. Their investments in others is never supplanted by occupation or ideology. Instead, as we have seen in the case of competence, work and belief are themselves constructed in relational terms. While changes in commitments that serve competence and ideology are significant, changes in relationship have far more profound consequences for identity.[2]

In a fundamental way, identity is expressed by joining others and taking a place within that community that is bound to others but uniquely one's own. The French existential philosopher Gabriel Marcel viewed identity as "being with," a state for which we have little language. But this is at odds with a culture that tends to locate identity in individuality and lone achievement.[3]

In our highly individualistic age, we have become wary of talking too loudly about connections with others, as though this implies self-abasement, self-denial, or self-abrogation. It is difficult in the vocabulary of the modern age to laud self-definition in the context of relationship. In seeking meaningful engagement with others, women do not look to depend or submit, but rather to form ever more articulated and multifaceted interconnections that allow for self-expression in a *responsive* exchange where both self and other are contained, recognized, empowered, valued, and enriched.[4] Love becomes a way of delineating the self. In the web of interconnection, a woman locates and expresses herself, knowing who she is in part through those for whom she "is." The yearning for connection is central, maintained through the activities of care and response.[5] Women long to be involved with others, to see themselves reflected in them, to be responded to. Identity is, in essence, a form of belonging, of embedding the self with others.[6] The quest for identity is the search for, in Carson McCullers' epic phrase, the "we of me."

The trick in managing a career, a family, and friendships all at the same time, said Clara, is to find ways of doing things that "respect *their needs and my needs at the same time.*" Identity in connection is *not* the same as selflessness. To find oneself *with* others does not involve obliterating the self any more than identity in competence means annihilating others. (Too often, however, I think that feminist writers fear that acknowledging relational identity in women risks banishing them once again to the kitchen.) Identity in women is an ongoing process of balancing and rebalancing needs of the self and investment in the needs of others, an intersection so interwoven that it is often foolhardy to ask, "Are you doing this for yourself or are you doing this for others?" The two are often inseparable. Psychological growth in *connection* involves finding more interesting and challenging ways of being with others, knowing them better (and simultaneously knowing oneself better), discovering more precise and meaningful forms of feeling known and validated as oneself, increasing moments of mutuality and bonds of trust, maintaining connection over time and distance, and grappling with the dilemmas of caring for another. Loyalty and fidelity to others become cornerstones of identity. In all these pursuits, for most of which we don't even have adequate language, women realize themselves. And they are who they are in different ways at different times with the different people in their lives, thus adding more threads and colors, more complexity and texture, to their overall identities.

Identity is, in part, composed of those who support and secure it. We are intertwined with those on whom we "fall back," those who are "there" for us, those to whom we are attached. We orient our lives, in part, to taking care of these relationships as well as of the people themselves, and this forms a crucial part of identity. As we have seen, the Guardians, early on, spun their identity around preserving those relationships that offered them safety and certainty. But the Pathmakers and the Searchers also concerned themselves with how to maintain old ties while creating new ones. On the other hand, the most diffuse of the Drifters, those who were the least well defined, were the same women who were most loosely connected to others. Poignantly,

Yvonne would like to locate herself in relationship, but fails: "My friends are very important to me because I need people to run to for problems with work or problems with relationships. I don't have any real long-lasting friends—friends from earlier times are all gone. I haven't seen them for a long time. I keep in touch—I have to do the calling. Most of my friends seem—if I don't pursue the friendship, there wouldn't be one. I'm basically a loner, I think." In this statement, we witness identity seeping away until Yvonne is left with the identity of "a loner."

Identity is also built out of people we admire, look up to, and take bits of to fashion ourselves. Who we choose to identify with both derives from who we already are and also influences who we become. Women who found mentors, for example, were most likely to achieve in the work world, but this had a complex interplay. Clara, adoring the women she apprenticed with to learn her craft, said that she often wasn't sure what mattered more—the work or her joy at being with her teachers.

We realize our identity only in sharing it with others, and the sharing itself confirms and strengthens our sense of who we are. Whether we look to others to reflect our sense of ourselves, to resonate with our experience, or to accept what we offer of ourselves, our identity remains lodged in the interconnection. Identity is the place we take *with* partners, children, parents, siblings, colleagues, friends, and all the others. This definition is a far cry from saying that a woman's identity is determined by the man she marries!

For this generation of women, however, constituting themselves in relationships has been more an act of creativity than ever before. Able to support themselves economically, allowed to "be a woman" in many different ways, these women had the freedom to locate themselves in a wide range of relationships—relationships in which their own needs and wishes could be powerful shaping forces. In this realm, these women have given intense thought to possibility, to choice, and to revision. Resisting forces that might subordinate them, these women have sought and worked for relationships of mutuality and empowerment.[7]

WOMEN AND PARTNERS

The most significant revolution that these women have effected in their lives has been the change in their expectation and experience of marriage. For their mothers, marriage was an economic necessity, a socially demanded life structure for financial survival when independent means of support was largely denied women. Their mothers grew up with the notion that their husbands would be providers while they would have charge of the family. Husbands were valued for their success in provision and cherished to the extent that they abstained from such upsetting and hurtful behaviors as abusiveness, gambling, infidelity, and so on. "He's a good husband," their mothers might have said. "He doesn't run around, he's good to the children and he comes home at night." But the daughters, the women of this study, witnessed their mothers' subservience and emotional isolation. They saw their fathers as largely absent or, when they were physically present, as relatively silent in the home. Many viewed their fathers as gruff and critical, as men who came home to be physically cared for but emotionally left in peace. Some women saw this pattern of dominance and control in reverse: a demanding, emotionally blackmailling, often-depressed mother who kept her husband constantly fearful of her rages and in her thrall. Regardless of which parent was in the ascendant, these women observed between their parents an economic and power arrangement from which flowed the complex dynamics of dependency, which always contain both exploitation and retribution. They may also have observed some affection, but few witnessed between their parents an emotionally engaging relationship of active resonant love. And they vowed to do better.

In their own marriages, the women of this generation were determined to have friendships. They sought men who seemed supportive, interested in them as people, and capable of mutual interchange. Both their own proclivities and the economic necessities of the 1970s led them to share the provider role; this set a framework for their equalitarian designs for their marriage. I was struck by how many of them in midlife described their husbands as their best friends, people they could count on to talk about their feelings and reactions in life, people they could trust for rock-solid support of their endeavors. "I think we've been incredibly well-suited, been unbelievable lucky," Clara said. "He's always been there and supportive and loving. I know he thinks I'm wonderful and beautiful. I know he cares enormously about the children. He's a wonderful companion, intellectually, emotionally. My emotions are very on the surface—I cry very easily—he's always been very indulgent. I feel so grateful to have this relationship which is so wonderful, this best friend that I live with, who I can talk to about anything." Clara is perhaps one of the most happily married, but her experience is not atypical.

None of these women told me that they valued their husbands as economic providers in the way their mothers might have done and none seemed to feel economically bound in their marriages. In fact, nearly half the working married women were earning as much or more than their husbands.

Economically capable of supporting themselves, these women valued their husbands as people with whom they shared interests and the ongoing saga of their emotional lives. They betrothed themselves to people with whom they could intertwine themselves but still remain—and be valued as—separate and unique individuals. These were women who shared an educational and occupational history with the men they married. Less segregated by social distance and differentiation of roles than any previous generation, they did not inhabit a different social universe from their husbands. Emily relies on her husband to read her legal opinions. Grace, the other judge, is married to a lawyer and their intellectual sharing is important to them both, despite trouble between them in other aspects of their lives. And Marlene, as a nurse-midwife, looks forward to swapping patient stories with her physician-husband. Although being in the same field can also raise difficulties, having an independent professional identity means that these women share rather than divide experiences in the public and private realms of life. Both members of the couple locate themselves both inside and outside the relationship, which forms an increased basis for mutuality.

As girls, these women often viewed their mothers as "dominated" or "submissive" in their marriages, as subservient to their husbands' authoritarian control. This, too, they categorically refused. Some women, trying so hard not to find themselves disempowered in their marriages, chose men who were mild-mannered, gentle rather than willful. Later in life, these women had to come to terms with feeling that, if anything, their husbands were too retiring or too unambitious. They were more likely to complain about their husbands being "couch potatoes" than despots in the home. These women had to make peace with what they later recognized as an unconscious longing to have it both ways, to have their husband be both lion and lamb. But, on reflection, they prized above all their husband's commitment to the family and their shared goals, even if that meant forgoing the fantasy of the all-powerful "prince" who protected them from the harshness and deprivations of life.

Clearly, these women have come a long way from being the chattel of husbands. Yet their identity stories cannot be told as tales of individual effort and choice; instead, they are narratives of taking care of relationships and picking paths contoured by both themselves and those they love. Maria regarded her work in a very different way once her disabled husband could no longer be a main provider for the family, and Betty had to adjust to the financial wealth her husband acquired. Andrea turned down a prestigious job in the interest of her husband, and Clara has shaped her career around her husband's career moves.

Their partners become part of them. "We've been together so long, I can't imagine life without him" was a sentiment expressed by Millie but echoed by most. Their lives have been stories of growing together and in tandem. In myriad ways, each woman speaks with satisfaction of learning mutual accommodation, of making decisions together.

On the other side, partners are central to these women's identity stories in terms of their support and encouragement. Betty recognizes that her lifestyle is made possible by her husband's financial resources, and Andrea acknowledges that she might never have made it to or through medical school without Arnold's reassuring presence. Clara speaks of her husband as always having been the one to push her to greater accomplishment. Their partners provide a secure base from which they explore their competence in the outside world.

Beyond support, partners delimit the personal qualities these women can express easily and what they have to stretch for, thus providing the backdrop for the expression of identity. Andrea, for example, fought her first husband's dependency and inertia by asserting her independence and wish for freedom and adventure. In those days, she desribed herself as an intrepid explorer, headstrong and reaching for the world. With a more spontaneous and extraverted second husband, Andrea finds herself the one who pulls for more togetherness in the relationship, who asks that they stay home for once. Now she begins to think of herself as someone who loves the pleasures of home and hearth. In part, she has changed, to be sure. But, in part, I think she experiences herself differently when her husband contains and expresses different parts of herself. Betty, a very able and resourceful woman, struggles to feel competent next to her gifted, successful husband who, in the early days of their relationship, she had felt she needed to guide. Maria works to maintain her respect for her less ambitious and now-disabled husband, and not allow her own competence to disable him further.

Although these women tried to select partners with particular qualities, for most of them, there were surprises. Partners have had their own growth and histories that, for better or worse, have much influenced the course of these women's lives. Being bonded in intimate relationship has meant having to try to change what was malleable and accept what was not. Natalie wishes her husband "was more social and had more interests," but adapts. Regina had wanted more equality in regard to child care and domestic tasks, but recognizes that for her husband to succeed in his career, he needs more time and fewer demands. She remembers the awful period when he was unemployed and doesn't want to risk inviting such misfortune again. Their relationship is not as she would have had it, but she makes the accommodations she feels are necessary. Integration of identity has meant not only putting the shards of themselves together, but also interconnecting their identity with the needs and foibles of someone else. Most emphasize that, over the years, they and their partners have come to understand each other more and more.

It would be easy—though false—to ask about whether these women act for themselves *or* for others. We could paint them as either selfish or selfless. We could express our sense of injustice when they take on more than their share; we could scoff at them for compromises. Look at all Regina is doing, we could say, managing an academic career, two young children, and an illness. She is exhausted—why doesn't her husband help her more? Why does she let herself be blackmailed by worry that he will lose his job? Or why isn't Natalie's husband more responsive to her needs? Why doesn't she go out more without him? But those women who come to create a clear identity, whether in college or later in life, have demonstrated an artfulness in blending and bending, putting themselves together with their partners, improvising solutions, figuring out what is essential to them, and doing the best they can with the rest. Identity also involves living with what you feel you cannot change.

All but two of the women in my study are in long-term committed relationships. Their husbands (or partners) become a part of them, but they are not subsumed into their husbands' or partners' identities. Their lives are knit together, interwoven in such a way that to think about themselves and who they are in their lives calls immediately to mind an image of their life partner. They experience themselves as moving in tandem with them, together in being and in greeting the future. They carry their husbands or partners "in mind" while having the conviction that their husbands or partners are reciprocally keeping them "in mind." They do not give themselves up to an Other but, more precisely, they add an Other to themselves. While experiencing their own feelings, these women often "feel through" their partners as well, responding to events on two simultaneous levels: their own emotional reactions and their knowledge of their partner's feelings. Given an invitation to a party, for example, they might feel *both* "Oh, that sounds like fun," and "He doesn't like to socialize with these people. He gets bored when they persist in 'talking shop.'" They take pleasure in pleasing their husbands and partners and in the knowledge that they enjoy pleasing them. "He loves to make me happy," said Emily. "He's really tuned in to my needs," said Marlene. "Now I have someone to please," said Natalie. The currency of exchange in these marriages is pleasing and being pleased, but this feels joyous rather than enslaving.

Bonding and commitment ensue from opening themselves to another person, softening their own edges to allow a continuous flow between them. Identity in this relationship requires adapting to the needs and interests of their partner while feeling their own contours complemented by their partners. Many regarded their husbands as stabilizers who checked their own emotionality; others saw their husbands as expressing more of the feelings in the relationship, relying on them for practicality and reason. Parts of a whole self are bartered, with each partner often carrying aspects of the other. One's own self is thereby lodged, in part, in one's mate. The challenge of relationship remains one of balancing self and mutual interests. This, of course, is an ongoing process of continual renegotiation, adjustments, and readjustments in a context of loyalty and mutual devotion.

When this harmony is sundered irreparably, these women have gone through the process of disconnection and divorce, and a few contemplate that they may yet divorce in midlife. One-third of those who were married a first time had divorced and remarried, most of them finding in a second try the mutuality they had missed in the first. Some women—Regina, Sandra, Nancy, Debbie, and Grace—one-sixth of all the women I have followed—continue to live in disappointing or unsatisfactory marriages, valuing the security of companionship, the stability of family, or the comfort of not having to face life alone. They agonize about how much they can compromise—how much they can mute their need for intimacy in the service of maintaining attachments. Like Debbie, they wonder what direction really serves their growth: "If I leave, is that giving up? If I stay, am I giving up? I just don't know."

Overall, I was impressed by how good most of these women felt their marriages are: companionate, loving, responsive—anchors to their sense of themselves. Their marriages are not without tension and dispute but, for the most part, these women experienced these moments as the exception rather than the usual ambience. I was often amused, in the course of these interviews, at how so many women seemed embarrassed at having so little dissatisfaction with their husband to report. Most men are jerks, they assured me, letting me know they are aware of how modern women are expected to regard men, but *they* found the only good one.

From an observer's point of view, we could debate whether or not these marriages represent some ideal of "true intimacy." Often, conflict and disappointment seemed to me to be sidestepped and denied, rather than met and resolved. But outsiders can never judge a marriage. Each marriage is different and some are more complicated and ambivalent than others. What one woman finds gratifying, another would undoubtedly find unbearable. External commentary or social definitions here seem intrusive, not illuminating. What is most important is that those women who are contented in their marriages have created a relational connection that by and large suits them, which they can wrap themselves around and find themselves within. What they share as a group is their common ideal of companionate equalitarian marriage, this generation's primary revolution against socially imposed role definitions.

SEXUALITY

I think that as a culture we have overstated the role of sexuality in marriage or, more precisely, have used sex as a metaphor for the intimacy that takes place. Life is not like the movies, and most women do not marry a man who sweeps them off their feet and carries them into an ecstasy of sexual surrender. Most women figure out early on that such men are either not interested in being husbands or, if they are, probably wouldn't make good ones.

Although I did not ask specifically about their current sexual behavior after the college interview, most of the married adult women I interviewed who were happy in their marriages mentioned that sex was important as a way of being close to their husbands and as a form of pleasure. But passion in marriage, if it had been present at all from the beginning, was quickly combined with other forms of relational interchange and absorbed into a larger framework of mutuality.[8] Where sexual rhythms or needs were out of phase or sexual desire was unequal, sex became problematic, but these difficulties were seldom fatal to the marriage itself. Some women—women who felt contentedly married—had marriages that were infrequently sexual or where there had been periods of lack of sexual interest from one or the other. Many women mentioned, for example, that in the early years of child-raising, when the demands of young children combined with the stress of work took their toll in terms of energy, they were often too tired to be interested in sex. Others spoke of husbands whose sexual interest disappeared, sometimes for long periods. These then became problems for the couple to resolve. But when women think of their marriages, sexual interchange is not the first aspect of their relationship with their husbands that comes to mind. Other forms of intercourse predominate and are more central to a woman's sense of self.

NEW DEFINITIONS OF FAMILY

The flourishing of companionate marriage seems also to have had important effects on these women's understandings of family. If marriage is an alliance of equals, of people who like and are interested in each other, women no longer need children for company. In so many novels, a childless woman is bereft, not because she is not fulfilling her role, but because she is lonely. 'If only I could have a child, I would not be so depressed,' was the idea. But women of today, if they have formed an emotionally enriching marital partnership, need not bear children out of loneliness. Several women I have studied declined children in part because they felt fulfilled with their partner, their work, and the rest of their lives. Psychological theories and social mythmaking that persist in linking "marriage and children" or assuming that the purpose of marriage is to procreate are simply outdated. Marriage and children are increasingly separate enterprises. They are different forms of relational investment and now there is the social recognition (and the technology) to separate them.

CHILDREN

For the women who do have children, their children form a central design in their weaving of identity. Motherhood is such a powerful framework for identity that the having or not having of children is the single most salient distinction among the adult women I studied. All the mothers, regardless of their occupational success or commitment, said that their children were the most important aspect of their lives, their self-realization, and their sense of who they are.[9] Aside from severe trauma and life-threatening illness, becoming a mother seems to be the most potent identity-transforming event in a woman's life.

All the women who became mothers reported undergoing a shocking and unexpected metamorphosis on the arrival of their first child. They felt both an intense emotional pull, more profound than they ever had imagined, toward their child. At the same time, they experienced more physical exhaustion and loss of moment-to-moment freedom than they had anticipated.[10] All in all, becoming a mother was cataclysmic, not just a change in role or an addition of duties, but a transformation of desire and emotional organization. All these women needed time to rearrange themselves and rework their prior sense of identity with their motherhood now an integral part.

Motherhood initiated these women into a new range of emotional expression, unexplored reservoirs of love and care, as well as uncontrollable phases of rage and frustration. They awakened to new experiences of themselves in relationship, now charged with the care of a cherished and dependent being. "I felt things I never knew I could feel," many of them said. And the task of sorting through these feelings, putting them in the perspective of their past and current lives, was a major developmental task. Women got to know themselves differently as mothers, finding wells of capability they never knew they had as well as confronting their limitations in new and painful ways. "I never knew the word guilt until I had children and had to deal with what I could or couldn't be for them," Donna said.

Mothers located their identity not "as someone's mother," but in their joy and concern for their child or children and in their particular way of mothering. Many discovered in themselves lost springs of playfulness or abandon. Child-raising was far from an experience only of caretaking and responsibility. Having their own complex lives, these mothers seemed to situate themselves *with* their children, rather than trying to live through them. I was struck by the lively, differentiated portraits women drew as they described their children, appreciating their uniqueness as they got to know who it was they were parenting.

Mothering brought a new and intense relationship into these women's lives. And the experience of being a mother occurred at two levels. On the one hand, there was the sense of responsibility and care, the often wearying and frustrating routines of looking after children. On the other was the larger sense of relationship, the meaningfulness of connection.[11] The women I interviewed emphasized both these aspects and their own struggle to bring these two sides of their experience into relation. Here is Jennifer at age 33, with three small children, articulately describing what mothering has meant to her: "Can I say that motherhood has enriched and diminished me? Sometimes I wonder who I am anymore—then, after eight hours sleep or a few hours away from the kids, I feel whole again. Three little ones are a handful. I don't read many books anymore. Our sex life is less often—but great when we have enough energy for each other or when the baby isn't fussing at 10 P.M. Constant demands, interruptions, needs of little ones. Nighttime waking. Unpredictablility. Illness. Trips to the pediatrician. Sibling rivalry—though this is improving. I feel like I'm running on reserve too often. I need my sleep as never before. I need time for my morning shower and hair washing, just to feel alert and together enough to manage through the day!"

Nevertheless, despite the tedium, intrusion, and routine, what has been most meaningful in Jennifer's life—what she has been most proud of—has been her effort "to raise secure, happy and self-directed kids." Her experience is echoed by all the other mothers—the paradox inherent in the often hateful daily tasks that are the very fabric of the soul-filling love for their children.

All these women defined their mothering in contradistinction to the mothering they had themselves experienced. All hoped not to repeat what they felt had been their own mothers' mistakes, but all had to struggle with the negative part of their mothers that they increasingly came to recognize was also a part of themselves. Most spoke with pride about how successful they felt they were in doing things differently. Most saw themselves as more accepting of feelings, more determined to maintain open communication, less critical, and less harshly punitive than their own mothers had been. These women grew up in a psychologically attuned age and all feel themselves to be more sensitive to the implications of their interactions with their children than their own mothers had been.

The identity aspect of motherhood is not the now-deprecated sense of being "just a mother," but an effort to become a particular sort of mother with carefully etched values and goals: a good mother, a loving mother, a mother who can offer unconditional love, a mother who tells her children every day that she loves them. Motherhood is as specific in its role requirements as the highest-level professional job, And each women sets these standards, which form an important new segment of her own identity, when she designs herself as a mother.

From what I learned in these interviews, this image of the mother she would like to be springs from deeply internal sources rather than social definitions. Certainly, women turn to their contemporary culture for guidelines about what good mothering means; they read the parenting manuals, talk to their pediatricians, and share dilemmas with friends who have children of the same age. But they don't simply appropriate some socially defined role called "mother." Instead, women, it seemed to me, set their ideals from their own experience, with mothering a way to give voice to desire, to their wish to experience themselves in a certain way in connection with their offspring. This meant very often struggling with the distance between their ideals of themselves as mothers and their observation of how they are in reality. Many worried over their occasional loss of control when they found themselves yelling at their children or slapping them or being impatient or unkind. For Harriet, a central focus of her struggle with herself at age 43 was to find a way to stop yelling at her 5-year-old daughter. Each day she wrestles for more patience, chastizes herself, and analyzes the roots of her anger. She desperately yearns to bring her behavior in line with her image of the mother she wishes to be. To a greater or lesser extent, each woman who has become a mother speaks of a similar quest. In this struggle, they learn about themselves, about their malleability, about what is core and basic. Having children sharpened their awareness of their own complexity, bringing them knowledge of loving parts of themselves they had never expressed as well as parts that they wish were otherwise.

The process of raising children also brought women to the edge of their own flexibility. Mothering evolves constantly as children grow and their needs change. The experience of self as mother, the identity piece of this relationship, was similarly transmuted. Identity as "mother of a toddler" feels very different from identity as "mother of an adolescent." Identity in connection with a child is highly nuanced (although as a culture and in our psychological theories, we have lumped all the phenomena of motherhood together in an undifferentiated mass). These women understand that having become a mother is indelible. They will never again not be a mother. But within that, the feeling of being the mother that they are of the children that they have has its own developmental history that washes over and through everything else that forms their identity.

WOMEN WITHOUT CHILDREN

Having heard all this about the centrality of motherhood in the identity of women who have children, I might have expected that the fate of women without children would be a tale of loss and absence. In fact, it is not at all.

Nearly half the women I interviewed did not have children, exercising the choices newly available to them to define themselves as women in other terms. I found little regret among this group. They, too, rooted their identities in connection, just not connection to their own children.

Most of the women without children did seek links to the next generation. Andrea, Emily, and Brenda all were intensely involved with their nieces and nephews, hosting them, caring for them, concerning themselves with their well-being. Gwen experienced her hundreds of students over the years as surrogate children; she made a point of maintaining contact with many of them. These women were able to fulfill their need to extend themselves into the next generation without becoming mothers. They also created in their lives the opportunity to enjoy the special kind of relationship one can only have with a child. But, in terms of identity, this clearly carried very different weight than for the mothers. These were important and valued relationships, but without the inescapable responsibility and the depth of intense suffusing love and conflict that the mothers reported.

We have been so immersed culturally in the idea that the natural course for women is to reproduce that it is difficult to find a neutral stance from which to observe the lives of the many women who choose not to do so.[12] As they spoke of their decision, they often sounded a bit defensive, as though they had to explain why they chose not to do something their culture so takes for granted. It was hard to tell if they were justifying themselves to the nameless cultural imperative (which I must have represented to them) or within the context of their own ambivalence. Probably there was a bit of both. Given pervasive cultural assumptions about women, it is a daring act to refuse to procreate, and most likely these women are frequently called on to explain and rationalize to astonished and often critical others. Carolyn Heilbrun observes that "marriage without children at its center, understood as a system of mutual support, has largely been beyond the imaginative reach of either biographers or living women."[13] Among my participants are several women who are living this plot, in Heilbrun's terms, but the larger culture remains reluctant to recognize its viability. I hope I wasn't being naive in believing these women when they said to me in effect that, yes, they knew there was a road not taken, and, yes, that road may have its pleasures that they will never know, but their own road had its rewards and they were content to pursue it.

Women chose not to have children for different reasons. Unlike the decision to have a child, which, once made and realized, is irrevocable, deciding not to have children is ongoing. The possibility for this major life change always hovers. Some made a clear choice, others adapted to a choice that seemed to befall them. A few, at age 43, are still somewhat feebly considering that they might yet conceive or adopt. The Searchers and Drifters, women for whom commitment was a more arduous task, were more likely not to have children than the Guardians and Pathmakers. (Half of the Searchers and Drifters were childless compared to just over a third of the Guardians and Pathmakers.) Some, like Andrea and Laura, took stock of their lives and their needs and decided that they did not wish to take on the responsibility of children, that their lives already contained the connections and pursuits they desired. Emily would have liked to have a child, but her husband felt that he was too old. Others were ambivalent and let nature decide. Brenda and Natalie found partners late in their thirties. When they were unable to conceive, they decided to let it be, recognizing later that the decision not to undergo fertility-enhancement procedures was itself a life-shaping choice. (Those women who really wanted to have children, despite fertility problems, managed to have them.) Nancy, who kept putting off the decision, recognized that never deciding to do it was a way of deciding not to. Sandra and Vicky were preoccupied with their own conflicts. The identity questions they were struggling with were unrelated to the issue of motherhood and they saw having a child as only making matters worse.

It is important to notice, however, that the process of deciding not to have children (or of not deciding to have them) evolved in the context of a relationship, and many of these women recognized that their choice was the product not only of individual inclination but also of the relational system of their marriage. Gwen, for example, whose first husband had fertility problems, told me that she probably would have tried harder to have a child if the marriage had been better. She was uncomfortable about her husband's abusive behavior and was uncertain of how he might be as a father. About to enter marriage again at age 43, she feels that she might have liked to have a child with the man she is about to marry (if they had met and married earlier), but their "plans for travel and for a shared life together don't include that experience." Similarly, Andrea, who had had a tubal ligation during her first marriage, wonders at age 43 if she would have made that decision if she had then been married to her second husband.

Sometimes the women who had not become mothers were wistful, sometimes they expressed a bit of regret, but mainly they believed they had made the choice that seemed best for them and felt their right to live that choice.

"I'M A DAUGHTER AND A SISTER, TOO"

Being a daughter to their parents and a sister to their siblings continues as a highly important identity component even at midlife. Here is another region of experience where the reality of women's lives is not represented well in psychological theory or cultural assumptions. We tend to depict relationships with parents as involving a struggle for independence at adolescence and then necessitating care of aging parents in midlife. But between these marker events there is a long period of adult interaction that the women I interviewed counted as significant in their identity.

Throughout her life, Betty had little emotional communication with her father. But one of her most cherished memories of the past ten years was a trip she planned for him to take him to his ancestral home in Russia. "It was a wonderful experience. I can't say enough about it. To grow up with this Iron Curtain image all your life as a child—this unknown—you just don't know anything at all about where your grandparents came from and what their life was like. Having this mental wall because you don't know where your roots are. You can't go see it or go meet the people. . . . We didn't know what we were going to experience. My cousins were there looking for us. My cousin Peter had been trying to learn English on his own, so he was there with a cousin from the other side of the family who was a nun and no one in the family knew she was a nun—did this under secrecy because of government pressure. They took us to the village in the mountains [where my grandparents were born], a village of 1,400 people. Only two cars and ten telephones in the village, outhouses, hand-dug wells, manual labor by the women. And to take my father back was just awesome for me. We both cried a lot." In taking her father to Russia, Betty experienced a closeness to him that she never had before. And she found a connection with her roots that changed her sense of her own history.

Similarly, Andrea spoke movingly of having taken her mother to the small town in France where she was born. Andrea was grateful to have shared that with her mother, to have had this time of closeness before her mother's sudden death.

All but three participants in my study still have at least one living parent. (Half have two living parents; the others have just their mothers, except for Nancy, who has just her father.) Only a few are caring for ill parents. Throughout their ascent from adolescence to midlife, most of these women have remained connected to healthy and active parents who have continued to be important forces in their lives. Most of the Drifters, as we have seen, are still making use of their parents as parents, in trying once again to locate a core of themselves. The others intertwine themselves with their parents in complex ways, preserving bonds of attachment with varying degrees of mutuality, attempting to enjoy in adult terms their connection with the people who raised them.

When I asked women to tell me about what had been most significant for them in the past ten years, many, like Betty, emphasized episodes of their continuing connection to their parents. In the years from 33 to 43, many strove to realize themselves and solidify their identity through a modified role in their families of origin, gaining acceptance as an independent adult. With pleasure, Millie noted that her parents regarded her and took her for granted as "a middle-aged lady," a triumph for her after having been "the weird one" from late adolescence through her twenties.

One of the sharpest distinctions I found in these women over the years was in their knowledge of their parents. As late adolescents, confronting the necessity of separating and individuating, they were preoccupied with coming to terms with their parents of childhood. Except for the Drifters, all were intensely concerned with their parents' approval, struggling with deep fears of being "disowned" if they were to cross the lines of what their parents could abide. The four pathways, in large part, reflected ways of dealing with the task of emotionally individuating from their childhood homes. The Guardians, in need of security, stayed psychologically close to home, while the Pathmakers wrestled for independence in the context of connection. The Searchers were caught in conflict, one foot in the past, the other in the future, afraid to let go, afraid to hold on. The Drifters had turned their back on their homes but lived with loss and emptiness. For all these women in their late adolescence, their parents represented childhood, both its comfort and its restriction, its support and its expectation. Parents were people to be clung to or disengaged from.

Through the maturing perspective of their adulthood, these women reached for greater understanding of who they are—and were—in relation to their parents and a greater understanding of their primary family in relation to the larger culture. Over time, their understanding of their families changed in concert with their understanding of themselves. And they regarded the necessity of maintaining bonds of love and involvement with their families as central to their experience of themselves. A piece of the "Who am I?" question remained rooted in the answer to "Who am I in relation to my parents?"

As they stand more firmly on their own legs and their path leads further and further away from childhood and home, most experience an intense need to share the self they have created with their parents. But, as was true in adolescence, this is not easy. It often involves struggling for communication across a wide chasm. Regina described this poignantly: "Whenever I'm with them, I always go through a period of sadness and a desire to withdraw from them because of my disappointment at the lack of emotional intimacy. When we are together, time is spent organizing meals, keeping track of the kids, talking about shopping trips and decorating, but they don't share my life where I feel I really live, and I don't share theirs either. . . . My parents always said 'whatever you want you can do,' but in terms of actually engaging with any of us around life choices, the importance of career or relationships or issues of balancing or making choices, I never remember a single conversation about any of those issues. In terms of religion, my parents have been involved in church for years, but they've never discussed what that means to them. Or I try to talk to my mother about my feelings of disappointment for my son because of the issues he will have to face, and my mother says 'He's doing just fine' and changes the subject. So I feel I've sort of flung my way away from a vacuum in many respects and tried to find ways of engaging with people on a different level and making choices in the absence of specific encouragement and support. Support in terms of giving a loan if we needed it or helping with moves. But I've had to do life decisions on my own. Yet I'm also aware that they will always be there for me—to provide what they perceive as support. So that's been an issue of tension for me in recent years—trying to reconceptualize my relationship with my family and how that feels." It rankles Regina that she cannot bring herself to tell her parents that her children were born through artificial insemination because her husband is sterile. Her close friends know, her in-laws know, but to tell them would mean to break through a long-term silence that she does not understand. Still, she was by her mother's side through her mother's recent surgery, spends holidays and birthdays with them, and dutifully calls each week to report on events.

This fundamental orientation to take care of the familial bond—and to keep wrestling with its limits and inevitable disappointments—plays itself out in different ways for different women depending on the unique family circumstances before them. Some women had invited their widowed mothers to live with or near them, which meant having to work out an adult relationship in close quarters. For Theresa and Sandra, the invitation to their mothers to live with them was itself a product of their identification with their ethnic background, a sense of "this is what you do in my culture." In their cases, managing issues of psychological distance and boundaries became a paramount challenge.

Other women, by contrast, primarily among the Pathmakers who left home early and the Searchers who explored for years before settling down, live physically distant from their parents and work to maintain bonds through phone calls, letters, visits, or shared vacations. If they have children, they enjoy (or struggle with) their parents as grandparents, working to achieve and conserve an experience of kinship and belonging.

For all the women I interviewed, disruptions in family well-being claim their attention and call them to the pursuit of repair. If someone in their family is sick or worried, they interrupt their other pursuits to agonize about an appropriate response. These women define themselves in part through their efforts to be generative toward their parents, to "be there" for them, to offer them relationship and comfort. They want, for the most part, to see themselves as "good daughters," and they anguish very often over what this entails.

Brenda, for example, strains to find a way to be helpful to her parents who recently had a hard time. "My father is a strange fellow. I guess that's where I got my being very private from. He doesn't really talk, even to my mother. The roles have changed. Whereas he was always the provider, when they ran into some financial problems, I helped them out, so I think that's kind of . . . he's very proud and I think it hurt him that he had to come for help. Now he talks to me even less."

Some women are beginning to confront the aging of their parents and preparing themselves to be caretakers. Natalie says, "I see them getting older. My mother's focus is on what she had for lunch or a golf game, and it's so boring to sit and listen to her. They're failing now and I can see them going downhill. It's very hard. They took good care of me, so I will take good care of them. My brother has a family and I don't. I can see that since I'm a girl, there will be more responsibility on me."

For many women, being a daughter-in-law has been an important part of their identity. Some mention closeness to mothers-in-law that provides some of the affection they didn't get enough of from their mothers. Many are caught up in the family conflicts of their spouses and spent a good deal of their interview describing how they have been negotiating through family battles on their spouse's side. Donna's life has often been taken up with the ongoing tension between her husband and his parents, whom he works with—and the problems of explaining to her children why "grandma and grandpa aren't talking to us" even though they live next door. Betty and Maria are involved in taking care of aging in-laws, and others anticipate this prospect in the future. They, too, see care of parents as falling to the girls—this, too, is an element of their identities.

MY MOTHER, MYSELF

For all these women, their relationship to their mothers continues as a central axis of identity definition. They embody the truth of Virginia Woolf's insightful axiom that "We think back through our mothers if we are women." Even into midlife, identity is cast against the background of their mothers.

In the consciousness of these women, mothers hover like an ever-present doppelganger in a corner of their minds, a ghost in the wings of the stage as they enact their lives. A woman's sense of herself is highlighted in counterpoint to her awareness of her mother's choices or style. "I am this way *like* my mother" or "My mother was this way, but *I* . . ." are two primary and pervasive forms of identity experience.(And these phrases recurred in just about every interview, at all ages, without my ever having to mention or allude to their mothers.) The sense of "a life as my mother" seems to have been the earliest template for the little girl's imaginings of her future. All else that occurs is revision.

The depth and complexity of this bond surpass all other connections a woman may have.[14] Women are always, in one way or another, coming to terms with their mothers, with their love for them and their disappointment in them, their admiration and their contempt, with their wish to surpass and their guilt about doing so, their longing for her approval and their wish to disavow their need for it.

In her autobiographical novel, *Fear of Fifty*, Erica Jong describes this experience: "My mother's frustrations powered both my feminism and my writing. But most of the power came out of my anger and my competition: my desire to outdo her, my hatred of her capitulation to her femaleness, my desire to be different because I feared I was much too much like her. . . . Womanhood was a trap. If I was too much like her, I'd be trapped as she was. But if I rejected her example, I'd be a traitor to her love."[15]

Many of the women in my study, especially in their twenties, saw themselves as embodying and living out their mothers' own unclaimed yearnings for worldly involvement and accomplishment, while at the same time recognizing that in the plan for their own lives they were rejecting her manifest traditional values. They may have felt that their own success was in some way "for" their mothers while having also to live with the feeling that it was in opposition to all that she stood for.

Most felt their mothers to be most intensely involved in their adult lives through shared concern about family members, particularly their children. Few women mentioned that their mothers were very interested in their work lives. Maria, for example, felt the glow of her mother's pride when her mother told her aunt that Maria's kids were doing fine. Her mother was, however, only mildly impressed when she won an award at work. ("Well, that's nice, dear. But how is Robbie's cold today?") Continued emotional connection with mothers moves along the synapses of relationships. But then, these are women whose mothers, for the most part, had little investment in the world beyond their families.

While women think through their own life patterning using the prototype of their mothers' lives, the more persistent and haunting identifications tend to be with a mother's ways of managing her emotions and her interactions with others. Growing up, these women were exquisitely attuned to their mothers' fearfulness, their flashpoints of anger, their ways of asserting their power with others, and their givingness and self-sacrifice. As adults, they compare themselves to their mothers in terms of their courage to take risks, in their forthrightness with feelings, in what they ask for—and tolerate from—their partners, in how they manage a household, in how much they lose their temper and yell at their children, in taste, in personal habits. These are the more intimate expanses of existence, the styles of reactivity and responsiveness that emanate from a core of the self, and their mothers were the people whose ways of daily being they knew best. Women remain in life-long internal conversation with their mothers about all these matters, sometimes only unconsciously, but with conscious manifestations fueling the process of discovering oneself in the context of this ever-present bond.

A woman's internal relationship with her mother, rooted in her early experience, is also central to her self-esteem. So many of the women I spoke to told me of never having felt "good enough" in their mothers' eyes and of their lifelong struggle to approve of themselves nevertheless. For some, this was the source of a sometimes compulsive need to achieve, often taking the form of a drive for perfection that they only later understood was derived from their mother's expectations. Nancy, for example, came to the realization in midlife that she was repeating with her husband the need to earn approval from a critical person. It was a silent triumph of her adulthood when "I could tell myself I don't have to work all weekend to make the house look spiffy. You know, who cares?"

Beyond this inner conversation about self-worth that women maintain with their mothers, women remain in ongoing outward affiliation with them. At age 33, half of my participants listed their mother as the person they felt closest or second closest to among all the people in their lives. By the time they reached age 43, mother had been surpassed in importance by their spouse and sometimes their children on the list of "people you feel closest to," but she still appeared most often in second or third position. The "separation" from mothers propounded by psychological theory is a highly relative matter for most women who, in reality, stay intensely connected.[16] Several of these women have mothers who have become increasingly psychologically disturbed as they have aged, developing depression or obsessive-compulsive disorders, and this has drawn them into worry and care but has not, in most instances, quelled their need to coax their mothers into continuing to be emotionally available.

While some women may report being estranged or emotionally distant from their fathers, all continue to engage fervently, even in the wake of conflict, with their mothers. A woman remains tempted to bring new self-awareness or subtle changes in perception or choice to her mother for her validation. Women, even in midlife, are absorbed in the project of correcting their mothers' perceptions of them, attempting to bring the relationship with their mothers in line with who they have become.[17] The earliest self emerges in the encompassing shell of a mother's embrace, and so it continues forever after. The intricacy of a woman's connection to her mother is so profound and far-reaching that I have come to the conclusion that one can learn more about who a woman "is" by knowing about her relationship to her mother than any other single aspect of her life. In any case, all else will flow from this source. Whatever a woman is, in a deep psychological stratum of her being, either pays homage to or disavows her mother.

FATHERS

Few women maintain emotionally intense relationships with fathers that approach their level of involvement with their mothers. Most have warm and affectionate relationships with their fathers, but few list them as someone they feel "very close" to or describe them as someone with whom they make efforts to share themselves deeply. Some women, particularly those in troubled relationships with their mothers, mentioned valued, loving connections to their fathers whose company they enjoy and whose support they cherish. These women were more likely to have clearly articulated relationships with their fathers, ones not mediated by the overshadowing presence of their mothers. Clara, who has largely given up on having a good relationship with her "difficult" mother, cherishes her father for the love and closeness he has always offered her and tries to repay him with her concern and involvement in his interests. Overall among these women, however, relationships with fathers tend to be simpler bonds, much less wrenching and tumultuous, much less emotionally piercing than connections to mothers.

Fathers seemed to have had a more important role in these women's identity in their adolescence. For many, fathers were the authorities in the home, the makers of the rules. Their adolescent struggle was to negotiate their independence from a father's control or to maintain his good opinion while making their own choices. Once this battle was past, the involvement with fathers seemed to diminish. Throughout their twenties and thirties, his influence dims and he seems to be subsumed into their mothers as part of "my parents." But Debbie, for one, never gave up on this struggle and has returned to her hometown in hopes of finally settling her lifelong bitter accounting with her father.

Many women at midlife report that they have begun to establish a relationship "as adults" with their fathers, venturing to have real conversations or share parts of themselves with their fathers that they never had before. For some women, growing into their forties has brought them to a place where they can try to know their fathers as people rather than distant and mysterious authorities. Betty, for example, regards the trip she took with her father—and crying together with him—as an indelibly important moment in her life.

Women who grew up with adoring fathers seemed to have higher self-esteem; this led them to work through identity issues with more confidence. The Drifters, most of whose fathers were critical and disapproving, had a harder time. Having their fathers' support remained important to all these women, and it seemed to be from fathers that they felt more investment in their work efforts. Natalie's father reminds her of her writing aspirations by pointing out that if she is going to write that novel before he dies, she'd better get at it.

SIBLINGS

Sisters and brothers may create a relational network that contains and supports identity, but this is atypical. None of the women I interviewed has erected in their adult lives anything resembling the extended family groups in which many of them grew up. For many participants, the family life of their childhoods encompassed aunts, uncles, cousins, and grandparents, all living close together. Many had three or more siblings. "Family" for them was a kind of community tribe of belongingness that they experienced, in most cases, both as loving and confining. The world has changed since then, and none of them has recreated such a family-defined universe. Most live geographically distant from most or all of their siblings, and, although they may try to maintain kinship connection through visits and shared vacations, none offers a "family compound" to their own children. This change has meant having to recast themselves in different terms of belongingness, rooting connections to others in different phrasing.

The greater openness of society and availability of choice has meant that sibling groups have often taken quite different paths. Some have brothers and sisters whom they feel are enough like them to have a deep interconnection based on mutuality—Laura's sister, for example, has been her best friend all her life. Some of the women I interviewed have developed real friendship with their brothers and sisters as adults and maintain bonded and meaningful, though usually infrequent, ties. Clara grew intensely close to her younger brother after his daughter's death—an event that pulled all the siblings into closer touch. Natalie feels close to her brother, believes she can really talk to him or could turn to him if she had a problem, but he is preoccupied with his own family and seems to have little time for her.

Those who have formed an adult identity that is very different from what they grew up with feel themselves often at a great distance from their siblings. Regina, for example, as a college professor, is the only one of the children in her family to have gone to college. "I don't think the members of my family process life the way I do," she says, "especially my sister who tends to be flighty and exuberant, and I doubt she has the same questions and concerns that I do. I have an older brother who still lives with my parents and he keeps very much to himself." Once her children were born, she found more to share with her sister who had herself raised four children.

Several of the women find themselves to have become the "successful" one in terms of stability and continuity. Betty and Maria both have siblings who have had a hard time making it in life and have endured a variety of problems. And they feel called on to help and advise.

Betty's three younger sisters have all experienced much turbulence in their lives. Her next younger sister is divorced, grossly overweight, and battling a severe depression. Betty often invites her nephew to live with them during summers and vacations to give her sister a break and provide something pleasant for him. Her next sister she describes as "mean and demanding" and in the process of endangering her third marriage. Her youngest sister, she says, is "a horrible mess" and Betty is not sure how to be of help to her.

Maria's brother has had massive financial problems and Maria worries that her parents' continuing to bail him out will leave them financially stranded in the future. There are always crises with him. Sometimes she feels that she is the only one who can talk to him, and she struggles with how to be of use. For these women, as for others, shared worry about a sibling becomes a focus of continuing family connection.

Some women have become close to sisters of their spouses and grow to identify themselves in a deep way as part of their husband's kinship sphere as well. Most, however, more or less mechanically and more or less affectionately, go through the motions of attachment with siblings whose lives have been patterned quite differently from their own, but who they continue to rely on to "be there" (and for whom they expect to "be there") in case of crisis or need.

Andrea, since her parents have both died, tried to stay in connection to her brother even though he is very different from her. He has been successful, but in a very traditional way, and finds it hard to understand her divorce, her career, and her not having children. Still, they have learned to tolerate each other better over the years and she is beginning to enjoy his children. He, in turn, takes care of her dog when they travel. So she has found a form of interdependence that makes them feel close, despite their divergence in values and lifestyle. The sense of kinship persists as an important anchor even if is not present as an everyday emotional reality.

Tragic events in their lives or their siblings' lives have served to draw them closer. Having children, the presence of the next generation, also serves to gather siblings into greater association. For many, an interdependency evolves among siblings that is based on attachment and shared history, but often does not involve mutual understanding or companionship. Still, being a sister remains an ever-reworked part of adult identity.

FRIENDSHIP

Friends are a source from which identity possibilities spring; they also provide an audience for the woman who wants to "try on" different ways of being. Friendship has most impact on identity when women are in the process of defining or revising themselves. Women need their friends in order to explore themselves, to envision who they might be. (Women may be who they "are" with men, but they "try out" who they might be with other women—at least, this is how it seems to me.) Friends are charged with being a sounding board and helping to painstakingly examine all the nuances of a problem or decision. And friends are there to compare and contrast the self: How are you? How am I? Within the bonds of friendship, women may achieve insight into themselves and discover courage to make changes. Together they may create solutions to problems that seemed intractable. They come away with another point of view from someone they trust to care about them.

Once launched on a path, women have less need of and less time for friendship. Enveloped in the tasks and primary relationships of their lives, women rely on friends more for companionship and recreation, and this is, in general, low on the list of priorities.

In college, friends seemed to constitute "the world." Locating themselves as funny, brave, wild, shy, open, snobbish, prudish, or honest—all this took place in the community of friendship. It was through friends that these women discovered who else was "out there," which, in turn, made it possible to know better who was "in here." Enjoying and enlarging themselves through the association with different types of people, people of different backgrounds and ways of thinking, finding themselves in those they could feel similar to, and distinguishing their own uniqueness in contrast to those who they could disparage or reject—these were the surfaces against which women honed and polished their identity. But this process begins to taper off after college and into adulthood. By the time they are in midlife, women tend to seek constancy and validation instead of stimulation and challenge, and therefore maintain stable, close, long-term friendships rather than welcome new connections. Where friends represented possibility for change and growth in the college years, in midlife, they were asked more to provide support and companionship.

In the realm of friendship, many of these women were also pioneers. Many spoke of having grown up in homes where their mother's friends were her sisters or sisters-in-law. Having real friendships from outside of the family was a novel—and sometimes radical—idea within the subcultures they came from. Theresa, for example, takes pride in having a wide circle of relationships, so much in contrast to the fear of strangers that dominated her family. Brenda, who counts her cousins among her closest friends, thinks of herself as having "branched out a little over my mother's age group where her friends are her sisters."

As women grow, they become more exacting in their requirements of friendship and more clearly delineate superficial friends from emotional, intimate, enduring ones. Although many say they have many acquaintances, most regard only two or three people as "friends." As Regina put it, "I place a much greater emphasis on emotional intimacy than I did in previous years. In adolescence and early adulthood, I had a much wider circle of friends than I do now. Yet the relationships I do develop tend to be enduring, meaningful ones." Some have maintained long-term friendships, from college or before, people whom they feel they have known and have known them for a long time, and they are therefore witnesses to each other's growth. These friends, although they often live far away, pick up the relationship as soon as they meet again and usually share fully with each other, keeping track of what they have become, what they have learned about life. In addition, these are friends my participants feel they could call on for help in a crisis, that they, like family members, would "be there." Other women develop friendships out of a common work situation, where daily struggles can be shared and explored. Still other women feel that they have retreated from friendship, some out of disappointment and a sense of betrayal, some out of lack of time, some because intimacy with sisters or sisters-in-law takes the place of closeness to friends. There is no common pattern, except that all the women I have interviewed say that friendship has been very important to them and that friendships are harder to develop as one grows older.[18] As women become more centered in family life, they often reflect nostalgically on time spent with friends, wishing they could make space for it but, with a sigh, let it lapse into the realm of what is postponed for later. "Maybe as my children grow up I'll have more time to foster deeper friendships. I feel like I see friends as I'm flying from one thing to another," said Millie. Some women make a serious effort to keep these connections alive, planning regular get-togethers with friends from distant states or scheduled lunches with those nearby. This requires effort and is seldom the spontaneous togetherness they had known in earlier days. Harriet had recently organized a "pajama party" for several of her close friends from work. "It was fun, but I miss having a best friend," Harriet said.

For Clara, crisis in friendship led to a rethinking of her values and identity—of how she wanted to live her life. The past few years had been overshadowed by living through the dying of her closest friend and trying to be consoling to her friend's 8-year-old daughter. And this worry and involvement occurred just as Clara was beginning to work in the rare books collection of the Yale Library, and was trying to balance her increased professional investment with the needs of her two young children. Clara took her friend to her chemotherapy, visited her, brought her meals, and was with her most of the week before she died. "It just seemed like the sort of thing you'd do for a good friend," Clara said. "One of the things that troubles me about the way the world has evolved is that women have so little time anymore to give to their friends and I have these moments of having nostalgia for the fifties when women had time. I can't even think of anyone to put down as an emergency backup person on my children's school cards. I was lucky at the time to have a job that was flexible. I'm a fiercely loyal person and it's very hard for me not to be there if my friends need me." And Clara has decided that she does not want to allow her work and family commitments to preclude being the kind of friend she wants to be.

Women who are without partners are more likely to turn to friends for companionship, and this often involves complex cycles in relationships with long-term friends. Gwen charts her life parallel to the life course of her closest friend, Edna. Raised on a farm, she looked to Edna, who grew up in the city, to expose her to "cultural things." "It was a very important part of my life," Gwen said of her friendship with Edna, "but we have had a very cyclical relationship. When I got married and she wasn't, we kind of strayed and then when we both were married, we came back together. Then she got divorced and we kind of separated, didn't have things in common, then when I was divorced we did a lot together. But now that I'm engaged I don't see her as much."

Women in a period of actively redefining their identity are most likely to turn to friends for input, feedback, response, and support. Marlene, when her first marriage was in tatters and she was full of dread and uncertainty about her future, turned to a group of women in a women's collective who supported her in mapping a plan for herself. Donna, a Drifter now in the process of trying to anchor herself, is similarly looking to other women to help her reorganize, to show her a way. She speaks of her search for the "wise woman" who could guide her toward her "feminine energy" and help her learn to nurture herself. Having renewed her attention to who she is, in quest of who she would like to be, she relies on friends for "seeing how I interact, seeing the effects of things I might say to people and really wondering why somebody said something and trying to receive what has been said and feeling it enough to respond and find a response, really trying to understand a lot about a person's intentions and their true actions, . . . finding a space to express myself." Donna felt drawn toward women who seemed to know how "to take care of themselves." From them, she hoped to learn how to take care of her own needs. She appreciated her new close friendships with women for the opportunity to explore "the differences in the way women have actualized who they are" and to "deeply look at things from all perspectives." Donna was turning to friendship, much as people did in adolescence, to help define herself.

Friends may also be identity-transforming in offering a new context for a woman to think through her life. Women often sharpen their boundaries against the experiences of their friends and may come to regard themselves in a new way. It was through a deeply intimate conversation with an old friend that Alice began to rethink her childhood and grasp the dysfunctional nature of her family. Similarly, Andrea came to the decision to divorce her first husband after vicariously going through the divorce process with a friend.

But these women were somewhat the exception in using the resources of other women in the quest for self-definition. The feminist ideal of women banding together to raise their consciousness of their roles as women and promote their shared interests has largely bypassed most of the women I studied. I was struck by how narrowly constituted most of these women's worlds are at midlife, how few doors are open for the entry of new ideas or alternate points of view. Most women choose friends who share their understanding of life rather than promise to radicalize or undermine it. Their friends support their lives as they have constructed them. In mirroring their lives, their friends make their identities more stable. At the same time, this relative isolation in small friendship networks leaves women substantially alone in tending their paths and dealing with obstacles along the way. Few see their difficulties with child care and social support for working mothers, with work discrimination or bureaucratic, hierarchical organization in larger social (or gendered) terms. They take each difficulty as their own individual problem, turning largely to their families or close (like-minded) friends for support, but shrinking from acting toward resolutions in shared terms—by joining larger communities or politically oriented groups to work for change.

SPIRITUALITY

Spirituality is another form of identity that is grounded in connection, a sense of embeddedness, larger and more ethereal perhaps, but a tie to some force greater than the self. This is a realm of experience that is rarely represented in psychological theories of development but forms for many a central core of growth. The movement from childhood's concrete forms of religiosity to adult spirituality is a profound process of renewed understanding of oneself in relation to others and to finding meaning for one's life. This forms an odyssey for some women that links them to purposefulness and an enriched context for the events of their lives. More than half the women I have interviewed define themselves in an important spiritual way. For some, like Fern and Millie, all their actions seem to emanate from some higher power. They feel "called" to be what they are. Some take up religious commitment as a form of community, joining with others in shared ritual, maintaining tradition, feeling an increased sense of belonging. Some define their spirituality in individualistic terms, working out their relationship to nature, to ethics, to higher forces in existential and universal terms, thereby articulating their identity as a person in the larger scheme of things. Spirituality serves as ideology, a moral force that grounds them and helps them define what is "good." For many of these women, this is an even more consuming quest than occupational self-definition.

In *Middlemarch,* George Eliot explores the growth of identity in her characters through the unfolding of their spiritual development. She says, "By desiring what is perfectly good, even when we don't quite know what it is and cannot do what we would, we are part of the divine power against evil."[19] This seems to give voice to what many of the more spiritually oriented women tried to tell me about their own effort to find themselves in relation to their desire for the good. The search to know what good is and the quest for the personal means to implement it, often in what Eliot later terms "unhistoric acts"—this, too is central to a woman's identity.

IDENTITY AND CONNECTION

Erikson says that identity is based in occupation and ideology, but this does not hold true for women unless we redefine both occupation and ideology to include connection. For women, identity is based in connection to others. The creative expression of the self leaves its mark on others, while the self absorbs the imprint of others in return. Occupational commitment, as we have seen, is itself most meaningful to the extent that it makes a woman feel connected with others. Similarly, women phrase ideology in interpersonal, interconnected terms.

By midlife, most women have built structures for their lives and are enlarging on what they have fashioned. The expression of identity consists of "being there" for the people they have made commitments to, either at home or at work. The deepest sense of identity is located in these ties to others who need them. This is not self-sacrifice. This is articulation of the self in relation to others, self-actualization in relationships. The self knits together all the threads of connection, creating from them a new whole. To question what is self and what is other asks that a woman untangle what she has woven together as though this self, this whole, were reducible to the sum of its parts. Women feel their own feelings and know their own experience against the counterpoint of the feelings and experience of those they love. A statement of identity that was true to what these women were trying to tell me would sound something like this: "I am who I am for and with all the people I have consecrated myself to and all these people being there, responding to me and renewing me even as they take what I give allow me a self to live in when I am alone." Women exist in process, in a dynamic flow of interaction. They cannot be defined in terms of any role or label: mother, doctor, teacher, wife; whatever the description, it reduces and names but does not reflect the core of a woman's identity. The vitality and creativity of identity derive from and are expressed in the flow of connection.

These connections, of course, are always imperfect and always changing. Clashes and misunderstanding, ruptures in intimacy and in family ties, changes in one's own and others' needs all unsettle a woman's understanding of her place with others and create new challenges of self-definition. Those who have lived through serious disruptions of close relationships are those who have most sharply defined their edges and their needs. By working through change or loss in relationship, these women achieve new self-understanding that they invest in new, richer, and more gratifying connections. The potholes and pain of relationships do seem to be, in the end, identity enhancing. Much of life becomes an epic of trying to more deeply understand one's interactions, and this is often the central theme underlying revisions in identity.

All theory, dear friend, is grey, but the golden tree of actual life springs ever green.

Goethe, Faust

10 REVISION

"Proportion is the final secret, [but] to espouse it at the outset is to ensure sterility," E. M. Forster says, in *Howards End.* The course of women's lives is a dialectic between extremes, between risk and rigidity, adventure and security, coming to rest in a sense of balance. There is no single trajectory of women's lives. Women rebalance and reshape themselves, striving for harmony of the parts, responding to the exigencies of living in society, and creating a whole where the pieces best fit.

The most visible of the revisions that women make as they mature are shifts in their expression of competence and connection. Changes in jobs, ambition, projects, partners, friendship, the advent and challenges of children—all these appear on the surface of the life tableau. They both reflect and herald rearrangements in the deeper strata of the self, the core, where identity resides. Over time, the women I have considered here have both changed and stayed the same. Some elements of their identities have remained constant, others have undergone steady metamorphosis, while others are fresh and brand new.[1]

Beyond what is most visible, identity reflects the inner organization of the parts of the self, where unconscious yearnings are joined to conscious realization and conflicting desires and experiences are recognized and held in some tolerable equilibrium. But this integration, this core, will only hold when a woman can assume the authority of this self she has authored in an interpersonal world that responds to her understanding of who she is by taking her to be that person she feels herself to be.

Making all these parts function in tandem—inner organization, authority, self-expression, and context—is the work of revision. But I don't think there is a fixed sequence here. I don't believe that there are definable "stages." Each woman fits these pieces in place in a sequence and pattern different from one another. Each learns different things at different times. Some women take up their competence first, then later focus more on their connection to others. Others need to feel that their connections are well established before exploring the limits of what they can *do* in the world. Still others attempt to work on both simultaneously. The lessons of life that one woman masters in her twenties become clear to another only in her forties. For some women, major losses or disappointments usher in a period of conscious efforts at revision. For others, arriving where they intended to go sparks a reenvisioning of identity for the next phase of life.

THE PULSE OF REVISION IN EACH PATHWAY

Women who began the search for identity passionately in their late adolescence, throwing off the mantle of who they were and seeking to remake themselves, spent their early and middle adulthood trying to anchor themselves. They were in search of constancy and purposefulness from which they could fashion an enduring sense of meaning. The odyssey of these women—the Drifters and some Searchers—was often filled with daring and trials as they experienced one mode of being after another, often finding themselves yet more lost and confused. More open to experience in their adolescence than the women of the other groups, they lived close to the danger of being overwhelmed by their own inner contradictions and mercurial feelings. They were later than others in taking seriously the task of structuring themselves. To tell the tale of their development, we would speak in terms of "settling down," sometimes "settling for," but the denouement of the plot involves coming to rest on decisions that feel relatively firm, and on a life plan that bounds and orders their lives. Their quest from late adolescence to midlife is for more control of themselves and their enterprises. Their growth is toward modulating their impulses, reining themselves in, and keeping the parts of themselves in balance rather than swinging from one to the other.

Those who were Guardians in college, on the other hand, move as they age toward greater courage and less control. They begin at the opposite pole, lashed to security and safety. Tightly organized in adolescence, their firm beliefs and clear goals came at the cost of silencing parts of themselves, keeping a firm hold on impulse and emotion. As they grew—and grew more certain of themselves—they opened themselves, gradually, to experience, to their own feelings, to closed-off aspects of themselves, as well as to greater awareness of possibility in their world. Theirs is a narrative of unfolding, loosening the tight bindings of the self, achieving proportion by allowing themselves to tolerate conflict and pain. Little by little, they part from their perfectionism and learn to live with their limitations and with what they cannot command.

The Pathmakers, some of whom had a long moment of crisis before they finished their college years, continue to oscillate between questioning and certainty but, having found balance earlier, their pendulums traverse a narrower span from age 21 to 43. Having discovered their own center early on, they tend to stay moored near it, resisting the sterility Forster warns against by remaining aware of choice and making incremental changes in themselves and their lives. The Searchers, as we have seen, either become in personality style and orientation to life more like Guardians or Pathmakers; in some instances, they get crippled by inner turmoil and their growth in identity is (however temporarily) derailed.

WHAT DOES A WOMAN WANT?

Toward the end of his life, Freud acknowledged that for him the great unanswered question was What is it that a woman wants? This has become a famous question, used very often by feminists to discredit him, asked by men frequently to join their own perplexity to that of a wise man. Women often regard it with amusement, pleased perhaps to feel mysterious and opaque, but most woman recognize the absurdity of trying to answer a question phrased this way.

In aggregating all women within one question, Freud could not see their enormous diversity. Each woman wants differently. But it is never easy for the individual woman herself to decipher clearly her own desire. The most fundamental quest of a woman's life is to decide what *she* wants for herself and to find a way to name and phrase that desire in terms that orient her to planning and action. In the past twenty-five years, we have, as a Western culture, awakened to increasing recognition of women's oppression and constriction by a society that was organized to direct and manage women's desire. How could anyone know what a woman wanted when her social world, from her earliest days, told her what she must do and must be? Until quite recently, women seemed able only to think in terms of what they "should want." But women born at mid-century and after came of age in a climate of choice and possibility. For the first time, the question of what a woman wants could be asked in an authentic way. At least in social terms, women had gained sovereignty over themselves.

Women's lives are no longer monolithic. As we have seen, among these thirty very homogeneous women—homogeneous in the sense that they are all white and educated—there are very different lives. Only some are mothers. Most are heterosexual and married, but not all. Most work, but only some have personally meaningful careers. Even with this small group of similar women, I can generalize only at great peril. These are women who have made use of their option to choose and have followed widely divergent paths.[2]

All women want a sense of competence and a sense of connection—that is one generalization I can make with some confidence. But these are abstract concepts, and women seek them concretely in differing modes and in different places. How to go about achieving them is often the enigma. Choice is a slippery process, as is self-knowledge. To "know what one wants for oneself" is not an easy matter and is often a lifelong quest. Freedom is liberating, but it can also be terrifying.

Our current construction of women, within both the media and feminist theory, assumes that women know what they want, but are kept from it by an oppressive society. What we don't depict is the anguish of trying to know desire, the false starts, the endless discussions with oneself about what might be right for us, about what parts of ourselves we most want to express. And all this in an ever-changing context in which the social world may or may not offer the objects of our desires.

In this study, we have seen women struggle to translate very inchoate longings—to "be someone," to "do something"—into realizable goals. And they have done this more or less on their own terms. Guardians begin with certainty, adopting in large part the dreams and values transmitted by their families or carrying unchallenged childhood fantasies into adult ideals. They choose with the weight of tradition propelling and buttressing them. Pathmakers and many Searchers, by contrast, wrestle through options and then make their choice, and they decide always with less conviction than the Guardians. Searchers (most of them) choose only after an extended period of self-examination and experimentation, and remain most aware of internal conflict and struggle, of desire never fully satisfied. Drifters are at pains to know their own desire among the shifting impulses and dreams of the moment. They struggle to find themselves within their own volatility, but are vulnerable to being appropriated by someone else's design.

What does it mean to decide on one's own terms? How can one be sure that the terms are one's own when we are always, to a greater or lesser degree, the product of our own individual histories? In part because we construct lives—our own and others—within the framework of a culture that values individualism and daring above social embeddedness and custom, we find it easier to laud those who take their stand against what has always been expected of them.

Dorothea, in *Middlemarch,* is a more sympathetic character than her sister Celia precisely because, within the confines of the limited choice available to her, she overrides what has been charted for her and chooses, however foolishly, to follow her own dreams. Celia, by contrast, eagerly accepts the readymade life that Dorothea spurns, wondering at her sister's stubbornness and oddity. Like Celia, the Guardians prized their adaptation to their heritage, delighting in the rituals that were passed down to them, pitying those who lost their way in the quagmire of possibility. Yet, in midlife, once they become more aware of having questioned so little and set about rethinking themselves, we are likely to applaud their insight and to feel that they are on the path to a truer identity.

The process of wanting among the Searchers and the Drifters has opposite pitfalls. For them, desire is often self-generated but short-lived. What feels like conviction often shows itself in a short time to be passing infatuation. Many experience an intoxicating hopeful excitement that may conceal a poorly conceived purpose. At any given moment, they may appear to "know what they want," but the certainty is transitory and soon transposes itself into yet another impulsive plan.

Women are often at pains to clearly name their own desire. There are so many self-deceptions attendant to the process of wanting. As we have seen, revision of the self is most often revision of desire, the recognition that what one seemed to want at an earlier stage of life was a false desire, a wish that felt at the time like it was one's own, but now seems to have belonged to someone else. Or what seemed like mission at an earlier phase of life is later revealed to be caprice. Women themselves are often not sure if their choices are their own—whether they have "fallen into" a way of being or fully and consciously chosen to do so. As life progresses, they may see that what seemed like a choice at the time was in fact determined by fear, passivity, impulsivity, unconscious wishes, or external pressure. Sometimes, the attainment of desire only gives rise to a new, more compelling longing. Recognition of desire is what impels a woman outward into the world. The course of revision for women, then, is learning, as we grow, more about the nature of our own desiring and more firmly grasping the reins.

THE MANY SELVES WITHIN IDENTITY

The process of wanting and desiring is further complicated by the the fact that people are composed of many discrete "selves." Women have multiple layers to their nature, and the solution to the riddle of identity formation is to include as many strands as possible.[3] The earliest identity choices often favor certain parts of the self and relegate others to the shadows. As women grow, they struggle to make space for these disused or disavowed parts of the self, widening the expanse of identity to encompass what was left behind. Many women, for example, after spending their twenties and thirties learning to adapt to work roles, to organizations in which they are employed, and to the demands of motherhood or marriage, find that they have shelved their creativity or their playfulness; refinding these becomes a quest of their forties. Others forfeit their spirituality in their passionate effort at worldly success, only to reawaken in this need later on.

Some women, in search of themselves, leave behind their heritage and the part of themselves that belonged to it, only to rediscover their roots at midlife. Marlene, for example, at adolescence, wanted nothing more than to be different from her immigrant, Holocaust-survivor parents. By age 33, although grieving their deaths, she was enjoying being fully a member of late twentieth-century America, free of the painful past. But by age 43, she had developed a fervent interest in the Holocaust, reclaiming her birth in this terrible phase of history, reconnecting with previously estranged relatives, and pulling this previously hidden and shame-filled part of herself into a prominent position in her evolving identity.[4]

Although new ideas, new skills, new relationships, and new meaning-systems make their way into identity as it grows from adolescence to midlife, some of the most important revisions derive from refinding what was there all along. Like slowly turning kaleidoscopes, the shifts in a woman's identity involve rearrangement of pieces, now accenting one aspect and muting another, now altering the arrangement once more. This flexibility and capacity to improvise are a source of both strength and surprise in the way in which women construct themselves.[5]

This capacity for realigning the emphases of life also makes it possible for women to move among their multiple roles, roles that highlight competence and those that highlight connection, both contemporaneously and at different times in their lives. For many women who are mothers, for example, devotion to children feels paramount when their children are small, but they keep their investment in their careers alive, recognizing that the structure of priorities of interest and purpose may shift.[6] Others begin to take their need for leisure and their avocational interests more seriously and look for time to develop in these areas. The dramatic tension in a woman's life occurs among these segments of self as she strives to keep them in balance. No wonder women so often feel like "multiple personalities."

Needs change as they develop over the life course, but not necessarily in predictable or generalizable ways. What offers exercise for faculties at one stage of life may become routine and lifeless at another, as different aspects of the self emerge to speak their part in desire. Virginia Woolf's image of Shakespeare's sister, of woman as artist, takes us only so far in understanding the lives of less unusual women. Most of us are artists only in small ways. Most women, those without genius or obsession, are less single-minded and lead multifaceted lives, doing our deeds unhistorically and often unheeded, making our mark more privately and individually.

The answer to the question of "What does a women want?" is "Not one thing." The search for a solitary purpose, except in cases of genius and rare gifts, is illusory. Does society expect women to have just one desire? The women of my study who seemed most content were those who were realizing themselves in multiple ways, who had work and relationships and interests and involvements, who recognized differing aspects of themselves at different times, and who resisted definition into unitary categories and found ways to express their own diversity.[7]

INTERNAL REVISION

Regina, at age 43, told me the following dream: "I dream that I'm in a big house where I've lived for quite some time. And all of a sudden I learn that in the center of the house—it's almost like between floors—there is a whole suite of rooms that I never knew was there—it's hidden from sight and the only way that you can have access to this suite of rooms is through a cobwebbed spidery staircase that's narrow and dark, but I go up through the staircase—or maybe it's going down, I don't know—and I find myself in this suite with huge rooms. Everything is suffused with this golden light and my reaction to all of this is delight. I think 'There's room for everyone here' and I never knew it was here. I've thought about that dream a lot lately. I don't yet know what these rooms are going to be like to actually live in them, but I know that they are there."

For me, this dream captures the essence of the process of revision, as I have understood it, in women's lives. Revision is like discovering rooms that have always been there, hidden inside, accessible through the previously darkened and unused regions of the self—but taking care to make room for everyone who matters.

Work and family commitments are the most visible parts of a woman's identity. This is the way we, as a culture, identify someone. Inevitably, as I write about these women's identities, I fall into the culturally determined habit of describing women in terms of what they do for a living and whether they are married or have children. But the most profound revisions of identity for the women I have studied are not visible at all. They are internal—the house with hidden rooms in the metaphor of the dream. The most important revisions involve making meaning and thinking about the self in new ways, effecting fundamental transformations in experiencing life. Women describe these moments of change as "awakenings," knowing in a new way what they have in some ways known all along.[8]

As Donna reflected on the unfolding of her life from age 43, dividing her life into chapters, she noted, "From chapter to chapter, there is an increasing consciousness." This seemed to me true of all the women I interviewed. Going through the process of thinking aloud about their lives, most women found themselves lacking the words to tell me about the deepest sense of their revision, but all spoke in one way or another about "increasing consciousness."

Clara, struggling for words that reflect on her experience of life, said, "[These experiences] have opened a window into what other people feel. All these experiences just make you *understand so much more.*" Understanding so much more, opening up more, having more confidence—these are the ineffable revisions these women tried to describe to me. The memorable turnings of their lives are ones that allowed them to look upon the world with expanding vision and to know better their own connection to it. For some women, this involved learning about the compromises and inevitabilities of life and finding a place within that—"an angle of repose" in Wallace Stegner's phrase. For many, as we saw, this revolved around coming to terms with disappointments in the work world, the recognition that one could not do all one wished, or that work itself was often dull or unrewarding. Many had to revise their goals and dreams as they better understood what was possible to accomplish, and some saw possibilities of effectiveness that they hadn't known were there. For others, a shift in or loss of an important relationship was a catalyst for revisiting their idea of themselves. Sometimes gaining a new relationship, as in motherhood, was the force that turned the kaleidoscope.

For some, the growth of psychological awareness led them to regard more seriously the importance of their own emotional needs. Having learned very often in childhood that feelings were to be put aside, controlled, or ignored, or that pleasing others took precedence over consideration of one's own desires, many women came to greater appreciation of the parts of themselves contained in their emotional responses to life. Although it arrived at different times to different women, this crisis of authenticity was an important part of identity revision. They grew to embrace their anger as well as their tenderness, their guilt, their sadness, their pain, and their joy. As Andrea tried to summarize the essence of her sense of revision, "I have grown to be more aware of myself and my feelings than ever before." (And here again, language is too flimsy to fully contain the experience.)

For other women, the increase in consciousness was more woven into their understanding of relationships. Many spoke of their quest to know better what love is, their effort to know if the feeling they had for their husbands, for example, was "really love" as it seems to be depicted by the culture. Some were aware of passionate longings that went unfulfilled, desire that they let themselves know about, but kept from acting on in order not to dislodge or jeopardize other commitments they treasured. Others spoke of growing into a greater understanding of motherhood, both its rewards and its limitations—all they discovered they could feel and the perfection they could not embody.

Most of these women, irrespective of group, believed that, as they aged, they could understand better their own life course and this felt like a central and valued piece of their identity revision. Many had to gain years of distance from their childhood to realize how it had shaped them. For some, this understanding involved becoming critical of how their parents raised them and seeing themselves as mistreated or oppressed in some way. Although this, in part, reflects the recent society-wide rush to claim victimization as well as cultural pseudopsychologizing about dysfunctional families, I think it also represented important rethinking for many of these women. In a deeper way, growing into a less idealized view of their families gave both Guardians and Drifters something substantial against which to define a carefully etched identity. In order to declare "I am," one must simultaneously state "I am *not that.*" Thus, Fern, once she was able to see herself as enslaved to a demanding mother, earned herself the freedom to choose as she wished. And Alice, coming to recognize herself as having grown up in a family where emotions were outlawed, set herself a course to reclaim her right to feel. The dialectic of identity requires such rethinking, sharpening the self against what is opposed to self, and this reknowing of the past is a major force in these women's revision.

The tide of criticism of their early life also allowed many of these women to claim the energy of anger. Behind what had seemed to be an idealization of the past was often a fount of dammed-up rage that, once released, could be converted into animation to make changes in the present. Thus, insight was not a passive knowing, but an enlivening vision, one in which the woman was able to resist and refuse what she had come to see had been imposed on her. Even the more disorganized and less certain women spoke of greater understanding of their early lives, and their mission to make a self that is not crippled by whatever the noxious conditions were. The image of the "inner child" was appealing to some as a way of reclaiming what felt authentic and unsullied, bringing forward an innocence that had not bent to their family's malforming influence.

On the other hand, insight also involved new understanding and forgiveness of their families of origin. Many of the women I spoke to mentioned that they were now at an age where they could remember their mother at the same age. This seems to be a critical moment in a woman's life. In fantasy, they could be a peer to her and, in some ways, imagine themselves mothers of themselves. Suddenly, their own mothers began to make new sense to them. They started to see their mothers as women in their own right instead of idealized embodied spirits of perfection or vilified images of imperfection. They seemed to conceptualize in a way newly possible the essential humanity and private subjectivity of their own mothers—"a woman just like me." Psychoanalysis has shown us the way that we preserve throughout life our infantile attachment to superhuman parental figures. An important challenge of adulthood, however, is learning to know these superbeings as real people. This doesn't supplant the inner longing for the perfect parent, but it does promote insight and adult connection to parents.

This greater knowledge of parents as "fellow adults" also allowed these women some emotional distance from their unprocessed childhood anger. Clara, for example, said that she was finally able to understand that her mother's unhappiness was not because she, Clara, was unlovable. In these instances, the decrease of anger was freeing. No longer bound to an inner lump of pain formed out of the sense of their mothers' earlier disapproval of them, these women were able to liberate their own consciousness, to embrace their mothers in forbearance and understanding, and claim their adult right to regulate their self-esteem on their own terms.

Insights such as these are the result of tortuous processes of self-analysis, discussions with friends, and grappling for understanding.[9] Because they are elusive, such insights are intensely prized as women go through the process of revising themselves. To know themselves better, to see themselves more clearly, to engender the courage to change themselves and their lives if need be—these seemed to me to be the true heartbeat of the revisions these women had been making.

Conflict, of course, is the parent of change, and the women I interviewed varied widely in how much internal conflict they could tolerate. Erikson points out that identity is transformed in periods of heightened vulnerability that carry with them the potential for change. Many, as we have seen, chose to silence whatever part of themselves might have been headed for such vulnerability, whatever aspect of themselves might have been reaching to be more or other than they were, if such a part even existed in them. Instead, they opted to build themselves a safe cocoon and live within it. These women, embracing peace and harmony, risk burying their vitality. Some even told me that they felt their lives were dull or ordinary, not likely to be of interest to anyone else. Was I sure I wanted to be interviewing them? they asked me. But they seem to have what they wanted—an absence of ambivalence, a sense of comfort rather than emotional turmoil, constancy and predictability instead of surprise. They live out their lives quietly in a small crevice of the world enjoying simple pleasures. They don't write magazine articles or go on television, so we, as a society, rarely hear about them.

Psychologists seldom believe in the well-being of such people. My former teacher, Elvin Semrad, a gifted and well-known psychoanalyst, used to say that a person was either mad or sad or lying. The women I have spoken to, many of them, are neither sad nor mad, but I truly do not believe that they are lying. Psychologists may pelt people like this with epithets of denial or constriction, but I think that this, too, is a way to live and seems to be a viable path among the panoply of roads that people travel.

Will these women have an awakening as their lives go on? Perhaps. Many women grow more spirited and courageous as they grow older. Many Guardians, after all, had their major emotional growth spurts in their late thirties as they discovered more complex and often painful ways of thinking about themselves and their histories. Internal revision is always possible, and the heralds of change may be greeted either with avoidance, getting past the hurdles as smoothly as possible without disturbing the status quo, or with eagerness, welcoming the moment to refashion one's experience of life.

SELF AND OTHER

As growth unfolds and life progresses, the most far-reaching modifications and revisions are in the way in which a woman positions herself in relationship to others. But these revisions exist in a felt sense of the self, an orientation to one's place in one's world, and they are inordinately difficult to put into words. We seem best able to describe relationships when they are in conflict, when someone is angry or feels wronged and mistreated. It seems to be nearly impossible to characterize the course of learning about relationships and developing satisfactory ones without sounding pious. This is in part because we have so little vocabulary for relationships, and the words we do possess have all taken on sentimental greeting-card associations.

Changes in orientation to relationships and the location of the self within them are even harder to articulate. These revisions involve a gain of knowledge about how people are together, an increase of complex awareness, an appreciation of the nearly unfathomable variability in the ways we humans orient ourselves with each other. They involve limitless struggle with the paradox inherent in women's relationships, that relationships are at the same time enabling and potentially imprisoning.[10] They are the stuff of life, yet they can claim one's life. Women spoke of this to me in terms of "keeping it all in balance," or "taking account of myself *and* others." What these women were undertaking was redoing their connections with an effort to keep both self and other in focus.[11]

In terms of actual experience, this was grounded in concern with what one could expect of others and what one could expect of oneself. What is reasonable and appropriate behavior from others, and how does one respond when someone's behavior crosses this line? And what about others' expectations of oneself? How does one say 'no' and maintain the relationship? How does one let another person know what one needs? So much of life revolves around the conflicting needs of people, and although we sagely pay lip service to compromise, simple compromise is often that which neither person wants. True compromise—balance between needs of the people involved, sharing of resources, taking account of everyone's point of view—requires perspective and energy and all of this matures as women grow. As Clara put it, the challenge was "to respect their needs and my needs *at the same time.*" Psychologist Carol Gilligan (1982) has described this inclusion of self in the ethic of care as the highest stage of female moral development.

This process takes place in minute interactions, gradual accretions of experience that slowly lead to change. The mundane quality of such experience makes it seem to disappear from view. It resides in a woman struggling with how to maintain herself in an argument, how to assert her point of view, and also how to modify her own requirements in the interests of someone else. She learns to listen to herself—her own needs, wishes, and feelings—while holding the Other inside.

The workings of such change are perhaps easiest to witness in the Guardians and the Drifters, for these groups are at the extremes. The Guardians begin as college students with an inner conviction that, if they are very good, the world will treat them as an adored daughter, approve of them, protect them, and cherish them. They present their conscientiousness, their moral purpose, their respect for rules and goodness to others in hopes of reward. They are both self-focused *and* selfless in their orientation. They are willing to put aside their own needs to be of service to others and to do right, and therefore are selfless, but, more deeply, they act in their own interest, their wish to be seen as lovably angelic, and they are highly aware of their own goodness.

All this is under pressure to change as these women move through their twenties. They find that few, if any, people in the larger world are willing to treat them as adored daughters, and many feel confused and frightened by this. Most of the Guardians found it difficult to make or maintain intimate relationships or friendships, although they managed to get by on their dutifulness. It is usually not until their mid-thirties that these women come to realize that relationships are not about "doing it right." (I recall here a college student patient of mine, much like the Guardians in personality style, who was desperate to know that she was "good at sex.") Instead, relationships involve the flow of needs and responsiveness, of feelings and irrational fantasy, of blending of capability and tolerance of eccentricity. But this is hard-won learning that necessitates leaving aside idealizations and coming to love people (as well as the self) for what they are, with all their limitations. It also involves recognition that others, unlike the idealized parents of childhood, operate from their own centers. Rather than existing to approve or disapprove of one's own actions, people act out of their own complex motivations, of which concern for the other is only a part. These women come to experience other people as more and more separate and distinct from them and as having a right to be so. Relationship takes place to a greater extent between clearly defined selves.[12] Fern, for example, was able to refrain from criticizing her son for enjoying Rome in an adolescent manner while, at the same time, understanding and allowing herself her own disappointment in his trip.

This revision is ongoing, it is not a process that comes to an end. Such learning continues, often daily, throughout life. In midlife, the Guardians, as well as the other groups, are each day refining this understanding, moving backwards and forwards, now churlishly demanding their own way, now resentfully doing what others want, but more and more articulating the self with others, struggling to maintain empathy, respect, and authenticity.

The Drifters, at the other extreme, lacking a clear sense of self from the beginning, find it easy to lose themselves in others. Their journey is one of trying to define a self by separating what they are from their merger with others. For them, the needs and interests of others form an overwhelming cacophony that they can escape only by fleeing the relationship itself. For them, growth consists of containing the self in relationships, erecting a boundary that can persist in the face of others' distinctiveness. Unclear about their own inner life, they persistently misjudge others, imagining them to be what they wish them to be. For the Drifters, growth involves greater clarity about both sides of this balance—who they are and who others are. As they grow, both they themselves and the people in their lives begin to emerge from chiaroscuro and take on more definite shape. And this, too, is an arduous and long-term project.

MORAL PURPOSE

Beyond the self and its relations with others lies the realm of purpose and dedication to something larger, something beyond immediate concerns. Those women who found purpose in their lives through allegiance to some cause or goal seemed to be among the most vital and engaged of all the participants in this study. Millie, for example, in her sense of religious calling or Fern's dedication to helping the underprivileged exemplified women consecrating themselves to some larger meaning system. But this kind of investment was rare.

While nearly all the women I interviewed stressed the importance to them of moral *values* (beliefs), few have engaged in moral *purpose* (action) that reflects concern for the larger social good. For those few, such commitment evolved out of their awareness of needs beyond the self, sometimes deriving from religious conviction, sometimes arising out of work tasks. And it seemed not to appear to these women until some time in their late thirties, after the occupation of tending to the self and others close at hand had waned a bit. Some were aware of such stirrings, wishes to commit themselves to causes that mattered to them, but the lack of time kept them away. Alice, for example, wants to devote herself to environmental protection but the demands of her teaching and her family already consume her time and energy. Perhaps this larger ethicality and breadth of vision still awaits many of these women who have yet to discover, like Millie, that "you truly find yourself by giving yourself away."

REVISION AND PSYCHOTHERAPY

For the women I have interviewed, revision in their experience of themselves and their lives took place in spurts across the twenty years I have known them. Sometimes, the process was incremental: harbingers of change percolated for some time before the actual change was noticed. For some women, there were dramatic moments of revision—rethinking following a crisis or a definable life transition. Many made use of psychotherapy to help this process along.

When they were college seniors, only two of these women had been in intensive psychotherapy (Clara and Evelyn). By the time they were in their mid-forties, eighteen of the thirty[13] had had at least some contact with mental health professionals. This finding was astonishing to me—that out of a

randomly selected sample of women in college so many should seek therapy. Some of my colleagues have suggested that perhaps the however-brief
contact with me may have made this option more salient for these women.
To this I say perhaps, but I have no evidence that this is so. No one ever discussed it with me or asked me for referrals. And the 1970s and 1980s were
a psychological age. As a culture, we turned to psychotherapy to explore our
discontent, and I suspect that among educated women this was a common
experience.

After college, all but one of the Drifters, two-thirds of the Searchers, and
half of the Guardians availed themselves of psychotherapy in one form or
another. Except for Nancy, the Pathmaker "blown off course," none of the
Pathmakers have sought such help. As a therapist myself, it was instructive
for me to view these women's experiences with psychotherapy from the perspective of an onlooker, and to ask about how it has served these women in
their growth.

Of the eighteen who had been in therapy, six had only very brief contact
for support in a life crisis: for help in family conflicts or problems with mood.
In these cases, the therapy addressed the immediate need, but did not
attempt to offer these women the opportunity to consider larger revisions of
themselves or their lives. Natalie, who I think could have profited from some
real help about her "writer's block," received only brief behavioral intervention that was not successful.

More intensive psychotherapy had a life-changing impact on eight others.
Emily used an intensive long-term therapy in her early thirties to help her
trace the origins of her difficulties with men to her relationship with her perfectionistic mother and to enable her to make a satisfying intimate
relationship. Grace and Gwen sought treatment to help them reorder themselves after their marriages ended. Debbie's extended therapy early in her
forties enabled her to set career goals, to pull herself out of what felt like suf-
focation in motherhood. Clara has credited her therapy after she dropped out
of college at age 19 with helping her out of a dangerously angry and rebellious adolescence and putting her on the path to finding herself in the first
place. Although she sought help for panic attacks, Theresa's therapy has
helped her to better understand her own origins and try to avoid the crip-
pling effects of her parents in her own mothering. Both Leslie and Sandra
have had long-term therapy to stabilize them and help them work through
early and unresolvable anger at their families. For all these women, psychotherapy was useful and productive, assisting them along the road toward
insight and planning and helping them to design their own paths.

The remaining four women who have been in therapy have had only
moderately successful or unsuccessful outcomes. Three are women I had

classified as Drifters. Evelyn, one of the most troubled women in the group, is being maintained on medication and therapeutic support for anxiety and depression, but the relationship of these symptoms to identity issues seems to have been only tangentially explored. Donna and Vicky have been in and out of therapy. Donna seems to have been abandoned by her therapist in a hurtful way, and it was difficult to know just how Vicky has been making use of her treatment. Nancy had some intermittent therapy related to her troubled marriage, recognizes her need for more help, but can't quite organize herself to pursue it.

In general, therapy has been of use to these women in their search for identity, but to some more than others. It has been most useful, not in the relief of symptoms, but in helping women get perspective on and insight into themselves. Therapy has served to enliven what in them seemed frozen or paralyzed, to help them draw on parts of themselves that had been dormant or underdeveloped, to free themselves of fetters from the past, and to help them envision new lives and find the courage to pursue them.

Psychotherapy can, and does, catalyze the identity formation process. It helps women to sort themselves out and supports them in doing what they want but fear to do. At the very least, it offers them new language and perspective with which to understand themselves. In our current culture (or at least the culture of liberal health insurance, including mental health coverage, for working people), a passage through psychotherapy has become a rather common rite of passage. But it is not necessary for successful identity formation. The Pathmakers work things out without professional help. Thoughtful revision of one's life always involves coming to a better understanding of oneself. As people grow, most begin to see their own repetitive patterns. And this consciousness illuminates the undergirding of past choices and liberates the future from the bondage of the past. People rethink and relinquish what they had previously lived without question. Therapy, at its best, helps some women do what others do without such intervention, to claim internally their right to fashion their own lives.

REVISION AND THE WOMEN'S MOVEMENT

Because these women came of age just as the women's movement was gaining momentum and force, we well might look from this angle and ask about how this social and historic force affected the course of their lives. Changing attitudes and expectations toward and for women inexorably reshaped the way in which these women lived their lives, but the influence of the women's movement occurred in subtle and indirect ways.

Only Marlene, Regina, and Grace, among these thirty women, participated in organized groups that were allied with women's interests, and this association was profoundly important and influential to them. For the rest, the effects of the women's movement made themselves known through the media and the culture that changed the values in the people around them. They absorbed the central tenets of the feminist protest, which centered around two major ideas: (1) equality—that women are not inferior to men and are capable of doing whatever a man can do; and (2) freedom—that women ought to be fully free to make choices in their lives.

In college, the changing role of women was manifest mainly in a young woman's vague sense that she would probably pursue some sort of career in addition to raising children. On the threshold of financial independence from their parents, many resisted the idea of becoming economically dependent on a man and wanted to feel capable of supporting themselves. In addition, most recognized their own joy in mastery and competence, and found it hard to imagine "just staying home."

As they continued to grow, these women increasingly began to ally themselves, at least intellectually, with the women's movement. They came to understand that a gendered analysis helped explicate some of the problems they were experiencing at work. They began to see that there was something systematic in the way in which men mistreated women in the workplace, but beyond some shared griping and doomed individual efforts at change, none were able to join with other women to take group action.

All three of the women I have been following who entered historically male-dominated professions eventually won "first woman" roles. (Emily and Grace were the first woman judges in their states and Andrea was the first woman appointed to the examining board in her specialty.) They saw their gender as being a benefit to them as they capitalized on being the first in line, aware of all the women behind them. These women thought deeply about taking up their roles as women, wanting to conserve aspects of themselves that they thought of as their femininity even as they showed that they could "do the job" as well as a man.

The right to control reproduction has been another aim of the women's movement that these women have intensely joined, in spirit if not in action. One-fourth of these women have had abortions, and nearly all mentioned concern about the right to abortion as the single political issue they feel most strongly about (and this includes two who are right-to-life advocates). Many who became mothers were very attentive to the process of childbirth and gave long and careful thought to their choices about where to have their babies and who would be in attendance. Many profited from the work of other women who had refashioned giving birth as a personal experience rather than a medical one.

All the mothers say that they are trying to raise their children without gender stereotypes. The mothers of daughters especially want to ensure that their daughters are raised to embrace freedom of choice and expansive goals. In this private way, they are carrying forward their understanding of feminist ideals, doing what they can to prevent gendered experience from creating inequality.

All these women felt affected by the women's movement in terms of their greater freedom to choose. None explained her life choices in terms of social expectations or seemed to understand her life as following a social prescription for women. Except perhaps for the ideal of being thin, these women could not define a clear cultural story that she felt obliged to make a prototype for her life. Experiencing the absence of social constraint, they felt free to try to define and follow their own desires. To that extent, more than any previous generation, these women believed themselves to be the authors of their own lives. Although only Marlene, Grace, and Jennifer used the word feminist to describe themselves, all these women gained freedom and possibility of choice through the efforts of the feminist movement.

REVISING LIFE STORIES

As our identity changes, so does our version of our life story. The present shapes the past. When I was 27, three months before I left my first husband, I was a participant in another psychologist's study and asked to fill out a "life experience" questionnaire. On a scale of 1 to 7, one question asked, How happy are you in your marriage? Without hesitation, I circled 6—very happy. And it was true. Just as there was truth in my decision to leave him. At the time, I had been living a comfortable identity as a forbearing and fundamentally contented doctor's wife, secure in a bond with a decent, loving man, who was also quite rigid and workaholic. I was busy decorating a home, planning vacations, and pursuing my own career goals.

Two months later, I had fallen wildly in love with another man and decided that what I most wanted in life was an intense and passionate connection. In a short time, I had mentally rewritten my life story to portray my first marriage as a dull, confined, lifeless world that I had entered because it was what I had always thought I was "supposed " to do. I was young, I now recounted, only 17 when I entered a committed relationship with him, and he was the man of my mother's dreams. I felt I had gained insight—that I had let myself know what I had in some way always known, but I knew it in a different way—a way I could now act on and use to change my life and assuage my guilt. Looking back on this, twenty years later, I ask myself which version of this story was the true one. And, from this perspective, I realize they both were—and that I would also tell yet another version of "truth" today.

As we listen to the stories of women's lives, we find that there are, in fact, many stories: the story that is lived at the time and the stories waiting down the road. Growth is a process of rewriting, revising, and interweaving these narratives.

As people develop, they revise the stories they tell themselves (and me) about their own growth. Identity, as the backbone of a life story, provides unity to a life as lived by choosing versions of one's history that "fit," often editing out what is incongruent.[14] The past is reconfigured to make our present identity seem inevitable—or, if not inevitable, at least meaningful. We smooth out the past, omitting those bits of experience that seem to have no import for what we have become. In retelling our lives, the past also absorbs aspects of the larger culture's narratives (so that we all feel like products of our times). I was astonished, for example, by the 43-year-old Guardians who told me about how college for them was a time of gaining independence and encountering new ideas when, indeed, their early tapes make clear that they were doing no such thing. But experiences of the past that were then in the shadows have emerged to prominence in light of later events. Having become comfortable with self-reliance later on, earlier experiences of independence that had been frightening and underplayed in their college-age identity later take on a new significance. In addition, this is the cultural story we tell of what happens during that age, and the fading of old states of personal awareness causes our own history to blend into the tale commonly told. Similarly, trauma and loss get worked into new configurations as time goes on, and their role in the evolving life story may change. Looking back on her late adolescent marriage now with a mother's eyes, Donna says, "I can't even remember my reasons for eloping."

Many shaping experiences seem to lose their edge as events are absorbed into the personality and the person moves on. Few of us can remember the vision we used to see the world with before we knew what we now know. Unless we think hard about our changes, we tend to be more conscious of our constancy. We usually think that how we are now is how we have always been. But in other states of mind, we may feel ourselves a stranger to the person we used to be twenty years ago, so aware are we of all that has changed—and this seems synchronous with our culture, which tends to pay more attention to change than constancy.[15] Only by tracking these women at different points in their lives have I been able to grasp both their continuity and their change—and it is a formidable task to keep both in mind at once. Yet this we all share: we change and we stay the same.

Some women live a single story; others live many. And some women seem to live a postmodern story with no clear plotline at all. Most women, because they have multiple facets, must tell their individual story in segments: the story of one's partner, the story of one's career development, the story of one's children or of not having children, the story of growing up and one's continuing relations with parents, the story of an important friend and how she or he may have influenced or shaped one's life, the story of an interest or passion or special talent that marks one's creative engagement in life, the story of a spiritual quest or turning away from one. And all these stories intermingle and influence one another. The "plot" of a woman's life is seldom linear. The self is dialogic, parts of the self in conversation with each other. Identity encompasses all these selves, forming a narrative that weaves them together.

As these women grow, their possible selves grow along with them. There are always shadow selves, potential selves, other ways of being that exist in the region of "some day" or "what might have been." As women revise their expectations of what life might be like for themselves and for others, their fantasies of possibility are reshaped as well. These secret hopes and desires become less tangible as they get older; for some, growing older means coming to terms with what will never be. We live in a society that at present tries to tell women that they can have it all, all that they might want, but these women know that this is not true. Using the Madison Avenue and TV images of "having it all" in midlife—looking beautiful, being thin, having a high-paid high-power career, a handsome, supportive husband, and well-behaved bright children—none of these women have it all. Do they hate themselves for it, as some have suggested?[16] I don't think so (although worry about weight is the most frequent and persistent source of self-condemnation). But media images of Superwoman do make it difficult to know how much they can realistically aim for, especially when so much that they hope for, so much of what really matters most—like health and safety for loved ones—seems increasingly out of their control.

Paradoxically, women whose lives have most unfolded according to their intention and plan are the ones who most feel the effects of luck and fortune. They see themselves as having had the good fortune to be in the right place at the right time. They take credit for having had the clear vision to take advantage of opportunity and the talent to make the most of it, but they regard their success as a combination of ability and luck. In thinking of the future, they beseech fortune once again to keep disaster at bay, to allow them opportunities to express themselves. By contrast, those women who have followed the more tortuous paths and suffered the most failure and disappointment are often the most forceful in declaring that they have created their own destinies, with luck having no role whatsoever. They see themselves as fully in charge of their own lives when, to an outsider, it seems more the case that they have not been. Some psychologists might view this as women's tendency to blame themselves for failure. I regard it more as part of the existential struggle to value ourselves in full recognition of how little ultimate control we have. Part of maturity is seeing this in balance; to some extent, each identity pathway leads ultimately to the same paradox.

Women forge their lives with more or less deliberation, more or less conviction, seeking more or less stimulation and challenge. As identity progresses, many forces, both internal and external, affect its revision. A woman may venture—indeed, must venture—but the outcome depends in part on fortune. As a woman creates her life, she may reach back for old threads or search for new ones. She may integrate some aspect of the past and give it new meaning, thus transforming both the past and the emerging present. She weaves together both her desires and her capacity to respond to the unforeseen twists, knots, and breaks in the yarn that come her way. She can overstitch what is already there, rework an old pattern, or create, sometimes by accident, something original. Revision is always possible. As these women look to the future, they do so with optimism, with hope of having more leisure to pursue the neglected parts of themselves, to deepen their relationships, and to forge new ones. They regard the future, as they look toward age 50 and beyond, as being less fettered, less hectic. Self-realization, never finally attained, continues to beckon on the horizon.

"We women have lived too much with closure," says Carolyn Heilbrun, "this is the delusion of a passive life. When the hope for closure is abandoned . . . adventure for women will begin."[17]

Sampling Methods and
Data Collection Procedures

PARTICIPANTS

Phase 1

Sample I: In 1971–72, I randomly drew names of senior-year college women from the student directories of three colleges or universities—every fiftieth name, every hundredth name, depending on the size of the school. I interviewed sixty women until I met the criterion of having forty-eight who would be distributed as twelve in each of the four identity status groups. At the time, Pathmakers were overrepresented—there were more Pathmakers than I included in the final sample. It was harder to find Drifters, in part because they were least likely to keep appointments and had to be pursued.

Because universities tend to have characteristics unique to themselves, I interviewed women from three very different kinds of institutions, all middle to upper range in terms of their academic standing: a large state university, a large private university, and a small women's college. Most students lived on campus but many resided at home. Many also held part-time jobs and paid for all or part of their own tuition.

At this time, participants were paid a small stipend for their participation.

Sample II: I interviewed twelve additional women in 1973. These women were randomly drawn from another large state university in another (somewhat more conservative) region of the country. In this group were primarily Guardians and Searchers, with a few Drifters and only one Pathmaker.

Phase 2

In 1983, I attempted to locate the sixty women I had interviewed in the previous decade. Because many had moved or changed their names, and their educational institutions had no record of them, I was able to locate only forty. Of these, two were deceased. Five refused to participate. Therefore, thirty-three people constituted this second group.

Phase 3

In 1993, I attempted to recontact these women. At this time, I was able to locate thirty. All agreed to participate.

METHOD

First data collection (Phase 1, Samples I and II): I contacted each woman by letter and then by phone, inviting her to participate. I described the study as an investigation of the psychology of women. Seventy-five percent of the women I contacted agreed to participate.

I interviewed each woman beginning with Marcia's Identity Status Interview (Appendix B), which took between a half-hour and an hour. Interviews were taped and later rated by myself and Susan Schenkel, an advanced graduate student also studying identity formation using the identity status format. We agreed on 90 percent of the ratings. Those on which we disagreed were rated by a third person and we grouped participants in the identity status that had received two ratings.

Following the Identity Status Interview, participants took an intelligence test and some other psychometric tests and were then interviewed for one and one-half to two hours using an open-ended semistuctured Personal History interview protocol (see Appendix C). This interview was intended to elicit material about the participant's early life, relationships with parents and friends, significant internal (and external) conflicts, as well as information about her experience of herself. I also asked about earliest memories, recent dreams, and, in some instances, requested Thematic Apperception Test stories.

Follow-up I (Phase 2—1983): Participants were sent and asked to respond to a comprehensive questionnaire (see Appendix C) either in writing or on tape. This was followed by a lengthy interview either in person or by phone. Most of the women vaguely remembered that they had participated in some study in college, but many did not. In the intervening years I had had no contact with them.

At this time, I often had to persuade and cajole them to participate—they were suspicious about revealing themselves to someone they weren't sure they knew. The times had changed as well—it was a less trustful age. Some were hesitant at the beginning of the interview, but then warmed to the task and seemed to enjoy the opportunity to reflect on their lives with an interested, empathic listener. Because of the demands on people's time to do this very comprehensive inventory of her life and experiences, the form of data collection varied for each woman to suit her needs. Interviews lasted three to five hours. I did the majority of face-to-face interviewing at this time, although two women were interviewed by my students.

Follow-up II (Phase 3—1993): Again, I contacted each participant first by letter and then by phone, announcing that I was, in effect, "at it again." At this time, all remembered me. In some cases, in the late 1980s, I had sent people who had requested it copies of a paper I had published about the study. Two or three had come across my book *Finding Herself* and read it. In 1984, a year after the first follow-up, I had sent each woman a Christmas card to thank her again for her participation and urge her to be sure to let me know of any address changes she might make. Beyond this, I had no contact with them in the interim. I was delighted to find that these women were not only willing, but often eager to participate once again. Some went to a lot of trouble to come for interviews. Others offered to meet in their homes, offices, or vacation houses. Again, I personally did most of the interviewing while seven of my graduate students did others. Some women were not available for face-to-face interviews, so again we worked by questionnaire, tape, and/or telephone. In-person interviews lasted four to five hours.

The overall principle in all these data collections was for me to get to know each woman as intensively as possible. Instead of following some rigid format, I modified both procedures and questions in the service of gaining as much knowledge of each one of them as I could. Each woman gave me written permission to use her material in my work. Nearly all asked me, at this last conversation, if I am coming back again in ten more years. I know these people so well now, have spent so much time trying to understand them—how could I not?

Presentation of Life histories:

All identifying information has been disguised, but the essence of each woman's life choices has been preserved. (You may think you recognize someone, but that's because there is much that is similar among us.) I have also chosen to refer to each woman by first name only, not out of disrespect or a wish to infantilize them, but because many women have changed their last names through marriage and divorce and it was logistically impossible to refer to them by full name. It is our first name that is most constant across our lives if we are women.

The Identity Status Interview*

INTRODUCTION

- Where are you from? Where are you living now?
- How did you happen to come to this college?
- Did your father go to college? Where? What does he do now?
- Did your mother go to college? Where? What does he do now?

OCCUPATION

- What are you majoring in? What do you plan to do with it?
- When did you come to decide on _____ ? Did you ever consider anything else?
- What seems attractive about _____ ?
- Most parents have plans for their children, things they would like them to go into or do. Did your parents have any plans like that for you?

* Source: Adapted from Marcia (1964) and Schenkel and Marcia (1972).

- How do your parents feel about your plans now?
- How willing do you think you'd be to change if something better came along? (What might be better in your terms?)
- Do you plan to marry? Do you plan to work after you marry? Why or why not?
- Do you plan to have children? Work after you have children? Why or why not?
- Do you expect to take time off from work when you have children?
- How do you plan to combine work and marriage and child-rearing? What problems do you think might exist? How do you feel these might be solved? Have you ever felt differently about this? How does the man in your life feel about these things? How important would it be to you that he agree about these things?

RELIGION

- Do you have any particular religious affiliation or preference?
- How about your folks?
- Have you ever been active in church (synagogue)? How about now? Do you get into many religious discussions?
- How do your parents feel about your beliefs now?
- Are your beliefs any different from theirs?
- Was there any time when you came to doubt any of your religious beliefs? When?
- How did it happen? How did you resolve your questions? How are things for you now?

POLITICS

- Do you have any particular political preference?
- How about your parents?
- Have you ever taken part in any kind of political action—joining groups, writing letters, participating in demonstrations, etc.?
- Are there any political issues you feel pretty strongly about?
- Was there any particular time when you decided on your political beliefs?

SEXUAL VALUES AND STANDARDS

- What are your views on premarital intercourse? What criteria do you use to determine your actions? Have you always felt this way?
- Have you ever had any doubts? How did you resolve them?

- What would your parents think about your sexual standards and behavior?
- Do you feel there is ever any conflict between your ideas, emotions, and behavior?
- Could you give an example? How do you handle the conflicts? How frequently do they occur?

The Personal History Interview

TIME 1—DURING COLLEGE

- If there's a person who you want to know you, what sorts of things would you tell them about yourself?
- What was most important in the last two or three years in terms of making you the way you are? What influenced you most? Before that—say, during high school? How about before that—like in elementary school?
- In the last few years, who of all the people that you've known during that time did you like most? Before that? (You've talked about boyfriends and pals. Is there someone that you liked in a different way?)
- Who of all these people did you most want to be like? Did you become like them in any way? Who of all the people that you know now would you most like to be like?
- Right now, what is the thing you like to do most? If you had a lot of free time, what do you put it to? (Is that what you'd put your life to?) (In a more general sense, what would you like to put your life to if you could arrange things any way you'd like?) (What would you do? Is it something you've seriously thought of putting your life to?) How much trouble would you really take for this? Would you delay status, marriage, money, take real risks?

- How do you imagine your future in the next year? In the next five years? In ten years?
- All of us have daydreams, even though we don't necessarily take them seriously. What kinds of things do you daydream about? Is there a daydream that you've had continuously, something you like to daydream about when you listen to music or are alone?
- What is the last night dream you remember?

Just on the spur of the moment, what is the earliest thing you can remember? (When was that?) What is the second earliest thing you can remember?

TIMES 2 AND 3—ADULTHOOD

Part I: Life History

1. Thinking over the past ten years, what has been most significant for you? What changes have there been?

2. What have been the major good experiences in your life in the past ten years?

3. What have been the major bad experiences in your life in the past ten years?

4. What have been the major turning points in your life in the past ten years? What have been the critical decisions you have made?

Part II: Occupational History

Please give occupational titles and dates:

Dates	Position (title)	Duties (what you do/did)

Please describe the reasons for any changes in the past ten years.

For periods when you have not held a job, please describe your pursuits.

Describe your current employment: What do you do? In what ways it is satisfactory to you? In what ways unsatisfactory? What is the most important gratification you derive from your job? Which aspects of your job do you find to be most difficult?

Have there been people (or one specific person) who have strongly influenced your career direction or goals? If so, please describe them, and how they influenced or guided you.

From an occupational viewpoint, what direction do you see your life taking in the future? What do you hope to be doing ten years from now?

Part II: Education

Have you pursued further education in the past ten years?

Institution	Program (course of study)	Degree	Dates
1.			
2.			
3.			

Do you plan to pursue further education? Please describe your plans.

Part III: Personal History

Family

_____ Single—never married   Please begin with Question 4.

_____ Married to the same person you were married to ten years ago
Please begin with Question 10.

_____ Separated or divorced in the past ten years   Please begin with
Question 1.

1. If you have been separated or divorced since 1983, please discuss the decision to end the marriage.

2. How did the separation or divorce change you or your life? Please describe your experiences after the separation or divorce.

3. If you have remarried, please describe the decisions involved in your remarriage. What events led to it? (Then go to question 10.)

4. Do you plan to remain single? Please explain

5. Are you currently involved in a love relationship? Please describe its role in your life.

6. Describe your current dating patterns.

7. If you are engaged or living with someone, do you plan to marry this person? Please explain your situation with regard to the decisions involved.

8. Please describe any other love relationships that have been significant in your life over the past ten years? How long have they lasted? What brought them to an end?

9. What do you want most in a love relationship?

PLEASE GO TO QUESTION 13.

10. How has your marriage changed in the past ten years? How do you fit together as a couple? How do you complement each other? In what ways do you clash?

11. How has your marriage fulfilled your needs? How has it not fulfilled your wishes? How would you like it to be different?

12. Have you had any serious marital problems? Have you seriously considered separation? If so, please describe the areas of difficulty.

13. Do you have children? If not, go to Question 21.

    Name   Sex   Age

    Are there particular ages of your children's development that you have found particularly enjoyable or frustrating? Why?

14. Please discuss how you came to decide to have your first child at that particular time in your life. How did you decide on timing of subsequent children?

15. Do you plan to have more children? If so, when and under what circumstances? If not, why not?

16. How has having children changed the person that you are? What aspects of your life (self, love relationship, career) have been enriched by motherhood and what aspects have been diminished?

17. How are your views about raising children the same or different from the way your parents raised you?

18. Please describe your children briefly. What are they like?

19. What has been the most difficult aspect about being a mother? What have you found hardest to adjust to? How would you like things to be different?

20. Describe the most challenging interaction or problem you've had to deal with with your children. How did you handle it?

21. Have you had any miscarriages, abortions, or stillbirths? What effect has this event(s) had on you?

22. If you do not have children now, do you plan to have them? Why or why not? Please explain.

Part IV: Religion

What religion do you practice?

How committed to your religion are you? What does your religious commitment involve?

Have your religious views or practices changed in the past ten years? If so, what brought about these changes?

Part IV: Politics

How involved in political issues are you? Which political issues do you feel most strongly about?

Did you vote in the last presidential election?

Are you active in local, community, or national politics? What do/did you do?

Have your political views or preferences changed over the past ten years? If so, how?

Part IV: Sex

How have your views about sexual morality—i.e., premarital, marital, or extramarital sex—changed over the past ten years?

What statement would you make to define your own *principles* in regard to your own sexual behavior?

What principles might you want your daughter to follow in regard to sexual morality? (Please answer this question even if you don't have a daughter.)

Part IV: General Circumstances

What has your financial situation been like in the past ten years? Have you had to struggle financially or have you been financially secure?

Describe your health over the past ten years. Describe your use of alcohol, tobacco, and drugs.

In what type of setting, city or country, have you lived during the past ten years?

How many times have you moved in the past ten years?

Have you ever been in psychotherapy or counseling? If so, when and for what reason?

If any of the above factors has been especially significant in your life, please explain.

Part V: Personal Growth

1. What is the very earliest thing you can remember in your life? Please describe in detail the very first memory you have of some specific event.

2. What is the second earliest thing you can remember in your life?

3. Try to see your life as a series of chapters, beginning as far back as you can remember. These "chapters" should group years that seem to belong together. What would be the main theme of each chapter in terms of the things

that mattered most to you, that you most wished for or were trying to accomplish? What were the most important things that happened in each chapter?

4. In what way has luck—or fortune—played an important role in your life? How much do you feel that you have been the architect of your own destiny?

5. Looking back, who have been the most important people in your life? Why?

List in order the ten people to whom you feel closest today:

Name	Relationship to you	How long known
1.		
2.		
3.		
4.		
5.		
6.		
7.		
8.		
9.		
10.		

Please put a star next to those people to whom you feel *very* close. Please put a circle next to those people to whom you would turn for help in a crisis.

6. Describe your current relationships with your parents and siblings. How have these relationships changed over the past ten years?

7. As you look back, how are you the product of your family? How are you different from them?

8. The next are some questions that we didn't know how to ask about in the past because we weren't aware of their importance for some people:

   a. The first is—as a child, did you ever have anyone in your family touch you in a sexual way that you could now consider abusive? If yes, at what age or ages? Please describe what occurred. How do you think this has affected your life and your feelings about yourself, others, your sexuality.

b. Did anyone treat you in a way that you would now consider to be physical abuse? If yes, at what age or ages? Please describe what occurred. How do you think this has affected your life and your feelings about yourself, others, your sexuality.

c. Have you had experiences of sexual and physical abuse in adolescence or adulthood? If yes, at what age or ages? Please describe what occurred. How do you think this has affected your life and your feelings about yourself, others, your sexuality?

d. Did either of your parents have a problem with alcoholism or other substance abuse? At what age or ages? Please describe. How do you think this affected you?

9. How important have friendships been in your life? How has the experience of friendship changed over the years?

10. How would you describe your college years? How have the experiences you had in college most affected your life?

11. If you had it to do over again, what would you change about your college years?

12. What are your major hobbies or interests and how important have they been for you?

13. What has been your philosophy over rough spots? How have you coped with stress?

14. What are your hopes, dreams, and plans for the future? How do you want your life to change in the future? In what ways do you hope to become different as a person in the future?

15. Imagine yourself at age 80 looking over your life. What would you be most satisfied to have accomplished or experienced in your life? What are the accomplishments in your life so far of which you feel most proud?

16. If there is anything else of unique significance in your life in terms of influences, experiences or relationships, please tell me about them here. (Is there anything I should have asked you in order to really know you—but didn't?)

This interview protocol served for both follow-ups except that the question with an asterisk (*) was only asked in 1993. In 1983, the questions were asked in a somewhat different order. That interview began with Part IV, which is a reprise of the identity status interview.

None of the interviews followed this protocol exactly. Often, a great deal of the material that would respond to the later questions was already discussed in Part I. I (and the other interviewers) used the protocol to touch all the areas of interest, but did it in an order that preserved the flow of conversation. The interview stance was reflective, trying to encourage each participant to share what was meaningful to her. We did not interrupt to go on to the next question.

NOTES

CHAPTER 1

1. See Erikson's paper, "Womanhood and the Inner Space," in *Identity, Youth and Crisis* (1968). For the larger theory of identity, see the other papers in this volume as well as *Young Man Luther* and *Gandhi's Truth*.

2. The quest plot was the essence of the male journey depicted by Levinson et al. (1978). Vaillant's (1977) longitudinal study of men also places career achievement in the center of men's life enterprise.

3. Heilbrun, *Hamlet's Mother* (1990).

4. Gergen (1990) points out that there is almost no space devoted to women at midlife in recent psychology textbooks. Even psychology of women texts tend to present only such topics as sexual development, marital relations, mothering, widowhood, and sexual crimes. Gergen sees the "basic story" of women's adulthood as told by psychology as a life narrowing to family concerns, following which a woman is permitted community involvement as long as she continues to meet her family's demands. Then there comes the loss of her children, followed by loss of her husband, and then she is alone.

5. See also Rossi (1980) and Neugarten et al. (1968).

6. This work belongs to what McAdams (1988) terms "the personological" tradition, evolving from the work of Henry Murray and Robert White, attempting to study people as wholes growing within a context.

7. Some of the interviewing, in various phases has been carried out by my superb research assistants under my supervision. I have, however, stayed in touch with each woman both before and after such interviews, calling to clarify what was unclear to me from the tapes.

8. The interview formats for each phase of the data collection are presented in Appendix A.

9. For a discussion of the problems in writing about real people, see Josselson (1996).

10. See Helson (1993) for a discussion of issues of stability and change as they have been treated in personality research.

CHAPTER 2

1. See Appendix A for a discussion of the sampling.

2. Ten were raised Catholic, seven Protestant, six Jewish, three Episcopalian, and four with no clear religious affiliation.

3. Of course, some were a year or two younger or older, depending on when their birthdate is in relation to the interview date and whether they were in Sample I or Sample II. For simplicity in this work, I group all the women in their early thirties as age 33 and all the women in their early forties as age 43. Their actual chronological ages at the time of the most recent interview range from 41 to 44.

4. At age 33, fifteen were married to their first husband and three had divorced and remarried. Of the rest, nine had never married, one was a widow, and two were divorced.

5. Two had law degrees, one an M.D., one a Ph.D., one an MBA, one a Master's degree in Library Science, and four had Master's degrees in education.

6. Of the three not in committed relationships, one was a lesbian in an ambivalent and uncommitted relationship, uncertain about whether she might really be bisexual, one had never married and one, who had been among those married at age 33, was divorced but engaged. All the rest of the women who had been married at age 33 remained married to the same partners except one who had divorced and remarried in this decade and another who had divorced at age 40 and was engaged at the time of the last interview.

7. According to census bureau statistics compiled in 1992, 24 percent of all white women between the ages of 35 and 44 who have earned a bachelor's degree do not have children. For women with graduate or professional degrees, 32 percent are childless. These figures indicate that my sample, in which 47 percent have no children, overrepresents childless women in comparison to the base population. See Bacha (1992).

CHAPTER 3

1. While Erikson inspired interest in identity within psychology, philosophers and sociologists have had much to say about this topic. Charles Taylor (1989) traces the history of our conceptions of the self and identity and explores the moral bases of what he terms the "modern identity." Roy Baumeister (1986), within psychology, also takes a historical perspective on our understanding of the self. A group of interesting papers about identity within contemporary philosophy has been assembled by Daniel Kolak and Raymond Martin (1991). For a sociological perspective on identity (although they don't call

it that), see Bellah et al (1985). Recent summaries of the identity concept in current psychology include Blustein and Noumair (in press).

2. *Young Man Luther,* p. 111.

3. Erikson (1968), p. 283. This has been a much-quoted passage from a much-derided essay. He has been criticized most for agreeing with Freud that anatomy is destiny. In fairness to Erikson, however, he was well aware of the social constraints on women and, in contrast to other psychoanalytic writers, expressed regret about the ways in which women held themselves back (and men held them back) from expressing their intelligence and creativity in public ways. In this essay, I believe that Erikson was describing social reality as he saw it at the time rather than inscribing how women *must* be in society. He was, in fact, rather idealistic about what women, with their unique proclivities, might bring to the sciences and to the world. From the same essay: "And if we grant that a woman is never not a woman, even if she has become an excellent scientist and co-worker, and especially when she has grown beyond all special apologies or claims, then why deny so strenuously that there may also be areas in science . . . where women's vision and creativity may yet lead, not to new laws of verification, but to new areas of inquiry and new applications" (p. 292). In 1968, this was a fairly radical thing to say.

4. *Writing a Woman's Life,* p. 21.

5. Marcia (unpublished manuscript) suggests that whereas men tend to resolve one identity issue at a time and then move on to the next, identity in women is more synthetic, more attentive to the shape and details of the whole, molding and reorganizing the parts.

6. In Marcia's work and in the professional literature, the four groups are known by different names from the ones I have given them here. In psychological research, the **Guardians** are called **Foreclosures,** the **Pathmakers** are **Identity Achievements**; the **Searchers** are **Moratoriums** and the **Drifters** are known as **Identity Diffusions.** I changed the names to make them more descriptive and less evaluative.

For reviews and discussion of identity-status research over the past thirty years, see especially the comprehensive *Ego Identity: A Handbook for Psychosocial Research* (1993) edited by Marcia and others. Also see Marcia (1980), Waterman (1992), and Kroger (1993).

7. In 1970 and 1972, I randomly selected sixty women from four different colleges and universities in two different states. All were between the ages of 20 and 22. Participants were initially contacted by letter and invited to particpate. Seventy-five percent of those invited agreed to be interviewed. Following the Identity Status Interview, each participant was interviewed in depth about her childhood, her family, her relationships, and her aspirations.

In 1983, I was able to locate forty of them and to invite them to be interviewed again. Two had died, both among the Drifters (one had committed suicide; I was unable to determine the cause of death of the other). Five refused to participate. Therefore, thirty-three women were available at the time of this first follow-up.

In 1993, I attempted to recontact these thirty-three women yet again. I was able to locate thirty, of whom all agreed to participate. Most were interviewed in person for 4 to 5 hours. Some others completed written questionnaires followed by telephone interviews.

See Appendix A for a more complete description of the methodology. The interview schedules for all three data collections are available in Appendix C.

8. Each subcategory was assigned a rating and then weighted in terms of its importance to the participant in order to form an overall rating. Therefore, some women who seemed to be constructing an identity around relational values but were drifting on occu-

pation would still be rated as Pathmakers. Most women were uninvolved politically, so this domain of identity had little weight in their overall ratings. In general, for women of this age, crisis and commitment in religious and sexual/relational values was more predictive of overall identity. See Marcia and Friedman (1970) and Schenkel and Marcia (1972). For the Identity Status Interview I used to make these assessments, see Appendix B.

9. There has been much debate in the research literature about whether these four groups represent waystations on the road to identity or are different personality types. Throughout college, there seems to be a good deal of moving about among the groups, especially from the less mature categories of Foreclosure (**Guardian**) and Diffusion (**Drifters**) into Identity Achievement (**Pathmakers**). Moratorium (**Searchers**) represents the most unstable state because sooner or later people have to choose. (See Waterman, 1993, for a discussion of the stability of the identity statuses.) On the other hand, those who are still searching as college ends seem to share characteristics that make decision-making more difficult. Recent thinking suggests that there may be both developmental and characterological aspects to each of these groups; that is, some people may be in each group while passing through to another; others may belong in the group because that is their deeper personal orientation. See Marcia (1989); Kroger(1995), Berzonsky (1985) and Archer and Waterman (1990).

Many of the studies that document movement from one identity status to another show that these transitions take place during the college years. Kroger (1995), for example, distinguished between "firm" and "developmental" Foreclosures, defining "firm" Foreclosures as those who remained foreclosed from the beginning to the end of their university years. Many studies document the increase in identity achievement over the college years (Waterman, 1993).

I chose to interview and classify my participants at the end of college, a time of maximum pressure from society to formulate identity. The Eriksonian Moratorium period was drawing to a close. I assumed that people were in the groups they were for deeper rather than transient reasons. The longitudinal data allowed me an opportunity to see that these groups defined at the end of college seemed to represent inner necessity, some fundamental personality characteristics, more than developmental transition for all but the Searchers.

10. There were no statistically significant differences in intelligence between the four groups of women in this study. There were, however, statistically significant differences in field independence, with Guardians and Pathmakers more field independent than the Searchers and Drifters (see Schenkel, 1975).

11. Helson, Stewart, and Ostrove (1995) were able to identify these four groups in three different cohorts of college women. The groups remained similar across cohort, although the older women, those born in 1928, were less likely to be in the paid labor force and more likely to be married and have children. The later-born cohorts, who graduated from college in 1958–60 or in 1964, were more likely to take advantage of opportunities to define their identity in vocational terms. Thus, the content of identity may change as a result of social changes, but not its underlying structure.

12. Some of these women, if they had gone to a psychological clinic, would have been diagnosed as having borderline personalities or serious depression.

13. One of the thirty women could not be assigned to an identity category—she simply didn't fit any of the criteria, but I have followed her nevertheless. For the remaining twenty-nine women, there was 90 percent agreement with two raters. In the disputed

cases, with a third rater and a two-out-of-three criterion employed, reliability grew to 100 percent.

14. Marcia takes a life-span developmental approach to identity-status research. He regards "identity integration at late adolescence as an initial formulation, subject to reformulation and reintegration throughout the life cycle" (1993, p. 21). See also Fraser and Marcia (1992) and Waterman and Archer (1990).

15. See Stewart (1994).

16. Jack Block considers the identity groups to be differentiated by "a fairly enduring pattern of ego resilience and ego-control, mixed with a little introspectiveness" (cited in Helson, 1993, p. 109). Helson (1993) adds that they may represent aspects of a self-system that affects the ability to change.

CHAPTER 4

1. Among the four identity groups, the Guardians (Foreclosures) show the highest levels of obedience to authority and the lowest levels of anxiety. See Marcia et al. (1993).

2. Using a different method, Helson, Stewart, and Ostrove (1995) were able to assess changes in identity status over time from college through midlife in three different cohorts of highly educated women. They regard women in this group as carriers of culture and found that they were very similar to one another across samples drawn from different historical times. These women grew into well-functioning traditional conscientious women who retained a high respect for rules. Mallory (1984) also found no evidence that this style of identity development was maladaptive for women.

CHAPTER 5

1. In this sense, the Pathmakers in this study were very much like the people Gail Sheehy (1981) identified as Pathfinders. She was surprised to find that they were action-oriented people, not very much given to introspection or self-analysis.

2. In a study of the earliest memories of women in these four groups, I found that the Pathmakers' memories were most likely to include "blends" of striving and attachment (Josselson, 1982). This finding was replicated in Orlofsky and Frank (1986).

3. Hanoch Flum (1993) defines another identity status category he calls "evolutive." This is a style of identity formation in which young people maintain close ties to their family, forming identity on their own terms without overt crisis or rebellion. In his terms, Andrea might fit this pattern.

CHAPTER 6

1. The Searchers, in college, are in the midst of a normative separation-individuation struggle. For further theoretical explication of these issues, see Josselson (1980, 1987), Blos (1967), Kroger (1989, 1992, 1993). Difficulties in separation-individuation, however, often underlie many of the emotional disorders of adolescence. For relevant work, see Armstrong and Roth (1989) and Rhodes and Kroger (1992) on eating disorders and deJong (1992) on suicidality.

2. Weintraub (1978), in his study of the history of autobiography, comments that this idea that salvation is to be found in an active life and only by losing oneself can one find oneself is an old one, dating back to St. Augustine. Although only Millie states this insight clearly, many of the women I interviewed seem to have come to the same discovery.

3. Another of the Searchers, Norma, also fit this pattern. In addition, of the three women I interviewed when they were 33 but could not locate at this most recent data collection, one was also a Searcher who "went home again" like Natalie and Laura.

4. Natalie's shifts of pronoun—her use of "I" and "you" are telling in this excerpt and suggest the ways in which she feels herself somewhat outside her own decisions.

5. In a six-year follow-up study of thirty men (the only other long-term longitudinal study of the identity statuses), Marcia (1976) also found that all the Searchers (Moratoriums) changed identity statuses over time. His findings were similar to mine. Some had become Pathmakers (Identity Achievements), some Guardians (Foreclosures), and some Drifters (Diffusions).

6. Relationships are, for women, critical as holding environments to undergird the search for autonomy. See Josselson (1992) and Winnicott (1965).

CHAPTER 7

1. I do not mean to suggest that all "hippies" were Drifters. Some were Searchers or Pathmakers, depending on what it meant to them to be living this lifestyle. (See Keniston, 1960, 1968.) But it was an easy avenue to drift into and along, since impulsivity, risk-taking, and restlessness were part of the norm (Braungart, 1980).

2. See Bourne (1978).

3. Two more from the private women's college were also in this group in the college-age sample. These women died in their twenties, one a suicide, the other under unknown circumstances.

PART III

1. Following a group of talented women from the Radcliffe class of 1964, Stewart and Vandewater (1993) concluded that "a range of different life patterns can be satisfying and that no particular pattern is a formula for mental health or happiness" (p. 246). Similarly, Brown and Pacini (1993), studying women who had graduated from Vassar in 1957 and 1958, found that women who had been nominated as "ideal students" in college were, by midlife, indistinguishable on measures of success and well-being from those who had not been nominated. See also the other studies in Hulbert and Schuster (1993).

2. David Bakan (1966) discusses similar polarities in his concepts of _agency_ and _communion_. My concepts of competence and connection are similar to his except that my idea of competence requires less individualism and separateness than Bakan's _agency_ and my understanding of connection includes disharmonious relational experiences as well as satisfying ones and requires less merging of self than does Bakan's view of _communion_. My view of competence is most similar to that of Robert White (1959).

3. In her study of midlife women, Terri Apter (1995) concludes that women of this generation no longer follow a "social clock" (Neugarten, 1968) that dictates the time frame for milestones of a life. New life patterns allow for launching a career, marrying, or hav-

ing children at different chronological ages. Apter points out that despite the unhappiness that may have attended the limited choice of women in previous generations, there was a "comfortable inevitability" about life patterns that has been replaced by the anxiety of choice for this generation. Helson (1984, 1994), however, argues that the social-clock concept continues to illuminate aspects of the women's lives who she has studied.

4. See also Stewart and Malley (1989).

CHAPTER 8

1. Mary and Kenneth Gergen (1993), in comparing men's and women's popular auto-biographies, similarly found that women's autobiographies center on their relationships with others and do not draw strong demarcation lines between their public and private worlds. In contrast to men, women's stories "highlight the interdependent nature of their involvements" (p. 139). The "ordinary" women of my study are in this sense much like the highly visible successful women whose autobiographies the Gergens analyzed. Similarly, Schuster (1990), in a longitudinal study of intellectually gifted women, found these women at midlife to place highest value on their relationships at work and to feel most vulnerable in the interpersonal sphere.

2. In previous studies, men's sense of competence has been represented as success-oriented (see, for example, Vaillant, 1977; Levinson, 1978). These reports suggest that men speak of their experience of competence and success in ways very different from what I hear from the women I have been studying. Whether or not men in fact *experience* their work lives differently from women or have been socialized to talk about them differently is an unanswerable question because we can only imply experience from speech. Many men, on reading about the experiences of the women in my study, have told me that they too have similar feelings and experiences and that the dissatisfactions about work expressed by my participants also hold true for them.

3. William James had the idea that self-worth is a function of success in those domains of life that the individual particularly values. Success itself, then, is not identity enhancing unless the person feels that the region of their success is central to their system of values. See James (1892).

4. Other longitudinal studies of women similarly find that women do not derive their central sense of self or of success from their work. Studying thirty-five women who had graduated from UCLA's Gifted Student Program in 1961, Schuster, Langland, and Smith (1993) found that none of their participants, interviewed twenty-three years later, equated success with income, social status, or professional accomplishment. Success was more in terms of personal goals. Similarly, Brett (1993), following one hundred fifty-one women who graduated from Radcliffe in 1969, found that, twenty-one years later, these women, most of whom had achieved a high level of professional success, did not usually name their work as their most important activity. They were more likely to stress the centrality of being with their families. See also James (1990).

5. See Horner (1972) and Heilbrun (1988).

6. Susan Chase (1995b), in her study of women school stuperintendents, was similarly surprised to find that her participants were proud to tell work narratives of power, self-confidence, and accomplishment. She points out, however, that the situation of an anonymous interview may invite women to claim their achievement more unself-consciously than other narrative contexts such as autobiography.

7. Helson and McCabe (1993) also found that women in search of new identity in midlife most wanted to achieve a status where they had something valuable to give others.

8. The idea of "relational work" is a radical one. Flax (1990) writes, "In a culture in which affective relations are considered "natural" and "female," and "work" is considered instrumental, serious and male, the very concept of relational work is an oxymoron. . . . Anyone could "mother" or relate. There is nothing "scientific" or "skilled" about such practices" (p. 87). This may in part account for the general derogation of "women's work." But this excludes the experience of women from our understanding of work. Miller (1986) points out that women tend to "find satisfaction, pleasure, effectiveness and a sense of worth if they experience their life activities as arising from, and leading back into, a sense of connection with others" (p. 1).

9. Marcus, Cross, and Wurf (1990) discuss the fact that, by midlife, most people have located themselves in environments that reflect their competencies. Thus, the sense of competence remains stable at this age unless there is some disruption in the life structure.

10. LaBier (1986) explores what he calls "Modern Madness," symptoms of malaise resulting from lack of fulfillment in work. Although he included both men and women in his study, most of his examples are drawn from men's experience. His work documents that men of the same generation as the women of my study experience a similar sense of lack of vitality or personal engagement in their work. I suspect, however, that women, who are less likely to define themselves by their work, are quicker to recognize the emptiness of the work world, less likely to be seduced by games of power or blind ambition. LaBier points out that the "new careerists"—those who now make up the majority of corporate workers—are demanding more personal development and self-fulfillment at work. The women of my study, however, seem rather to be asking for more meaningful interconnection with others, more sharing of tasks, more sense of having direct effects on others.

11. See also Apter (1995) and Marshall (1993).

12. For Erikson, the crisis of generativity versus stagnation is the central dilemma of adult development. But just as intimacy seems merged into the identity question for women (see Josselson, 1987, and Patterson, Marcia, & Sochting, 1992), so generativity seems also to be at the heart of identity. There are no women in my group who seemed to define the competence pole of her identity separate from her sense of generativity. McAdams (1988), studying people's life stories, similarly concluded that generativity cannot be separated from identity.

13. See Waterman (1993) for a discussion of the relationship between identity and personal expressiveness.

14. Kathleen Hulbert (1993), summarizing a series of longitudinal studies of women, suggests that women may demand more of work because they are more aware of what they are giving up to be at work—they feel the tug of "alternate possibilities."

15. In a recent thirteen-year longitudinal study of 81 high school valedictorians, of whom 46 were women, Arnold (1995) found that talented women without female models, faculty mentors, or contact with practicing professionals rarely developed a strong career identity.

16. In a study of women in helping professions, Grossman and Stewart (1990) found that the principle gratifications experienced by these women at work were relational, and that these relational experiences were also the source of strain in their work. O'Leary and Ickovics (1990), studying women in low-level clerical jobs, also found that women said that relationships at work were the most satisfying aspect of their work.

17. At the same time, conflict in the workplace, where it leads to greater understanding of others and of people in groups, can be a positive force in personal development (Sinnott, 1993).

18. Inglehart and Brown (1987) found that, among medical students, women performed better in the more "relational" clinical years than in the more competitive academic years where men excelled, despite equal academic ability. They understood this as women's proclivity to learn and express themselves in person-oriented situations where their skills are used in personal contact.

19. See Gilligan (1982). Baruch, Barnett, and Rivers (1983) distinguish between experiences of "mastery" that derive from paid work and experiences of pleasure that grow out of arenas of intimacy, thus working with a disjunctive categorization of these experiences as though there is no mastery in intimacy or interpersonal closeness in work.

20. Hulbert (1993), in summarizing sixteen longitudinal studies of women's development, concluded that emotional support from significant others appears to be crucial to a woman's achievement. Similarly, Bateson (1989) comments on the centrality of support from significant others in maintaining achievement orientation.

21. Conflicts between work and nonwork demands differ depending on the particular career a woman pursues. Most of the women in this study are in service-oriented occupations. Studies of women in other fields suggest that women in high-level technical and managerial fields may find the most incompatibilities between their wish to pursue a career and enjoy a private, relational life, given the long hours and decision-making load required in these occupations. (See Etzion, 1988, and Barnett, Biener, & Baruch, 1987.)

22. Other studies indicate that there may be positive psychological consequences for women engaging in multiple roles. See, for example, Pietromonaco, Manis, & Frodhardt-Lane (1986) and Crosby (1991).

23. LaBier (1986) chronicles the disillusionment that "careerist" men feel in their work, documenting the ways in which status, position, and possessions are illusory compensations for boring work and lonely, disconnected experiences in the workplace. Women, perhaps, recognize these pitfalls more instinctively than men and find ways not to fall into the same traps.

CHAPTER 9

1. Miller (1987). See also Miller (1984, 1988).

2. Many theorists have written extensively about the relational basis of identity in women. The most widely cited have been Carol Gilligan, Nancy Chodorow, and Jean Baker Miller, all of whom have called attention to and tried to articulate the ways in which women realize themselves in connection to others. More empirical work has located the same phenomena. Summarizing many longitudinal studies of primarily gifted and privileged women, most of whom went on to outstanding professional success, Hulbert (1993) concludes that the development of a network of relationships is what is central to a woman's identity.

3. See Gergen (1991) who maintains that "relationships make possible the concept of the self. . . . We appear to stand alone, but we are manifestations of relatedness" (p. 170).

4. This understanding has formed the core of the work of many women writers (of literature) who have given voice to female experience. Some recent work in the social sci-

ences, however, has also begun to explore the ways in which relational identity configures a woman's life. See, for example, Paul (1994).

5. See Gilligan (1984).

6. See Josselson (1992, 1994) and Blustein & Noumair (in press).

7. For an exploration of the processes of mutuality and empowerment, see the work of members of the Stone Center at Wellesley College, including Jean Baker Miller, Janet Surrey (1987), and Judith Jordan (1986).

8. When I read the *Sex in America* study which showed that ours is a much less sexually active society than we have supposed, I was not at all surprised, given what these women have been telling me over the years—and given my experience with women patients. Of the twenty-three married women, three volunteered that their marriages were asexual, but these were all women whose marriages were highly troubled.

9. Mothers stress the central importance of their children, but they also stress the importance of their mates. Children, during the active mothering years, seem to "feel" more important than husbands, I think, because mothering engages both their competence and their connection and forms an active, insistent part of their lives. Husbands, by contrast, have centrality in being part of the framework rather than the foreground. But I don't think these women ever ask themselves which is more important. Both are utterly defining, but in different ways.

10. See Kaplan (1992)'s discussion of this. Also Oberman and Josselson (1996).

11. Mary Boulton (1983), in her study of the experience of motherhood, points out the difference between the experience of looking after children and the sense of meaning and significance of having them. The latter emerges on reflection, not so much in the immediate response to the interactions of caretaking that may be frustrating and difficult. Similarly, in their cross-cultural study of motherhood, Minturn and Lambert (1964) point out that "few tasks are as harassing as caring for small children and the increased responsibility of other [work-related] duties is compensated for by the respite from child care" (p. 91). This may in part explain why mothers who work outside the home may have more joy in motherhood than those who do not.

12. See Ireland (1993) for a thoughtful discussion of the decision not to have children and the issue of separating motherhood from female identity.

13. Heilbrun (1988), p. 77.

14. Hancock (1989) also found that transforming the tie to their mothers was the critical factor in women's maturity. See Chodorow (1978) for a theoretical analysis of the mother-daughter bond.

15. P. 28.

16. Kaplan and Klein (1985) discuss the intense connection late adolescent college women retain with their mothers. Despite conflict, most college women continue to regard their mothers as their "best friends."

17. See Apter (1990) for a deeply perceptive analysis of the mother-daughter relationshp in adolescence and beyond.

18. See O'Connor (1992) for a complete review of research on friendship among women.

19. P. 393.

CHAPTER 10

1. Other studies of midlife development similarly document both stability and change from adolescence to midlife. Helson and Moane (1987) studying a cohort of women ten

years older than the women I studied, from ages 21–43, using personality inventory scales, found that, over time, these women showed increases in self-discipline, commitment to duties, independence, confidence, coping skills, and ego development. While other longitudinal studies have found role changes that might have been strongly influenced by concurrent changes in social roles available to women, they also found personality changes in the direction of greater psychological mindedness and increased coping capacities (Block, 1971; Haan, 1981).

For other reflections and research on midlife women, see Apter (1995), Strayer (in press), and Rossi (1980).

2. Dan McAdams, in his complex and penetrating study of identity, *Power, Intimacy and the Life Story,* similarly concluded that one can only "remain dazzled by the splendid diversity in the forms that identity may take" (p. 210).

3. In their work on female authority, Young-Eisendrath and Wiedemann (1987) stress that such authority rests on legitimizing conflicting needs and desires and finding flexible responses to each new environment rather than aiming for consistency.

4. This particular struggle also characterizes women who, through their education, move from working-class backgrounds to more middle-class orientations. Worldviews that typify the differing social classes affect how women understand their lives. For a discussion of these issues, see Ostrove and Stewart (1994).

5. Carl Jung (1933) called this process individuation; he suggested that the hallmark of midlife is a deepening sense of self as people examine themselves in a new light. Jung also suggested that women in midlife move toward greater separateness and agency, which made sense in the culture within which Jung was writing. More likely, people move, at midlife, to reclaim lost parts of themselves; what has been easiest to express before midlife is largely dependent on cultural and institutional factors.

6. Some psychological theorists (Gutmann, 1980), following Jung's ideas about individuation and the eventual integration of the yin and the yang, have suggested that there is a midlife "shift" where women pick up their lost "masculine" aspects while men reclaim their lost "feminine" parts. My observations suggest that this is only clear in cultures that rigidly define gender roles. The women I have studied, at midlife, tend to strengthen whatever part of themselves seemed most in danger of atrophying. Thus, those women who did not have children, who had devoted themselves to work and career in the earlier part of their lives, in midlife are striving to emphasize either nurturing, creative, or leisure pursuits. Fiske (1980) in her study of adult transition, similarly concludes that adult development is best understood as a process of shifting priorities among what she conceptualizes as four basic commitments: interpersonal; altruistic (including ethics and religion); mastery/competence; and self-protection. To this I would add leisure, a dimension of experience that the women I have studied have felt is most likely to be shortchanged.

7. See Baruch, Barnett, and Rivers (1983) who found that the women who were most content were working married women—that is, women with multiple investments.

8. In a retrospective study of adult identity, Kroger and Green (in press) investigated events associated with identity change between the ages of 40 and 63. They found that people were more likely to attribute identity shifts to "internal change"—new awareness or shifts in perspective—than to external influences. Thus, their findings are consistent with my own.

9. Gisela LaBouvie-Vief has conducted a number of studies that document the growth of representations of the self and others across the life cycle. She has found empirically

that, looking at people (cross-sectionally) across the life span, there is a peak at midlife of recognition of the unique individuality of parents as well as of more complex representations of the self (LaBouvie-Vief et al., 1995; in press). She understands these changes in a cognitive-developmental framework in which greater cognitive complexity and the ability to think in terms of transformation is associated with cognitive maturation.

10. Gilligan (1990).

11. In summarizing the lessons they learned from their intensive studies of women's lives, Franz, Cole, Crosby, and Stewart (1994) conclude that interconnection is the foundation of identity. Women are distinct from one another in creating a unique constellation of relationships to other people. This has, of course, been observed by nearly all researchers who have studied women. See Gilligan (1982), Miller (1976), Chodorow (1978), Hulbert and Schuster (1993) among others.

12. Helson and McCabe (1994), in a longitudinal study, found that where women in their twenties had clear ideas about what others expected of them, women in their fifties thought that other people no longer had expectations about what they should be doing and thus felt free of interpersonal fetters in planning their lives.

13. Included in this calculation is the woman I could not classify into one of the identity categories. Sexually abused as a child, she has had a long history of therapy that has been helpful, but she is still left with a vague and shifting sense of identity.

14. Mary Catherine Bateson, in _Composing a Life_ (1989), says that "composing a life involves a continual reimagining of the future and a reinterpretation of the past to give meaning to the present, remembering best those events that prefigured what followed, forgetting those that proved to have no meaning within the narrative" (p. 29). A similar point is made by McAdams (1988) and by Grotevant (1993). See also Spence (1982) for a discussion of the relationship between narrative and historical truth.

15. Within psychology, however, longitudinal personality research has tended to overemphasize findings on the consistency of personality, often treating change as "error variance" (Helson, 1993).

16. See Sidel's (1990) analysis of women's response to cultural mixed messages.

17. 1988, p. 130.

REFERENCES

Apter, T. (1990). *Altered loves*. New York: St. Martin's Press.

Apter, T. (1995). *Secret paths*. New York: Norton.

Archer, S. L., & Waterman, A. S. (1990). Varieties of identity diffusions and foreclosures: An exploration of subcategories of the identity statuses. *J. Adolescent Research, 5,* 96–111.

Armstrong, J. G., & Roth, D. (1989). Attachment and separation difficulties in eating disorders: a preliminary investigation. *International J. Eating Disorders, 8,* 141–155.

Arnold, K. D. (1995). *Lives of promise: What becomes of high school valedictorians*. San Francisco: Jossey-Bass.

Bacha, A. (1992). "Fertility of American Women: June 1992." Washington, DC: U.S. Dept. of Commerce, Bureau of the Census.

Bakan, D. (1966). *The duality of human existence*. Boston: Beacon Press.

Barnett, R. C., Biener, L., & Baruch, G. K. (1987). *Gender and stress*. New York: Free Press.

Baruch, G., Barnett, R., & Rivers, C. (1983). *Lifeprints*. New York: Signet.

Bateson, M. C. (1989). *Composing a life*. New York: Atlantic Monthly Press.

Baumeister, R. (1986). *Identity*. New York: Oxford University Press.

Bellah, R. N., Madsen, R., Sullivan, W. M., Swidler, A., & Tipton, S. M. (1985). *Habits of the heart*. New York: Harper & Row.

Berzonsky, M. D. (1985). Diffusion within Marcia's identity status paradigm: Does it foreshadow academic problems? *J. Youth and Adolescence, 14,* 527–538.

Block, J. (1971). *Lives through time.* Berkeley, CA: Bancroft Books.

Blos, P. (1967). The second individuation process of adolescence. *Psychoanalytic Study of the Child, 22,* 162–186.

Blustein, D. L., & Noumair, D. A. (in press). Self and identity in career development: Implications for theory and practice. *J. Counseling and Development.*

Boulton, M. G. (1983). *On being a mother.* London: Tavistock Publications.

Bourne, E. (1978). The state of research on ego identity: A review. *J. Youth and Adolescence, 7,* 223–252.

Braungart, R. G. (1980). Youth movements. In J. Adelson (Ed.), *Handbook of Adolescent Psychology.* New York: Wiley.

Brett, B. (1993). The Radcliffe class of 1969: Women on the cutting edge. In K. D. Hulbert & D. T. Schuster, *Women's lives through time.* San Franciso: Jossey-Bass.

Brown, D., & Pacini, R. (1993). The Vassar classes of 1978 and 1958: The ideal student study. In K. D. Hulbert & D. T. Schuster, *Women's lives through time.* San Franciso: Jossey-Bass.

Chase, S. (1995a). Taking narrative seriously—consequences for method and theory in interview studies. In R. Josselson & A. Lieblich (Eds.), *The narrative study of lives, Vol. III: Interpreting experience.* Thousand Oaks, CA: Sage.

Chase, S. (1995b). *Ambiguous empowerment: The work narratives of women school superintendents.* Amherst: University of Massachusetts Press.

Chodorow, N. (1978). *The reproduction of mothering.* Berkeley: University of California Press.

Crosby, F. (1991). *Juggling.* New York: Free Press.

deJong, M. L. (1992). Attachment, individuation and risk of suicide in late adolescence. *J. Youth and Adolescence, 21,* 357–373.

Eliot, G. (1972). *Middlemarch* [1871]. London: The Folio Society.

Erikson, E. H. (1958). *Young man Luther.* New York: Norton.

Erikson, E. H. (1968). *Identity, youth and crisis.* New York: Norton.

Erikson, E. H. (1969). *Ghandi's truth.* New York: Norton.

Etzion, D. (1988). The experience of burnout and work/non-work success in male and female engineers: A matched-pairs comparison. *Human Resource Management, 2,* 163–179.

Fiske, M. (1980). Changing hierarchies of commitment in adulthood. In N. J. Smelser & E. H. Erikson (Eds.), *Themes of work and love in adulthood.* Cambridge, MA: Harvard University Press.

Flax, J. (1990). *Thinking fragments.* Berkeley: University of California Press.

Flum, H. (1994). The evolutive style of identity formation. *J. Youth and Adolescence, 23,* 489–498.

Franz, C. E., Cole, E. R., Crosby, F. J., & Stewart, A. J. (1994). Lessons from lives. In C. E. Franz & A. J. Stewart (Eds.), *Women creating lives: Identities, resilience and resistance.* Boulder, CO: Westview Press.

Gergen, K. (1991). *The saturated self: Dilemmas of identity in contemporary life.* New York: Basic Books.

Gergen, M. (1990). Finished at forty: Women's development within the patriarchy. *Psychology of Women Quarterly, 14,* 471–493.

Gergen, M. (1992). Life stories: Pieces of a dream. In G. Rosenwald & R. Ochberg (Eds.), *Storied lives.* New Haven: Yale University Press.

Gergen, M. M., & Gergen, K. J. (1993). Narratives of the gendered body in popular autobiography. In R. Josselson & A. Lieblich (Eds.), *The narrative study of lives, Vol. I.* Thousand Oaks, CA: Sage.

Gilligan, C. (1982). *In a different voice.* Cambridge: Harvard University Press.

Gilligan, C. (1984). The conquistador and the dark continent: Reflections of the psychology of love. *Daedalus, 113,* 75–95.

Gilligan, C. (1990). Joining the resistance: Psychology, politics, girls and women. *Michigan Quarterly Review, 29,* 501–536.

Gould, R. (1978). *Transformations: Growth and change in adult life.* New York: Simon and Schuster.

Grossman, H., & Stewart, A. (1990). Women's experience of power over others. In H. Y. Grossman & N. L. Chester (Eds.), *The experience and meaning of work in women's lives.* Hillsdale, NJ: Erlbaum.

Grotevant, H. (1993). The integrative nature of identity: Bringing the soloists to sing in the choir. In J. Kroger, *Discussions on ego Identity.* Hillsdale, NJ: Erlbaum.

Gutmann, D. L. (1980). The postparental years: Clinical problems and developmental possibilites. In W. H. Norman & T. J. Scaramella (Eds.), *Mid-life: Developmental and clinical issues.* New York: Brunner/Mazel.

Haan, N. (1981). Common dimensions of personality development: Early adolescence to middle life. In D. Eichorn, J. Calusen, N. Haan, M. Honzik, and P. Mussen (Eds.), *Past and present in middle life.* New York: Academic Press, 117–151.

Hancock, E. (1989). *The girl within.* New York: Fawcett Columbine.

Harter, S. (1990). Causes, correlates and the functional role of global self-worth: A lifespan perspective. In R. J. Sternberg & J. Kolligian (Eds.), *Competence considered.* New Haven: Yale University Press.

Heath, D. H. (1991). *Fulfilling lives: Paths to maturity and success.* San Francisco: Jossey-Bass.

Heilbrun, C. G. (1988). *Writing a woman's life.* New York: Ballantine.

Heilbrun, C. G. (1990). *Hamlet's mother and other women.* New York: Ballantine.

Helson, R. (1984). Personality and patterns of adherence and nonadherence to the social clock. *J. Personality and Social Psychology, 46,* 1079–1095.

Helson, R. (1993). Comparing longitudinal studies of adult development: Toward a paradigm of tension between stability and change. In D. C. Funder, R. D. Parke, C. Tomlinson-Keasey, & K. Widaman, *Studying Lives through time.* Washington, DC: American Psychological Association.

Helson, R. (1994). Has the social clock run down? Paper presented to Symposium on women growing older: An integration of theroretical perspectives. B. Turner & L. Troll (Chrs.), Gerontological Society of America, Atlanta.

Helson, R, & McCabe, L. (1994). The social clock project in middle age. In B. Turner & L. Troll (Eds.), *Growing older female: Theoretical perspectives in the psychology of aging.* Newbury Park, CA: Sage.

Helson, R., & Moane, G. (1987). Personality change in women from college to midlife. *J. Personality and Social Psychology, 53,* 176–186.

Helson, R., Stewart, A. J., & Ostrove, J. (1995). Identity in three cohorts of midlife women. *J. Personality and Social Psychology, 69,* 544–557.

Horner, M. (1972). Towards an understanding of achievement related conflicts in women. *J. Social Issues, 28,* 157–176.

Hulbert, K. D. (1993). Reflections on the lives of educated women. In K. D. Hulbert & D. T. Schuster, *Women's lives through time.* San Franciso: Jossey-Bass.

Hulbert, K. D., & Schuster, D. T. (1993). *Women's lives through time.* San Franciso: Jossey-Bass.

Inglehart, M., & Brown, D. R. (1987). Gender differences in values and their impact on academic achievement. Paper presented at the Tenth Annual Meeting of the International Society of Social Psychology, San Francisco.

Ireland, M. S. (1993). *Reconceiving women.* New York: Guilford.

James, J. (1990). Employment patterns and midlife well-being. In H. Y. Grossman & N. L. Chester (Eds.), *The experience and meaning of work in women's lives.* Hillsdale, NJ: Erlbaum.

James, W. (1892). *Psychology: The briefer course.* New York: Henry Holt.

Jong, E. (1994). *Fear of fifty.* New York: HarperCollins.

Jordan, J. (1986). The meaning of mutuality. *Work in progress.* Wellesley, MA: The Stone Center.

Josselson, R. (1973). Psychodynamic aspects of identity formation in college women. *J. Youth and Adolescence, 2,* 3–52.

Josselson, R. (1978). *Finding herself: Pathways to identity development in women.* San Francisco: Jossey-Bass.

Josselson, R. (1980). Ego development in adolescence. In J. Adelson (Ed.), *Handbook of adolescent psychology.* New York: Wiley.

Josselson, R. (1982). Personality structure and identity status in women as viewed through early memories. *J. Youth and Adolescence, 11,* 293–299.

Josselson, R. (1992). *The space between us: Exploring the dimensions of human relationship.* San Francisco: Jossey-Bass.

Josselson, R. (Ed.), (1996). *Ethics and process in the narrative study of lives: The narrative study of lives, Vol. 4.* Thousand Oaks, Ca: Sage.

Jung, C. (1933). *Modern man in search of a soul.* New York: Harcourt, Brace.

Kaplan, A., & Klein, R. (1985). The relational self in late adolescence women. *Work in progress.* Wellesley, MA: Stone Center Working Paper Series.

Kaplan, M. M. (1992). *Mothers' images of motherhood.* London: Routledge.

Keniston, K. (1960). *The uncommitted.* New York: Harcourt, Brace and World.

Keniston, K. (1968). *The young radicals.* New York: Harcourt, Brace and World.

Kolak, D., & Martin, R. (1991). *Self and identity: Contemporary philosophical issues.* New York: Macmillan.

Kroger, J. (1989). *Identity in adolescence: The balance between self and other.* London: Routledge.

Kroger, J. (1992). Intrapsychic dimensions of identity during late adolescence. In G. R. Adams, T. P. Gulotta, & R. Montemayor (Eds.), *Adolescent identity formation.* Newbury Park, CA: Sage.

Kroger, J. (1993). *Discussions on ego identity.* Hillsdale, NJ: Erlbaum.

Kroger, J. (1995). The differentiation of "firm" and "developmental" foreclosure identity statuses: A longitudinal study. *J. Adolescent Research, 10,* 317–337.

Kroger, J. (in press). Identity, regression and development. *J. Adolescence.*

Kroger, J., & Green, K. E. (in press). Events associated with identity status change. *J. Adolescence.*

LaBier, D. (1986). *Modern madness.* New York: Touchstone.

Labouvie-Vief, G., Chiodo, L. M., Goguen, L. A., Diehl, M., & Orwoll, L. (1995). Representations of self across the life span. *Psychology and Aging, 10,* 1–12.

Labouvie-Vief, G., Diehl, M., Choiodo, L. M., & Coyle, N. (in press). Representations of self and parents.

Levinson, D., et al. (1978). *The seasons of a man's life*. New York: Knopf.

Mallory, M. E. (1984). Longitudinal analysis of ego identity status. Unpublished doctoral dissertation. University of California, Davis.

Marcia, J. E. (1964). Determination and construct validity of ego identity status. Unpublished doctoral dissertation, Department of Psychology, University of California, Davis.

Marcia, J. E. (1976). Identity six years after: A follow-up study. *J. Youth and Adolescence, 5*, 145–160.

Marcia, J. E. (1980). Identity in adolescence. In J. Adelson (Ed.), *Handbook of adolescent psychology*. New York: Wiley.

Marcia, J. E. (1989). Identity diffusion differentiated. In M. A. Luszaz & T. Nettelbeck (Eds.), *Psychological development: Perspectives across the life-span*. North-Holland: Elsevier.

Marcia, J. E., & Friedman, M. (1970). Ego identity status in college women. *Journal of Personality, 38*, 249–262.

Marcia, J. E., Waterman, A. S., Matteson, D. R., Archer, S. L., & Orlofsky, J. L. (1993). *Ego identity: A handbook for psychosocial research*. New York: Springer-Verlag.

Marcus, H., Cross, S., & Wurf, E. (1990). The role of the self-system in competence. In R. J. Sternberg & J. Kolligian (Eds.), *Competence considered*. New Haven: Yale University Press.

Markus, H., & Oyserman, D. (1989). Gender and thought: The role of the self concept. In M. Crawford and M. Gentry (Eds.), *Gender and thought* (pp. 100–127). New York: Springer-Verlag.

Marshall, J. (1993). Patterns of cultural awareness as coping strategies for women managers. In S. E. Kahn & B. C. Lang (Eds.), *Women, work and coping: A multidisciplinary approach to workplace stress*. Montreal: McGill Queen's University Press.

McAdams, D. (1988). *Power, intimacy and the life story*. New York: Guilford.

Merriam, S. B., & Clark, M. (1991). *Lifelines: Patterns of work, love and learning in adulthood*. San Francisco: Jossey-Bass.

Miller, J. B. (1976). *Toward a new psychology of women*. Boston: Beacon Press.

Miller, J. B. (1984). The development of women's sense of self. *Work in Progress, No. 12*. Wellesley, MA: Stone Center Working Papers Series.

Miller, J. B. (1986). What do we mean by relationships? *Work in Progress, No. 22*. Wellesley, MA: Stone Center Working Paper Series.

Miller, J. B. (1988). Connections, disconnections and violations. *Work in Progress, No. 33*. Wellesley, MA: Stone Center Working Papers Series.

Minturn, L., & Lambert, L. W. (1964). *Mothers of six cultures: Antecedents of child-rearing*. New York: Wiley.

Neugartern, B. L. (1968). Adult personality: Toward a psychology of the life cycle. In B. L. Neugartern (Ed.), *Middle age and aging: A reader in social psychology* (pp. 137–147). Chicago: University of Chicago Press.

Neugarten, B. L. et al. (1968). Women's attitudes toward the menopause. In B. L. Neugarten (Ed.), *Middle age and aging* (pp. 195–200), Chicago: University of Chicago Press.

Oberman, Y., & Josselson, R. (1996). Matrix of tensions: A model of mothering. *Psychology of Women Quarterly, 20*.

O'Connor, P. (1992). *Friendships between women: A critical review*. New York: Guilford.

O'Leary, V. E., & Ickovics, J. E. (1990). Women supporting women: Secretaries and their bosses. In H. Y. Grossman & N. L. Chester (Eds.), *The experience and meaning of work in women's lives*. Hillsdale, NJ: Erlbaum.

References

Orlofsky, J., & Frank, M. (1986). Personality structure as viewed through early memories and identity status in college men and women. *J. Personality and Social Psychology, 5,* 580–586.

Ostrove, J., & Stewart, A. (1994). Marginal identities: Social class at Radcliffe in the 1960s. In C. E. Franz & A. J. Stewart (Eds.), *Women creating lives: Identities, resilience and resistance.* Boulder, CO: Westview Press.

Patterson, S. J., Sochting, I., & Marcia, J. E. (1992). The inner space and beyond: Women and identity. In G. R. Adams & R. Montemayor (Eds.), *Adolescent identity formation.* Thousand Oaks, CA: Sage.

Paul, E. L. (1994). The complexities of a young adult woman's relational world: Challenges, demands and benefits. In C. E. Franz & A. J. Stewart (Eds.), *Women creating lives: Identities, resilience and resistance.* Boulder, CO: Westview Press.

Pietromonaco, P., Manis, J., & Frohardt-Lane, K. (1986). Psychological consequences of multiple social roles. *Psychology of Women Quarterly, 10,* 373–381.

Rhodes, B., & Kroger, J. (1992). Parental bonding and separation-individuation difficulties among late adolescent eating disordered women. *Child Psychiatry and Human Development, 22,* 249–263.

Rossi, A. (1980). Life span theories and womens' lives. *Signs, 6,* 5–32.

Ruddick, S. (1989). *Maternal Thinking.* New York: Ballantine.

Schenkel, S. (1975). Relationship among ego identity status, field independence and traditional femininity, *J. Youth and Adolescence, 4,* 73–82.

Schenkel, S., & Marcia, J. E. (1972). Attitudes toward pre-marital intercourse in determining ego identity status in college women. *Journal of Personality, 3,* 472–482.

Schuster, D. T. (1990). Work, relationships and balance. In H. Y. Grossman & N. L. Chester (Eds.), *The experience and meaning of work in women's lives.* Hillsdale, NJ: Erlbaum.

Schuster, D. T., Langland, L., & Smith, D. G. (1993). The UCLA gifted women, class of 1961: Living up to potential. In K. D. Hulbert & D. T. Schuster, *Women's lives through time.* San Franciso: Jossey-Bass.

Sheehy, G. (1981). *Pathfinders.* New York: Bantam.

Shotter, J., & K. Gergen. (1989). *Texts of identity.* London: Sage.

Skoe, E. E., & Marcia, J. E. (1991). The development and partial validation of a care-based measure of moral development. *Merrill-Palmer Quarterly, 37,* 289–304.

Sidel, R. (1990). *On her own: Growing up in the shadow of the American dream.* New York: Viking.

Sinnott, J. (1993). Use of complex thought and resolving intragroup conflicts: A means to conscious adult development in the workplace. In J. Demick & P. M. Miller (Eds.), *Development in the workplace.* Hillsdale, NJ: Erlbaum.

Spence, D. (1982). *Narrative truth and historical truth.* New York: Norton.

Stephen, J., Fraser, E., & Marcia, J. E. (1992). Moratorium-Achievement (MAMA) cycles in lifespan identity development: Value orientations and reasoning system. *J. Adolescence, 15,* 283–300.

Stewart, A. (1994). The women's movement and women's lives. In A. Lieblich & R. Josselson (Eds.), *The narrative study of lives, Vol. II: Exploring identity and gender.* Thousand Oaks, CA: Sage.

Stewart, A. J., & Malley, J. E. (1989). Case studies of agency and communion in women's lives. In R. K. Unger (Ed.), *Representations: Social constructions of gender.* Amityville, NY: Baywood Publishing Co.

Stewart, A. J., & Vandewater, E. (1993). The Radcliffe class of 1964: Career and family social clock projects in a transitional cohort. In K. D. Hulbert & D. T. Schuster, *Women's lives through time*. San Franciso: Jossey-Bass.

Strayer, J. (in press). Trapped in the mirror: A psychosocial reflection on midlife and Snow White's queen.

Surrey, J. (1987). Relationship and empowerment. *Work in Progress, No. 13*. Wellesley, MA: Stone Center Working Paper Series.

Taylor, C. (1989). *Sources of the self: The making of modern identity*. Cambridge: Harvard University Press.

Vaillant, G. (1977). *Adaptation to life*. Boston: Little, Brown.

Waterman, A. S. (1992). Identity as an aspect of optimal psychological functioning. In G. R. Adams, T. P. Gulotta, & R. Montemayor (Eds.), *Adolescent identity formation*. Newbury Park, CA: Sage.

Waterman, A. S. (1993). Developmental perspectives on identity formation. In J. E. Marcia, A. S. Waterman, D. R. Matteson, S. L. Archer, & J. L. Orlofsky (Eds.), *Ego identity: A handbook for psychosocial research*. New York: Springer-Verlag.

Waterman, A. S., & Archer, S. (1990). A life-span perspective on identity formation: Developments in form, function, and process. In P. B. Baltes, D. L. Featherman, and R. M. Lerner (Eds.), *Life-span development and behavior, Vol. 10*. Hillsdale, NJ: Erlbaum.

Weintraub, K. J. (1978). *The value of the individual: Self and circumstance in autobiography*. Chicago: University of Chicago Press.

White, R. (1959). Motivation reconsidered: The concept of competence. *Psychological Review, 66*, 297–333.

Winnicott, D. W. (1965). *The maturational processes and the facilitating environment*. New York: International Universities Press.

Young-Eisendrath, P., & Wiedemann, F. (1987). *Female authority: Empowering women through psychotherapy*. New York: Guilford.

INDEX